The Fly Fisherman's Bible

The Fly Fisherman's Bible

Jim Bashline

Drawings by George Lavanish

Broadway Books
New York

BROADWAY

Broadway Books titles may be purchased for business or promotional use or for special sales. For information, please write to: Special Markets Department, Random House, Inc., 1540 Broadway, New York, NY 10036.

BROADWAY BOOKS and its logo, a letter B bisected on the diagonal, are trademarks of Broadway Books, a division of Random House, Inc.

Visit our website at www.broadwaybooks.com

First Broadway Books trade paperback edition published 2001.

The Library of Congress Cataloging-in-Publication Data has cataloged the previous edition as:
Bashline, Jim.
   The fly fisherman's bible/Jim Bashline.—1st ed.
      p.   cm. — (Doubleday outdoor bibles)
  ISBN 0-385-42242-3
  1. Fly fishing.   2. Fly tying.   I. Series.
SH456.B296   1993
799.1'2—dc20   92-29445
                             CIP

18 17 16 15 14 13 12 11 10

Contents

Introduction   vii

Part I: Freshwater Fly Fishing

   1. Choosing Tackle   11

   2. The Trouts   34

   3. Fly Casting   42

   4. Flies for Trout   55

   5. Fishing the Dry Fly   68

   6. Fishing the Wet Fly   79

   7. Fishing the Nymph   88

   8. Fishing Streamer Flies   99

   9. Fly Fishing for Bass   108

  10. Panfish   124

  11. Pike, Muskie, and Pickerel   131

  12. Atlantic Salmon   145

  13. Pacific Salmon and Steelhead   158

Part II: Saltwater Fly Fishing

  14. The Big Ones   169

  15. Fly Fishing the Flats   182

  16. Other Saltwater Species   199

Introduction

Fishing with artificial flies, the name given to man-made imitations of insects, crustaceans, and minnows, has a 2000-year history. Presenting the flies to the fish was once done with long wooden rods and a line constructed of braided horsehair. The early fly fishing outfits did not include reels. The fly was simply tossed or lofted onto the water. Fly casting as we know it today could not be done with such primitive gear. With the tackle at hand in those early days it's a wonder the sport survived. To have some idea of what pioneer anglers were faced with, try tossing a nearly weightless fly tied to twenty feet of kite string which is attached to the end of a fifteen-foot pole. It's maddeningly difficult.

For more than a few would-be fly fishermen the mechanics of casting a small hook wound with feathers and fur appears extremely difficult. It seems even more so if the novice begins his investigation of the sport by reading a few pages of one of the many advanced books dealing with flies and fly tackle. The Latin names of the insects and the lengthy dissertations about lines, leaders, reels, casting techniques, and everything else connected with fly fishing lead

many budding anglers to the unfortunate conclusion that this sport is too complicated for them. It isn't and that's what we hope to prove in these pages.

We fish with flies because it's an effective way to catch fish and it's a lot of fun. It's effective because practically everything a fish eats can be closely duplicated or suggested by an artificial fly. It's fun because few other recreational pursuits offer such direct contact with wild creatures. Fly fishing can be enjoyed by both sexes, and can be taken to any level of expertise the participant chooses.

Most artificial "flies" designed for freshwater are made to resemble insects. The most popular of the species pursued by fly fishermen, the various trouts, eat a huge quantity of insects, as do bass, sunfish, and many other common fishes. Freshwater fish also eat other fish, mostly small minnows, and some saltwater species feed almost exclusively on other small fish. Small fish are also the models for hundreds of flies that suggest this food source. The challenge of fly fishing is to cast the fly to a spot where a fish is expected to be with the hope of having the fish take it into its mouth. The nearly weightless fly cannot be delivered with other types of tackle. The longer fly rod and the weight of the fly line make it possible.

The foregoing covers about all there is to the theory of the sport. After that, casting, selecting the fly, deciding where to cast, and a dozen other considerations enter the picture—but these matters need not be terribly complex.

All forms of angling are productive at various times, but when fish are actively feeding on insects, fly fishing is the most efficient way to catch them. In fact, much of the time it's the *only* way to catch them. Fish usually ignore metal and wooden lures when they are eating easy-to-catch insects that are drifting along or just under the surface. Fishing with a dry fly— one that floats—is a commonsense approach when fish are making rings on the surface as they gulp floating insects.

When the fish's preference happens to be submerged insects, a wet fly or nymph—one that sinks—is called for. At other times, streamer flies, which suggest small minnows, will be highly effective. Hundreds, perhaps thousands, of fly patterns have been created that resemble grasshoppers, crickets, snails, crayfish, beetles, and every other creature that fish have been known to eat. The beginning fly fisher has many options to choose from, but he or she should approach the sport step by step. It's frus-

trating and self-defeating to attempt to digest the entire lore in one gulp.

In addition to the fun and excitement of the sport, fly fishing is attracting new followers each year for another sound reason. It makes good sense from a conservation standpoint. Real insects that gamefish choose to eat are swallowed quickly. The flies designed to imitate or suggest these creatures are seldom swallowed. When a fish seizes a fly it quickly discovers that it is not the real thing and tries to eject it. A live or natural bait is often gulped deeply, making an injury-free release much more difficult. There is no harm in keeping a few fish for the pan, but the more fish released to grow and be caught another day leads to more productive angling for all of us. The late Lee Wulff, a pioneer spokesman for catch-and-release angling, summed it up most eloquently: "A gamefish is too valuable to be caught only once."

This book is exclusively about fly fishing, and I'm happy to share the knowledge I've acquired during a lifetime of practicing the sport. My first fishing pole was a fly rod. I was six years old. At nine, I was tying flies with materials from a mail-order kit. Now, dozens of rods, thousands of flies, and fifty years later, I'm delighted to confess that the thrill of seeing a fish, any fish, rise to take a fly has not diminished in the slightest.

I

FRESHWATER
FLY FISHING

Walking the aisles of a consumer show is a good way to get acquainted with fly tackle. Rods, reels, and lines can be cast and evaluated, prices compared, and valuable fishing information exchanged. This show in Somerset, New Jersey attracted over 25,000 fly fishing enthusiasts.

1

Choosing Tackle

Walking the aisles of a recent Fly Tackle Dealers' Show in Denver, Colorado, I was overcome by a sense of awe mixed with a wave of nostalgia. Awe, because of the vast assortment of high-quality tackle and nostalgia because in my youth, choosing a rod, reel, and the other necessary components of the sport was a relatively simple task. There wasn't all that much to choose from. Today, quantity rod makers number in the dozens, and if we toss in the custom and semicustom shops, we're talking about hundreds of rod options. And it's the same with reels, lines, leaders, fly boxes, vests, waders, and other equipment that could be considered necessary or useful. Some items are neither, of course, but we find them fun to own or examine.

If a fly angler from the last century were transported to a fly-tackle shop of today, he'd be speechless. Most beginners find themselves in the same situation. As a way of sorting through the tackle options for fly fishing, let's consider the good all-around outfits for trout, panfish, bass, and saltwater species. Some choices discussed will not suit certain experienced anglers, who choose to make the game more challenging

through the use of lighter rods and finer leaders, but these folks must remember that they too had to start at the beginning.

THE ALL-PURPOSE TROUT AND PANFISH ROD

The nomenclature in use for more than thirty years rates fly rods by the line weight they are best suited for. Standard line weights are available in designations 2 to 13, with the smaller number being the lightest in weight and the smallest in diameter. Most fly rods are marked on the butt section with a line number or numbers. Therefore, when you see a rod marked "5 weight," "7 weight," or some combination of numbers such as "5-6 weight," keep in mind it has nothing to do with the length of the rod.

While fly fishing in general and choosing tackle in particular is, more often than not, subjective instead of objective, I'm going to begin the rod discussion with an unqualified declaration. The best choice for an all-around rod intended for trout, panfish, and a wide assortment of other frequently encountered species is

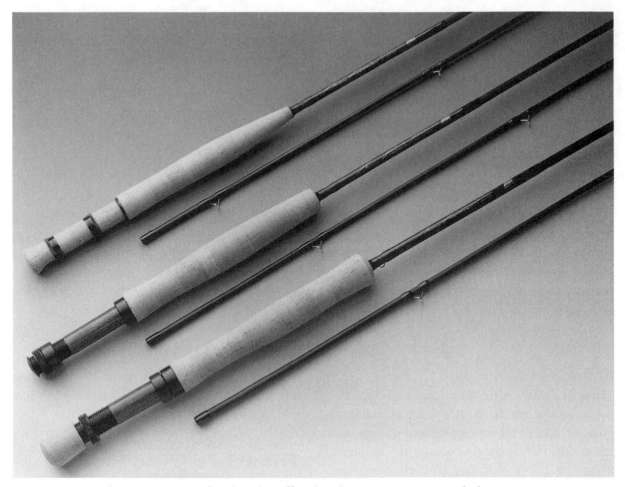

The assortment of rod styles offered today may seem overwhelming to the novice. Lengths, weights, reel seat designs, and grip configurations present nearly unlimited options. Tubular graphite, however, has passed all other material in popularity.

an 8-footer designed to cast a 6-weight line. Equipped with such a rod, the fly fisherman could approach well over 90 percent of the world's trout streams with a high level of confidence. As one's experience and travel plans increase, other lengths and weights will be considered and probably added to the tackle collection, but seldom will the trout angler be ill served with an 8-footer tossing a 6-weight line.

The recommendation of the 8-foot, 6-weight combination is not nearly as dogmatic as it sounds. An 8-foot rod is easily capable of casting a fly well beyond 60 feet and can also

deliver a fly softly at ranges under 20. Suitable leaders for both casting ranges and all distances between must be considered, but this choice of rod is not merely a compromise. It's the ideal casting tool for novice and experienced angler alike. Note: For some unknown reason, not all rod makers offer an 8-foot, 6-weight rod. But they should. You'll probably do just as well with one 6 inches shorter or 6 inches longer. If you're under 5 foot 8 inches tall choose the shorter one. If you're taller go with the 8½-footer.

Choosing a first or fiftieth fly rod can be fun and frustrating at once. No enthusiastic fly rodder ever outgrows the test "wiggling" that must be done when a new fly rod is being examined. However, shaking and flexing a prospective rod doesn't provide a lot of information. Considering the proliferation and popularity of graphite rods, today's buyer can be even more in the fog than was the case three decades ago when bamboo and fiberglass rods were the major choices. Glass and bamboo are softer, more flexible actually, than most graphite or graphite composite shafts, making it easier to second guess how they'll perform.

A graphite rod feels stiffer, or less "whippy," which prompts some questions about its casting performance. In order to discover the real "feel" of a graphite rod requires that it be strung up with reel and line and taken outdoors for some test casting.

Even the less experienced caster can feel the quick recovery time of most graphite rods. They

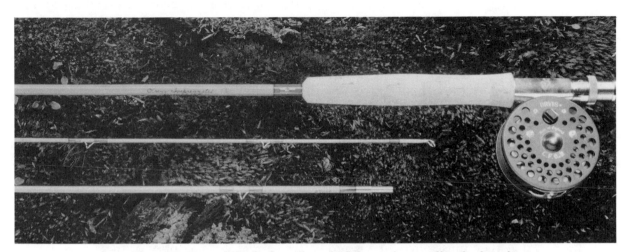

Bamboo rods are available from nearly fifty makers. All split-bamboo fly rods are handmade, thus insuring that no two are exactly alike. While cane rods are more fragile than graphite rods, many anglers appreciate their slower but extremely vibrant action.

Graphite rods are extremely light in relation to their casting power. While they can be broken if handled carelessly, they are practically impervious to the elements.

bend as the weight of the line is cast back and forth, just like bamboo and glass do, but they snap back to a straight attitude in a micro-second. This is what is meant by "fast recovery time." They simply respond faster to bending or stress. Graphite is also a lighter material than the other two mentioned, and this, combined with the fast recovery time, makes them much less taxing to fish with. It's fair to say that 90 percent or more of the fly rods that will be sold this year will be graphite or graphite-composite rods.

ROD ACTION

Now that we've settled on an 8-foot, 6-weight graphite rod, what more must be factored in? What about the cryptic designation known as "rod action?" In vintage tackle catalogs fly rods were described as having "wet fly," "dry fly," or "bass bug" actions. Today, three other words are used: slow, medium, or fast, with hyphenated combinations such as medium-to-fast. The rod makers have not joined in a plot to confuse the novice by throwing in still more options. They have learned that they must offer various rod actions to suit the casting styles and fishing preferences of individual rod buyers. As with golf clubs, tennis rackets, and baseball bats, not all rods perform the same when used by different people. Since human beings vary widely in size, strength, reflex time, and personality it follows that different tools chosen to hit different size balls will also vary. This is very much the case with fly rods.

The best choice for most beginners, and the kind of rod that fishes easiest for almost everyone, is a rod that is sensitive (bends easily) in the tip section and is less bendable in the butt section. When such a rod is flexed it should bend in a progressive curve instead of a semi-circle. This is referred to as a parabolic action. This sort of rod doesn't require the lightning-fast reflexes that some quick-action rods do and can help immensely when fighting a fish on a

small-diameter leader. We'll get into how rods bend during casting and fish fighting in another chapter, so for the time being, take my word for this: Buy a 6-weight rod with a slow-to-medium action. The clerks at most fly tackle shops will have several rods of this style for your examination.

Rods of the above configuration are available in all price ranges. While they vary tremendously in cosmetic style, quality of grips, guides, and reel seats, most rods on today's market are basically serviceable products. The old axiom of "getting what you pay for" is still true, but the rod shafts themselves are generally well made. This is not a blanket endorsement of all fly rods—sure, there are a few clunkers out there—it's just that it would be difficult to buy a rod from an established tackle company that would not perform adequately. In addition to the well-known rod makers, many custom shops and "boutique" suppliers turn out outstanding rods. These tailor-made rods usually begin with blanks (rod sections) supplied by a major manufacturer and are then fitted with all other accouterments. The price of these rods is usually determined by the fame and skill of the person doing the assembling.

Serviceable fly-rod outfits containing rod, reel, line, and a leader or two, from Cortland, Martin, Shakespeare, and several other makers can be found for under $75. As beginning equipment, they'll do just fine. The famous mail-order firms such as Orvis, L.L. Bean, and Cabela's also sell such outfits at slightly higher prices. Rods that sell between $100 and $200 are as "fishable" as the most expensive rods in the world. When rod prices are listed above $200, you're paying for nicer finishing, better hardware, and reputation.

Among the better known rod suppliers are: Fisher, G. Loomis, Orvis, Sage, Walton Powell, Winston, Thomas & Thomas, Deerfield, Cortland, Scott, Fenwick, Berkley, Eagle Claw, Hardy, Talon, Daiwa, Browning, Shakespeare, Garcia,

L.L. Bean, Cabela's, and St. Croix. I'm sure there are others that deserve mention, but I've examined or fished with rods made by these firms.

HARDWARE AND COSMETICS

All fly rods will cast better if they wear at least 10 guides, not counting the tip guide. An 8-foot rod with less than 10 guides may indeed be a fine rod, but it simply won't deliver the line in a smooth manner. A shortage of guides will also cause the rod to flex imperfectly when fighting a fish.

Good-quality metal guides are found on most rods today with special care being given to the butt, or stripping guide—the first one the line makes contact with as it leaves the reel. This is usually made of specially hardened metal or lined with ceramic. This guide and the tip-top are under constant friction and abrasion while casting and fighting fish and should be examined frequently for nicks and roughness. They should be silky smooth on a new rod. A damaged or poorly made stripping guide or tip-top will tear the finish from a fly line in short order.

The vast majority of fly rods designed for trout fishing are of the two-piece persuasion. Where they join is referred to as the "ferrule," and when assembled the rod should feel like a one-piece shaft. There should be no looseness or rocking. There seldom is, but if the rod you choose makes a perceptible noise when flexed or the hand detects a trace of movement, don't buy it. A rocking ferrule will soon wear out.

Rods that break down into three, four, or more sections have become very popular among anglers who travel a great deal by airplane. Short rod cases are also much easier to pack in small auto trunks. Multi-piece rods have not always been the fine casting tools they are today. Better designs now prevail, and so-called pack rods fish as well as any. If such a rod appeals, go ahead and buy one. I've used several of them for many years and those made by the better known manufacturers are totally reliable.

ROD GRIPS

Discussions of rod grip shape and length have filled many pages of fly-fishing books, and while some grips are more stylish than others, the overall shape really doesn't matter much from a functional standpoint. What does matter is the diameter and how you hold it. The only

Four-piece pack-rods are becoming increasingly popular among traveling anglers. Most casters find them comparable in performance to two- or three-piece rods.

way to discover which grip style feels best to you is to test several.

In measuring the circumference of rod grips that feel right to most experienced casters, I've discovered that $3\frac{1}{8}$ inches, or close to it, is a good compromise. This circumference translates into about $1\frac{1}{16}$ inches in diameter. If the grip tapers from front to rear, or is cigar-shaped, the hand can be slid back and forth until the best spot is found.

Most casters find it more efficient to place their thumb directly on top of the grip, aligning the thumb with the spine of the rod. The thumb is the strongest finger and provides much of the power needed for control. Some casters, out of preference or physical necessity, place their forefinger on top of the rod. If this feels comfortable, there's no reason not to do it. If you only fish on weekends, using the forefinger as the "power" finger can be tiring. For short range fishing, however, the finger on top proves to be very accurate for many anglers. Obviously, gripping a handle this way requires that the front end of the grip taper down to nearly nothing where it meets the butt section. If the thumb is placed on top, a grip that flares or is thick at the front end will feel much better at the end of the day.

A too-thick grip is an abomination. It will tax the wrist and cause the rod to eventually twist in the hand after an hour or so. Rod makers shudder to think of their finely tuned shafts being worked on, but sanding one a bit here and there is recommended if the grip doesn't feel comfortable. Begin with medium-grit sandpaper, sanding and testing until it feels right, and then finish it off with fine-grit paper. After all, it's your rod and you're the one it should satisfy. Remember, take off a little at a time and test it—you can easily sand off more cork but you can't put it back!

What's known as "specie" cork is the only acceptable fly-rod grip material. Synthetic foams and such feel terrible when casting and soak up water like a sponge. All good cork comes from Portugal and is graded by ladies who learn how to do it by trial and error. Rod makers and anglers must depend on them to choose well since they have a corner on the market.

REEL SEATS

There are three basic types of reel seats: up-locking, down-locking, and sliding rings. The locking styles are more secure and are used by most rod makers. Sliding rings are most often seen on bamboo rods where reducing hardware weight is desired. If reels are attached and removed frequently, wear will occur on the cork or wooden reel seat base causing the reel to drop off at some inopportune moment due to loose rings. This can be solved by applying a few wraps of electrical tape around band and reel foot. Few problems occur with locking reel seats.

Anglers who grip a rod near the rear will prefer up-locking reel seats. If the threaded ring is at the front, accidental unscrewing can happen with annoying results. A wrap of tape here can help matters, but an up-locking reel seat solves it forever. There are all sorts of materials used in reel seats, with strong aluminum alloys and stainless steel being the best. Wooden inserts look nice and seldom cause any problems unless dropped on a hard surface or otherwise abused.

REELS FOR TROUT AND PANFISH

The late Vince Marinaro, a fly-fishing guru, once said, "It's the rod that delivers the fly but the reel that fights the fish." That he was right is now accepted by most angler-writers, but it wasn't always. Even into the 1960s, some well-traveled anglers were still repeating the worn shibboleth that a fly reel merely provided a place to store the line when it was not being cast. In spite of some excellent fly reels being available a hundred years ago, other tackle items were not nearly as efficient. Until the creation of nylon, gut leaders were famous for failing at critical moments, fly lines were difficult to cast beyond thirty feet, and the rods which delivered them were, for the most part, short-range instruments. The catching of large fish was far more the result of good luck rather than good tackle. Fly rodders today scarcely raise an eyebrow when they hear of someone catching a 5-pound trout on a leader that tests 2 pounds or less. Of course, a measure of skill is involved but such a feat would not be so regularly reported if we didn't have good tackle and, particularly, such wonderful reels.

Fly reels designed to hold a 6-weight fly line and an adequate amount of backing are made by just about every quality reel manufacturer. A few makers specialize in larger-capacity, more rugged reels for saltwater, but even some of these are made in small sizes that work perfectly

for trout. These huskier reels, by the way, usually have wonderfully smooth drags, which is the reel feature that helps so much when fighting a large fish on a very fine leader.

Drag, durability, and design are the three "Ds" to look for in a fly reel. There's a fourth "D" to consider if you're concerned about your tackle's eye appeal—decoration. How does it blend with the cosmetics of the rod you chose?

The first three "Ds" are functionally joined. That is, if the reel was well thought out in the first place (a good design) it will probably have a smooth drag and last a long time as well. Its overall "good looks" is, of course, an entirely subjective matter. Some anglers for example, are not fond of gold- or silver-colored reels, while others think basic black is too plain. A smooth-working drag is not a subjective matter, and it's the first quality one should consider.

In the vernacular of fly fishing, there are two

Orvis CFO fly reel has become an American standard in less than twenty-five years. Rugged, lightweight with a dependable drag, it's an excellent choice for all trout fishing.

System 1 from Scientific Anglers is a good trout reel at a reasonable price. The drag knob is especially easy to grasp and adjust.

Fly fishing reels from Hardy of England have been around for nearly two centuries. Their simple spring-and-pawl drag system has proven itself worldwide.

Venerable Pflueger Medalist is America's best-known fly reel. It seems to last for an angling lifetime and then some. The ingenious drag system has never been successfully copied.

New reel names with innovative features appear (and vanish) every year. Among the latest of these are the unique yet traditional-appearing reels from Ryall Machine Works. The drag system makes full contact between the axle of the reel frame and the axle housing of the spool. An extremely smooth reel; the figured wood disc adds nice cosmetic touch.

definitions of the word *drag* and they are not related. A floating fly and the leader attached to it are said to "drag" when the current moves either of them so that the fly floats unnaturally. When applied to reels, *drag* refers to the tension or pressure applied to the reel spool which prevents it from rotating too rapidly. As more drag is applied, more effort on the part of the fish is required to pull line from the reel spool. At what tension point to "set the drag" is determined by the breaking test of the leader. Therefore, it must be set so a sustained pull will not break the leader. Obviously, the finer the leader, the lighter the drag setting. *Note:* With leaders

testing less than 2 pounds, all that's needed is enough drag to prevent the spool from rotating backwards, or "backlashing."

Regardless of how slight or tight the drag adjustment is applied, the reel spool should begin to turn without stutters or jerks when line is pulled from it. This smooth release of line is what protects a small-diameter leader from breaking as a fish begins a run or shakes its head. If the line pays off the reel in a herky-jerky manner, a sizable fish will probably be lost in short order. All the tackle shop talk about smooth drag is not idle chatter. When a fish takes off on a fast run, the reel spool jumps from idle to high-rotational speed in a heart-beat. A drag that can do this without chattering or hanging up is what we're looking for.

It's easy to determine the drag efficiency of the reel that catches your eye. Wind a few feet of line onto the spool and pull it out—in jerks—at different drag settings. Pulling out at a constant speed won't prove much. Instead, pull it out in fits and starts, fast, then slow, then jerk-jerk-jerk. There should be no stickiness or rough spots. If there are, consider another reel.

FLY LINES

To the novice caster the thick fly line, as compared with monofilament or braided line, appears to be a disadvantage in delivering the small and delicate artificial insects we call flies. Exactly the reverse is true. In order to make the fly rod flex and carry the much thinner leader along with the air-resistant fly, the fly line must have considerable heft. The weight of a fly line is indicated on the box or factory spool by a number. The numbers commonly used by most manufacturers run from 2 to 13 with the largest number being the heaviest. The numbers are determined by how much the first 30 feet of each line weighs in grains. All major fly-line makers share this numbering system.

Along with the numbers used to identify fly lines are two or three letters which tell us if the line is designed to sink (S) or float (F), and for what purpose the line is best suited. Fly fishing for trout and panfish is best done with a dou-ble-tapered, floating fly line. Double-tapered lines are of equal diameter at both ends and much thicker in the center portion. Such a line, if it is a 6-weight line, will be labeled DT6F. A 5-weight line of the same configuration would be a DT5F, and so on. A weight-forward line is thin for the first 8 or 10 feet, thicker for 20 to 25 feet, and then back to thin for the balance of the line. Such lines are more efficient for long distance casting or for casting large, wind-resis-tant flies. The usual combination of letters and numbers for a weight-forward, number 6 line would be WF6F (floating) or WF6S (sinking) or WF6ST (sink-tip). With the last designation, only the front 6 feet or so of the line is designed to sink.

The letter L indicates a level line which is of equal diameter over its entire length. Level lines are perfectly suitable for fly fishing at ranges under 30 feet. They will also work reasonably well for casting heavy bass bugs and flies when using longer rods.

Within these combinations of letters and numbers some special factory designations crop up such as bass-taper, rocket-taper, bug-taper, and saltwater taper. Basically, these are modifi-cations of the weight-forward (WF) designa-tion. A look at the accompanying illustration of fly line types will answer most questions about the taper code.

One could argue whether the rod, reel, leader, line, or fly is the most important compo-nent of the quintet needed for fly fishing, but it's the line that blends the parts into a func-tional unit. Put another way, without a suitable line, successful fly casting is difficult at best.

A 3-weight line used with a rod designed to cast an 8-weight line isn't heavy enough to flex (bend) the rod. Conversely, a 9-weight line on a rod rated for a 3 line will overburden the lighter shaft by causing it to flex too much. How the fly line joins with the rod to deliver the fly will be covered in more detail in the chapter on casting.

Most fly lines made today are coated with a form of PVC (polyvinylchloride), which is applied to a core of braided nylon. The coating can be applied in varying thicknesses. The resulting diameter(s) is what produces level, double-tapered and weight-forward designa-tions. The braided core is the same diameter throughout the length of the line. "Secret" machines apply the PVC coating, and if you think it's tough to get into Fort Knox, just try to get a peek at one of them!

Configurations of fly lines vary considerably from maker to maker, but they follow these general taper styles. Most trout fishing can be done with a double-taper line if you usually cast less than sixty feet. Beyond that, a forward-taper line will work much better.

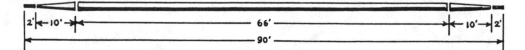

Double Taper. For casting trout flies and small popping bugs where extreme distance is not required. The larger body section provides weight for casting; the tapered ends assure a light presentation. Line can be reversed for longer use.

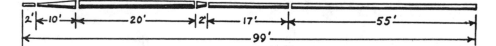

Weight Forward. For casting large, bushy flies, large streamers, and popping bugs. This line begins like the double taper, with 12 feet of tapered line. But instead of a long level section, there is a 30-foot section of heavy level line, then a quick taper down to a thinner running line for the rest of its length.

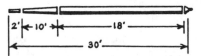

Shooting Taper. For long-distance casting. Behind the 12-foot taper, there's an 18-foot length of heavy level line with a factory-installed loop at the end to which a monofilament or floating line is attached.

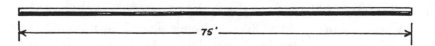

Level Line. For fishing live bait or situations where long casts or delicate presentation are not required.

Fly lines are available in a huge assortment of configurations, colors, and performance characteristics. While the beginner won't go far wrong with any well-known brand, a certain line may perform much better on one rod than it will on another. Stores that cater to fly rodders have trial lines to test. Take advantage of this service.

One or two fly-line makers do not use PVC or braided cores, and the future may see some totally new coating materials appear. In the meantime, PVC gives us a long-lasting product. Simple maintenance requires wiping the line with a soft cloth coated with mild soap and water and a final wipe with line dressing. Leon Chandler, legendary line maker with Cortland for fifty years, says, "Modern fly lines will last twice as long with frequent cleaning. I'm amazed at how few anglers take time to do it."

Should color be a factor in selecting a fly line? This debate has been softly simmering for many years and probably will for many more. It's a harmless argument because the fish are not likely to tell us what they think. With monofilament line (when the lure is tied directly to the line) or with monofilament fly leaders, color can be a factor, but with fly lines color is only important in the eye of the angler. When the fly is separated from the line by several feet of mono leader, which it usually is, it doesn't appear to matter much.

A floating fly line, regardless of color, appears dark gray or black on the water when viewed from beneath (at least it does to human eyes because I've checked this out in a wet suit). For this reason, any sort of fishing that requires a floating line could be done with any color line. Many tests have proven that with a 6-foot or longer leader, the fish don't seem to care. In dry-fly fishing, factors other than line color are much more critical.

Conversely, the color of a sinking line may be

important in a number of situations because the line is down there in the fish's field of view. That's why sinking lines are generally forest green, dark brown, or gray.

Choosing a fly line from most of today's established makers should not cause the beginner any loss of sleep. They're all "fishable" products and can be used with confidence. As with other tackle items, the subtleties and nuances of which product is best for your kind of fly casting and fishing will be discovered. As your experience and fishing horizons expand, you'll find certain equipment to be better suited to your skills. What a wonderful way to learn!

LEADERS

It seems logical to assume that the term "leader" came to be because it "leads" to the fly and also "leads" the fly through the water. The leader's primary purpose is to create the impression of the fly being unattached to the line. We're trying to fool the fish into believing that our offering is just there, all by itself. While I'm convinced that the fish can always see the leader (no matter how thin it is), it's quite obvious that simply tying the fly to the thick fly line won't work. You can't pass the line through the eye of small fly hooks!

Monofilament nylon is the only material presently considered to be suitable for fly-fishing leaders. Prior to about 1940, silkworm gut was the preferred material for nearly 200 years. In Shakespeare's time, hairs from white horse tails were the only choice. Current knowledge concerning the qualities of horse hair is limited, but plenty of anglers are still alive who fished extensively with silkworm gut.

Silkworm gut was actually obtained from the innards of the silkworm. Some forgotten genius discovered that by removing the silk gland from the larval form of the silk moth and stretching it, a strong, flexible strand could be obtained. By soaking the "worm" in varying amounts of vinegar and water, different diameters could be obtained. Not a very scientific process to be sure, but one that provided enough different "pound-tests" for making tapered leaders.

In truth, silkworm gut leaders worked quite well, and for several years after monofilament arrived some veterans were reluctant to switch. They thought gut was more flexible (when wet) and less visible than mono. But gut leaders had to be cared for. Gut was brittle and wiry when dry and had to be well-soaked before using. All fly anglers used to carry little flat tins with damp felt pads in them. These tins kept the leader ready for use when fishing commenced. Gut leaders are recalled with a small measure of nostalgic reverence—but that's about all. Modern monofilament is so superior there can be no comparison.

Tapered leaders are the best choice for all forms of fly fishing. They not only cast better but allow a smoother presentation of the fly.

Store-bought leaders are better today than a few years ago. Most leaders were an abomination to cast and some were so poorly tied they couldn't be depended on to last the day. Those now available are well made and well designed and will serve the fly angler adequately until his skills and experience demand more.

As the last mechanical link between angler and fly, the leader determines what sort of "landing" the fly will make. How well the angler makes his cast depends heavily on skill and compatibility of line to rod. But if the leader doesn't perform well it can mess up the entire plan. If it hits like a rock or doubles back on itself unpleasant things happen. A leader that behaves itself is a delight.

All leaders work better when the heavy butt end is stiffer than the slimmer tippet end. They do because the heavier line transfers its moving energy into thick material with more force than it does to thin material. Not being a physicist, I don't know why this is so, it just is.

Leaders with thin butts seldom straighten out as the cast unfurls.

Some ready-made tapered leaders will require the addition of a longer butt section in order to make them cast well and, of course, the addition of a new tippet or end section will be necessary as flies are changed. The diameter of leader material is measured in thousandths of an inch or millimeters, and these numbers are usually printed on the packages. The pound-test of the material is there too and so is the "X" rating. All of this information varies slightly among the various brands, but these differences are not significant. From 8-pound test and higher, the pound-test rating is enough to remember and below that the "X" rating will suffice. Here's a chart that shows what the terms mean from 7 pound to the smallest practical fishing diameters.

Tippet Size	Diameter	Pound-Test	Suitable Hook Sizes
1X	.010 in.	7	4, 6
2X	.009 in.	6	6, 8, 10
3X	.008 in.	4.5	8, 10, 12
4X	.007 in.	3.5	12, 14, 16
5X	.006 in.	2.5	14, 16, 18
6X	.005 in.	1.5	16, 18, 20
7X	.004 in.	1	18, 20, 22

Tippet material of less than 7X is useful at times when flies smaller than size 22 are needed, but great care must be taken when tying knots in such gossamer strands and even greater care

applied when playing the fish. A gentle hand on the rod is called for here. Even the most expert of fly fishermen don't land all fish hooked on fine tippets.

We need a tapered leader for fly fishing for two important reasons. First, it's impossible to push some sizes of leader material through the small eyes of fly hooks. The leader diameter must be appropriate for the size hook being used. Second, the weightless fly can't be cast delicately without having a gradual transition from thick fly line to the thin diameter leader that's attached to the fly. The mechanical process of fly casting depends on all of the components working together and the leader is an equal partner in the process.

TYING YOUR OWN LEADERS

Tying your own tapered leaders is not nearly as difficult as it may seem. The sections can be tied together with either the blood knot or surgeon's knot, and unless you have some physical handicap, you can learn to tie them quickly. Check the illustrations for directions and then practice. Yes, you'll be a bit awkward at first, but once you get the knack the skill will never leave you.

The illustration showing the lengths and diameters of the segments in two basic leaders can be used as a guide for making leaders of any length. A 7-foot is about as short as you'll ever need for even the tiniest of streams, but there are times you may want a much longer one.

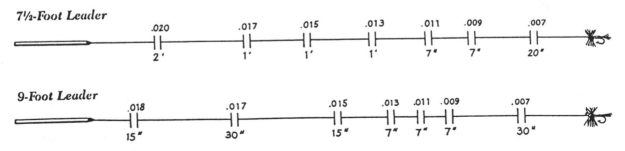

Two basic fly leaders suitable for trout or salmon fishing.

With either formula, add a proportional amount of that leader diameter to each section; 6 inches added to what was a 1-foot section means adding an inch or so to a 7-inch section. Be advised: this isn't brain surgery so if you're off a few inches here and there it won't matter. The important thing is to build a leader in such a way that the transition from thick to thin is done in a gradual manner. When using heavier flies—say, wet flies or streamers of size 8 or larger—some of the short sections can be eliminated. If the tippet end desired is .009 inch or thicker, use longer sections of the two diameters behind it and go with a 30-inch section of .009.

The two leaders illustrated will work well with most outfits for trout fishing. For Atlantic salmon, steelheads, bass, and other species where larger flies and bugs are more often the standard fare, some modifications will have to be made. Similarly, fish with formidable teeth in their jaws such as northern pike, muskellunge, and many saltwater species require different leader arrangements. Leaders for these purposes will be discussed in the appropriate chapters. In the mean-time, tie a couple of these basic leaders and become familiar with the knot tying procedures.

It's a good idea to always have a couple of spare leaders tied and ready to go—and carry them while on the stream. Most of the time merely tying on a new tippet will see one through a fishing day, but when disaster strikes and a leader becomes hopelessly tangled, frayed, or broken, the spare will be welcome.

RIGGING UP

Now that you have a rod, reel, line, and leader, you have to learn how to rig a fly outfit. The first thing you have to do is attach anywhere from 50 to 100 yards of 20-pound-test braided dacron backing to the fly reel. The backing serves as insurance in case you tie into a big fish that runs off with all your fly line. It also serves to fill up the reel spool. Attach the backing to the fly reel with a *slip knot*. Then attach the other end of the backing to the end of your fly line with a *nail knot*. Attach your leader to the end of the fly line with either a

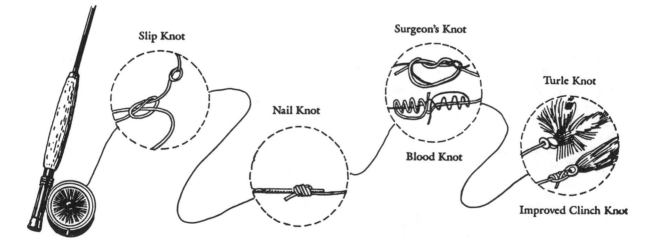

Here's how to rig a fly outfit. Tie the backing to the reel spool with the *slip knot*. Tie the other end of the backing to the fly line with the *nail knot*, the leader to the fly line with either the *nail knot*, or with the *loop-to-loop* knot. Leader sections are connected with the blood knot or the Surgeon's knot. Tie the fly to the leader with the turle knot or the improved clinch knot.

loop -to-loop knot (see drawing of the surgeon's loop), or a nail knot. If you need an extra tippet at the end of the leader, attach it with a blood knot or surgeon's knot. Finally, tie the fly to the end of the tippet with an *improved clinch knot* or *turle knot*.

NAIL KNOT

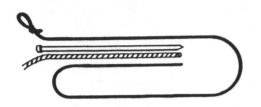

1. Lay the leader, a finishing nail, and the line side by side, holding them in your left fingers. Then form a large loop, bringing the point of the leader under the line, and grasp it, too, with the left fingers. (Loop is shown much smaller than in actuality.)

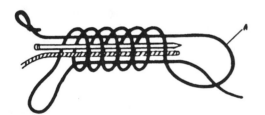

2. Grasp the loop in the right hand at about point A and wind it around all the strands toward the left hand— about five turns.

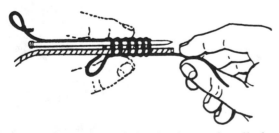

3. Grasp the point of the leader and pull the entire loop through the coils, holding line, butt, and nail as shown. Then carefully remove the nail, and tighten the knot by pulling on both the butt and the point at the same time.

SURGEON'S END LOOP

Use this knot to tie a loop in the end of a line for attaching leaders or other terminal tackle quickly.

1. Double end of line to form loop and tie an overhand knot at the base of double line.

2. Leave loop open in knot and bring doubled line through once more.

3. Hold standing line and tag end and pull loop to tighten knot. Size of loop can be determined by pulling loose knot to desired point

SIMPLIFIED BLOOD KNOT

This is used for tying monofilament line to leader or one length of leader to another. It works best with lines of equal or nearly equal diameter.

1. Take the two lines' ends and tie a simple overhand knot (which will be clipped off later). Then tighten to combine the two lines into one.

2. Form a loop where the two lines meet, with the overhand knot in the loop.

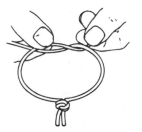

3. Pull one side of the loop down and begin taking turns with it around the standing line. Keep point where turns are made open so turns gather equally on each side.

4. After eight or ten turns, reach through center opening and pull remaining loop (and overhand knot) through. Keep finger in this loop so it will not spring back.

5. Hold loop with teeth and pull both ends of line, making turns gather on either side of loop.

6. Set knot by pulling lines tightly as possible. Tightening coils will make loop stand out perpendicular to line. Then clip off the loop close to the knot.

SURGEON'S KNOT

This knot joins a leader to line just like the simplified blood knot, but is used with lines of different diameters.

_____

1. Lay line and leader parallel, overlapping 6 to 8 inches.

2. Treating the two like a single line, tie an overhand knot, pulling the entire leader through the loop.

3. Leaving loop of the overhand open, pull both tag end of line and leader through again.

4. Hold both lines and both ends to pull knot tight. Clip ends close to avoid foul-up in rod guides.

IMPROVED CLINCH KNOT

This is a dependable knot for tying a fly with a straight-eye hook to the end of the leader..

TURLE KNOT

This is a good alternative to the clinch knot. With it you get a straight pull on the fly.

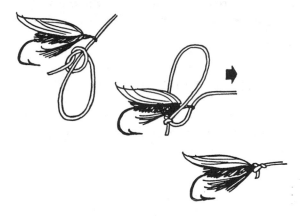

ACCESSORIES

Vests

Fly fishing in streams requires carrying your tackle and accessories on your person. The best way to accomplish this is by wearing a vest or jacket that has a lot of pockets. Over the years, manufacturers and designers have tried just about every imaginable pocket combination with varying results. Selection of the right vest may seem like an insignificant matter to the beginner, but as one logs more time on the

water this angling item becomes very important. It is a kind of traveling workshop.

The most annoying discovery I can think of, when wearing a new vest, is that the pockets won't accommodate the fly boxes, leader packages, and assorted sundries that I want to carry. If the most convenient outside pocket isn't large enough to hold a favorite fly box, that particular

Buttons, zippers, snaps and Velcro closures are all acceptable on fishing vests. Which way the zippers open and the placement of them are important considerations. Some pockets and closing devices are not well placed on some vests. Be sure to experiment by trying on the garment.

vest will not be a joy to use. If the zippers open the wrong way or the pockets are so shallow that everything falls out when you bend over, there will be more unhappy moments. By all means, measure your fly boxes and all other gear you intend to carry to be sure that the vest you plan to buy will accept them. The best plan is to try on the vest before buying it to discover if the fit and pocket arrangement are right for your purposes. If you order one from a mail order house be sure they have a return and exchange policy.

Muted colors, such as tan, gray, olive, etc., are the best choices for vests. Avoid bright colors unless you're posing for a cover shot. White vests and hats should be avoided for stream fishing where the local scenery usually includes some greenery and generally dark backgrounds. The white-clad angler will stand out like a neon sign and may spook the fish. Florescent orange should also be avoided for the same reason. If you carry a lot of gear, try to find a vest that has a padded yoke and shoulders. This will ease the all-day strain on the back muscles.

Vests come in several lengths and the kind of water you fish most of the time is the determining factor. A waist-level model will be suitable for most trout fishing. A chest-high style is a better choice for those who expect to do a lot of wading for salmon and steelhead.

Waders and Hip Boots

As with the length of the wading vest, the choice between waders and boots is largely determined by water depth. At least 50 percent of the trout streams in the world can be fished in hip boots. They are easier to get into and also much cooler during hot weather. Waders, especially the flexible Neoprene kind, will be appreciated when the water and the air temperature are on the chilly side. Waders are also more comfortable for sitting down on a damp stream bank or wet log. If your budget can handle it and you expect to be doing a lot of fishing in a variety of waters, owning "hippers" and waders is good insurance.

With either hip boots or waders the choice of

Felt soles on wading shoes, boot-foot waders or hip-length boots are the best choice. Some wading soles are flat, but for more comfortable walking, a prominent heel is preferable.

sole materials is extremely important. In some fast-moving streams there isn't much algae or mud coating the rocky bottoms. A molded rubber sole will suffice here and such soles are easier to walk in if a lot of hiking is necessary. On the other hand, if there is the slightest chance that slippery rocks will be encountered, felt soles are strongly recommended. The absolute compromise sole for nearly every bottom situation is a felt sole equipped with metal studs firmly attached to the sole of the wader or boot foot.

The choice between boot-foot and stocking-foot waders should be based on what is most comfortable and how much walking is expected. If you have weak ankles or expect to do a considerable amount of hiking, stocking foot waders combined with wading shoes will be the best choice. Boot-foot waders are easier and quicker to get into but do not provide much firmness about the ankle. Experience is the best teacher here, so the beginner should choose which kind feels best at first and try them for a season or two.

Neoprene waders are the most popular at the moment because of their excellent flexibility and insulating properties. They are a bit on the heavy side (although not so heavy as the rubber-coated, fabric jobs), but this is offset by the comfort factor in cold water. The super-light, nylon shell waders are great for walking and warm weather, but they do not offer much protection against the cold unless long underwear bottoms are worn beneath them.

Wading shoes come in dozens of styles, colors, and materials. Leather wading shoes are the most comfortable but they require more care than do fabric or fabric and leather combinations. When not in use, leather shoes should be periodically dried and treated with the leather preservative recommended by the maker. If lacing shoes is a problem, several companies offer shoes that feature Velcro closures. Shop around. The choice of wading gear is wide and you're sure to find something you'll like.

Landing Net

Since more and more anglers are releasing their trout to swim another day, landing nets are being used selectively. Small trout often get caught in the webbing and become injured. So when landing a trout under 15 inches, it's safer to run your hand down the leader, twist the

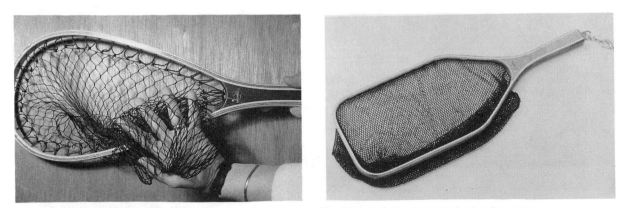

A landing net (left) is necessary for large fish. For fish under 15 inches, it's safer to slide your hand down the leader and back out the hook without touching the fish. Model at right is one of many new shapes designed for catch-and release angling.

barbless hook out of the fish's mouth, and set it free without touching it. Larger trout may be too scrappy for this treatment and you'll need your net to get them out of the water. Special landing nets are now sold for catch-and-release fishing. The frame is oblong and the netting tight so the fish can be easily unhooked and released.

Fly Boxes

If an angler carries a wide assortment of flies there's no question about the kind of fly boxes to buy. They should be the plastic "shell" variety. These weigh practically nothing and come in a nearly unlimited number of sizes, styles, and compartments. Every fly fishing shop and catalog offers them and practically all of them are of near equal quality. If used a great deal, the hinges will eventually give up but their low cost makes replacement a small matter. If dropped in the water, they will float, unlike the metal boxes that usually sink at the precise moment they

drift over the deepest part of the pool you happen to be fishing in.

Good-looking, long-lasting metal boxes, the ones with little metal clips for streamers and wet flies, also have advantages. They are nearly indestructible and allow instant examination of the contents. They are also heavy. Nevertheless, they have their admirers.

Some extremely good-looking fly boxes are now being offered that are formed from highly figured walnut, maple, cherry, and exotic woods such as bubinga. They are lined with a durable synthetic foam and hold all types of flies in a secure manner. If you want to dazzle your pals, these boxes are sure to do it. Less expensive, molded-plastic boxes lined with the same material or featuring dry-fly compartments are another choice. Whichever boxes you choose, remember, be sure they fit the pockets of your vest.

Wet flies and streamers used to be carried in fly "books." These were usually made of leather with several "pages" of felt, sheepskin, or other soft fabric into which the hooks were impaled.

Fly boxes are available in many sizes, materials, configurations and, of course, prices. The inexpensive plastic models are excellent choices for dry flies and they weigh next to nothing. The metal boxes featuring metal clips are ideal for wet flies of all sizes, including salmon and steelhead flies. They are, however, quite heavy if more than three of them are in front pockets.

Anglers with a hankering for the good old days still use them, but beware. If you stick a damp fly into one of the leaves you run the risk of having a rusty hook the next time you use that fly.

Hardware

An essential tool is a pair of fingernail clippers. Ideally, they should hang from a thong tied to one of the D rings on your vest or on a retractable string holder. They're used for cutting monofilament. Buy them three at time. You will lose at least two and the third one will be dull by the time the season is over.

With catch-and-release being standard procedure these days, forceps, hemostats, needle-holders, or some sort of small pliers have become necessary for hook removal. Nothing

A knife of some sort should be carried by every angler. Two knives are not out of place, but one of them should be equipped with a pair of scissors. Tweezers are also handy.

Clippers will be used more than any other tool hanging from a fly fisherman's vest. The quality of these varies. The best ones are but a dollar or so more than the worst ones.

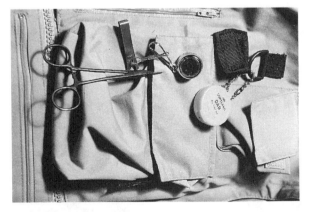

The left breast pocket of the author's vest always wears these three items: fly dressing, clippers and a hemostat for removing hooks from fish and pinching down the barbs.

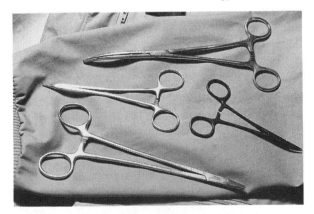

Hemostats, needle-holders, hook removers, whatever you wish to call them, have become essential for all fly anglers. The best ones are surgical-grade tools and will last forever.

beats the cross-hatched jaws of surgical needle-holders, but the pliers made specifically for anglers are serviceable and cheaper. (If you know a surgeon, beg a discarded needle-holder.)

The need for a pocketknife and scissors occurs often enough when fly fishing to warrant carrying them. The best plan is to carry both in a multi-bladed, Swiss-style knife. There are many models of these ranging from those large enough to build a log cabin to tiny ones that are difficult to hold in an adult hand. Check them out at the tackle store and select one that contains scissors, a blade of 2 inches or more, and a built-in pair of tweezers. These can also be carried on a thong, but be careful not to overload the front of the vest with too many dangling tools.

You don't really need a thermometer, but it's nice to know the water temperature at times. If a check reveals that the water is less than 50 degrees, for example, you may elect to use a streamer or wet fly instead of a dry fly for your first cast. Identifying a cooler stretch of stream during hot weather or warmer water when the air is nippy will frequently pay off. Most well-stocked tackle shops carry thermometers that are protected by a metal sheath, with an attached pocket clip.

Fly Floatant

For the very first cast over a large or selective fish, some anglers elect not to use any "dope" on their dry fly. Once the fly becomes water-logged or coated with fish slime you'll need some. The concern used to be the oil-like ring on the water surrounding the fly that came from some liquid dressings. Many of the paste forms of fly floatant don't form a ring and for that reason are the best ones to buy. Before applying the paste, be sure the fly is dry and don't rub on so much that the hackles become matted. Carry a few folded paper towels for squeezing the moisture out of the fly. When the fly is dry, rub the end of the forefinger into the paste container and massage the fly gently with floatant.

Miscellaneous

Extra paper towels are handy items in all fishing vests for a number of reasons, as are toilet tissues. A pack of matches in a waterproof container, a candy bar, a whistle, a couple of adhesive bandages, and a small tube of antiseptic won't take up much space and should be considered.

A paste or liquid fly dressing (floatant) is another necessity, even if you only fish with dry flies a few times each season. The liquids seem to last longer on the fly itself, but the paste forms don't evaporate as quickly.

2

The Trouts

BROOK TROUT

The brook trout, *Salvelinus fontinalis*, is an all-American fish. The obligatory reminder that the brook trout is not a trout at all, but a char, matters little to most anglers. Of more importance is the fact that *none* of the true trout is indigenous to that part of North America which lies east of the Rocky Mountains. The brookie was all there was. It has been transplanted to waters around the globe and done well, but the lion's share of them, and certainly the largest, are still found on the North American continent.

The record class brookies are in Labrador, Ontario, and Quebec. The Appalachian mountain streams and ponds, from Maine to Georgia, hold tens of millions of them. A brook trout of 5 pounds is not unusual in Canada (14 pounds, 8 ounces is the world record), whereas a 2-pounder is considered a nice fish anywhere else. But most brook trout are spoken of in inches instead of pounds. The average? Impossible to state for sure, probably less than 10 inches.

What the brook trout lacks in size is compensated for by its beauty, its willingness to take

flies, and its availability. Wherever the water remains cool and there's enough of it to cover its back, the brook trout can survive. Tiny rivulets that can be stepped across are often great brook trout producers. Autumn and early winter spawners, brook trout are able to maintain strong populations without much help from man if the water remains uncontaminated. They are also easily produced in hatcheries for stocking in waters that don't provide suitable spawning conditions. They are the fish that taught many of us what this angling business is all about.

Although no freshwater fish is as beautiful as a male brook trout, the species is not terribly smart. Brookies are much easier to catch than are the other trouts. In small streams they will come to the surface in very cold weather to grab a dry fly. They will strike baits and lures that are too big to swallow and are seldom as selective as other trout when a hatch of flies is present. Conversely, where the fish are born in the stream at hand, they can be extremely cautious. They'll run for cover at the slightest movement or shadow. Drop a fly into a tiny pool without spooking

Stream-born brook trout from a Quebec river—handsome fish with prominent white-edged fins. Veteran angler Jim Cox contemplates his dinner. Even in remote waters, four is enough to keep.

These are pan-size native brookies that taught so many youngsters how to fish for trout. Bluish-gray sides with red spots ringed with blue halos are typical brook markings. Brook trout have no black spots.

A 4-pound brook trout is a trophy almost anywhere. This fish is an old-timer among trout and is probably between 8 and 9 years old. It's an egg-laden female and was released as the camera clicked.

A typical river rainbow. Plenty of black spots peppering the sides with a distinct pink band extending from gill covers to tail. Rainbow trout have no red spots.

A two-foot rainbow about to be released in the correct manner. Note that this fish is heavily spotted on the gill covers; usually the sign of a stream-reared fish.

look for small red spots set in halos of pale blue and the vermiculations or "turkey track" markings on the back. The fins, especially during late summer and fall, are reddish orange rimmed with white and black lines. Even the brook trout that run to sea (yes, some of them do) take on bright colors when they enter freshwater for spawning chores. At sea, they look like bars of stainless steel.

RAINBOW TROUT

This fish, recently reclassified as *Oncorhynchus mykiss* (was *Salmo gairdneri*), has a dual personality. It is the ordinary rainbow trout of streams and lakes and is also the anadromous or seagoing steelhead. One variety or another has been transported from the western coast of America to every continent on the globe.

They grow to trophy size in New Zealand, southern South America, and a number of lakes in Great Britain and Europe. Widely distributed in the United States, the largest rainbows are found in Alaska, British Columbia, the Pacific drainage states, and in the Great Lakes. The steelhead strains that spend feeding time in the

them and you're almost sure to hook one.

Identifying brook trout is not difficult if the beginning angler remembers one positive clue. Brook trout have no black spots. After that,

A handsome rainbow of over 10 pounds with the well-defined line just above the middle of the flank. The back is grayish-green, often seen on lake-dwelling trout.

ocean are the giants of the clan. The all-tackle record, caught in Alaska, weighed a whopping 42 pounds.

The fly-caught fish of the world average around the 1-pound mark, maybe less. But that doesn't mean that plenty of big rainbows aren't taken on flies. Fish of over 20 pounds are caught every year, with 5- to 10-pounders being quite common on the West Coast and in the Great Lakes. Generally rainbows average smaller, with a 4-pounder being considered a trophy.

Rainbow trout are somewhere between brookies and brown trout on the intelligence scale. They are not usually as skittish as brook trout and seldom display the hyper-selectivity that browns are famous for. There are, however, some exceptions to this generality. In hard-fished waters, rainbows of all sizes are more cautious, and the sea-going steelhead goes through periods of "angler contempt."

In most waters the rainbow is a spring spawner, and as mating time approaches, the males become vividly marked with a band of bright pink or red that extends from gill covers to the root of the tail. The females also have a somewhat less brilliant stripe. Steelheads take on this spawning stripe after being in freshwater for a week or so, but when they enter the rivers they are as silver on the flanks as newly minted coins. Their backs at this time are steely-gray. Rainbow trout have only *black* spots.

CUTTHROAT TROUT

This fish, *Oncorhynchus clarki,* is to the Rocky Mountain states what the brookie is to the eastern regions. It is the native trout of the high country and can be found (like the brookie) in very small creeks as well as in lakes and large rivers. It's a willing taker most of the time but, like the rainbow, can wise up when fished for extensively.

In some waters, the cut may be confused with the rainbow because they do interbreed. But if you see a slash of red or bright orange at the lower edge of the gill covers it's a cutthroat for sure. There are many strains of cutthroats that vary in average size, number of black spots, and area of rosy-red on the gill covers. A rule of thumb is, if it looks a lot like a rainbow but doesn't have quite so many black spots, it's probably a cutthroat.

BROWN TROUT

Without question, the brown trout, *Salmo trutta,* is the fish most responsible for lifting fly fishing to its loftiest level. It was the trout of Izaak Walton's time and the one that British and European anglers tied their flies for. It was the trout that dry-fly fishing was made for, or perhaps, the other way around. The British took brown trout fry and eggs just about everyplace they visited over a century ago and the places they didn't stock them, others did. It appears that John P. Creveling received the first brown eggs from the Netherlands at his hatchery near Marietta, Pennsylvania, in 1883. Other fish soon followed from England, Scotland, and Germany. Within forty years, brown trout were well established from coast to coast.

Some anglers were not happy about the introduction of the brown trout to U.S. waters. The fish grew fast and in many waters soon replaced the native species. They were labeled "cannibals" by fisherman who hated to see their beloved brookies, rainbows, and cutthroats vanish. Overlooked was the fact that timbering, pollution, and water degradation of all sorts was doing far more damage to the native fish than the brown trout were. The happy part of the story is that brown trout are hardier and able to live and thrive in less than perfect habitats. The brown trout is here to stay.

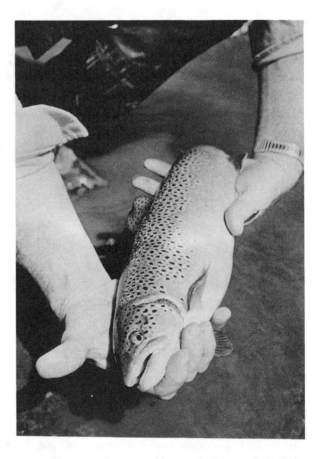

A healthy, well-formed brown trout of slightly over 23 inches. Some browns, like this one, are heavily spotted with dark brown and black spots from head to tail, including the dorsal fin. A scattering of red or rusty spots may appear on the sides. Fins are usually creamish or yellow.

Unlike the brookie, many of the brown trout's adopted homes produce larger fish than their original waters ever did. The brown trout of the Great Lakes reach prodigious size as they do in the lakes and rivers of New Zealand, Chile, and Argentina. The cool tailrace waters of a few southern impoundments in the U.S. have recently produced several fish of 30 pounds and more. Practically every state that boasts of a brown trout population has recorded 10-pounders with fish of 4 pounds being almost common.

Realistically, a 4-pound brown trout (a 20-inch fish, at least) is a trophy for most fly fishermen. The average brown trout caught anywhere in the world is much smaller than that but somewhat larger than most trout. While this fish is highly democratic about what it eats, many of the really *big* trout taken on flies are

Small stream-born or native brown trout. This little one doesn't wear many black spots but does display a neat row of red spots precisely on the lateral line (the midpoint of the flanks). The mixed genetic backgrounds of brown trout in North America produce many spot-pattern variations.

A well-spotted female brown trout showing white edges on ventral and anal fins. This is not an unusual characteristic among stream-reared trout. When held gently beneath the belly, as shown, trout will pose for the camera for about twenty seconds. Don't squeeze!

Another brown trout with an entirely different spot pattern. Fewer large spots than the previous fish but more of them are red. The fish is very dark on the back, indicating a shaded environment.

A well-fed brown trout that has "shoulders." This is typical of lake-dwelling fish that enjoy an abundance of food. Sides of such fish are usually highly iridescent or silvery.

browns. Where insect life is plentiful, many brown trout never lose their urge to come to the surface for a morsel of mayfly. And therein lies the magic of brown trout for the fly fisherman.

This is the genius of the trouts. An intelligence test has yet to be devised that can be applied to fish, but if one were, the brown would win. Even small brown trout will rise for naturals with an angler standing a few feet away, and show utter disdain for any and all artificials. Occasionally, they close in to an inch or so for a critical inspection of a well-cast fly. But will they take it? Not a chance—unless everything is just right. Oh, a freshly stocked brown trout may do something stupid, but if it's released or escapes on its own it won't make the same mistake for a while.

As the name suggests, brown trout are usually of a brownish color on their backs. Because of mixed ancestry, the spot patterns vary but generally consist of black spots on the back, brownish on the sides, with some individuals wearing a band of red spots on the lateral line. On some fish the spots may be auburn or a dark magenta. The fins are usually dirty yellow or olive, with some fish (especially at fall spawning time) showing a whitish edge. Like all trout, the adult males usually develop a "kype," or hooked lower jaw. This is especially true of fish over 2 feet long. The brown trout is the only trout that has both red and black spots.

Dolly Vardens, golden trout, arctic char, and a number of more obscure species such as the Apache and Gila trout are available in corners of the trout fishing world. When confronted with them the traveling angler is usually accompanied by someone who knows what they look like. Special flies or techniques are sometimes needed, but one or more of the methods described in this book will catch them. For the most part, a trout is a trout and will respond in the same ways trout do anyplace they're found.

3

Fly Casting

Nearly every company that makes or sells fly fishing tackle has offered a "How to Fly Cast" pamphlet at one time or another. At least 50 books have been devoted totally to fly casting and well over 300 general fly fishing titles include a chapter or more about the subject. It would seem that the fundamentals have been well covered and that there isn't much more to be said about it. Happily, there *is* more to be said because every good caster does it differently.

All fly anglers eventually develop their own style. But we have to start somewhere. Let's begin by stringing up the fly rod and using it over grass, artificial turf, or real water whenever and wherever the chance presents itself. The best golfers, foul-shooters, quarterbacks, marksmen, and pool hustlers have long known that to keep the hand-eye partnership functioning at top form requires practice.

It's a biological fact that some individuals are born with special physical abilities—strength, endurance, grace, fleetness of foot, unusually keen reflexes, and other wonderful endowments, whereas some are not. But no one is born knowing how to cast a fly line. It must be learned and constantly practiced. Yes, some will always do it better than others, but the important thing to remember is that fly fishing is seldom considered a competitive activity, except between the angler and the fish. You and I must think such a gentle competition is fun or you wouldn't have read this far and I wouldn't be writing about it. Let's learn more about it together.

THE FIRST CAST

It's a safe bet that before anyone picks up a fly rod for the first time he or she has seen someone casting on TV, at a sportsman's show, or on the stream. It's a wonderfully graceful way to fish, the observer decides, and something worthwhile learning. The quickest way to begin is through private lessons or at one of the many casting schools offered by local shops, tackle manufacturers, and mail-order houses. Attend one of these if you can, but if that's not possible don't despair. The vast majority of experienced fly casters working the water today didn't attend

one. The schools speed the process a bit but anyone with somewhat higher than room-temperature IQ can do well on his own.

Assuming that you've acquired that 8-foot rod, DT6F fly line, reel, and leader mentioned in the first chapter, pull about half of the fly line from the reel and pass it through the guides. Tie an old fly (with the hook point removed) or a small hank of brightly colored yarn to the leader. A 7- or 8-foot leader is a good length to begin with. Lay the rod on the grass and stretch the line by grasping it at four foot intervals and pulling it between both hands until you get to the tip of the rod. The stretching process can be speeded up by having a pal hold one end while you pull the other end. Stretching removes the kinks and curls (memory) that the line has acquired by being on the factory spool or reel. After being stretched the line will cast much better.

Reel up the line until twenty feet of it, plus the leader, is straight in front of you. Hold the line between fingers and rod grip firmly, not in a death grip. Raise the rod in a brisk but fluid movement with your hand rising in an arc just beyond your shoulder. Keep the hand going until it barely passes your ear. At this point, try to achieve a controlled pause in the rod's swing. The word "pause" is used because a sudden stop

The basic cast is a back-and-forth movement within certain limits. The rod should not travel much beyond the ear during the backcast nor beyond the 10 o'clock position of an imaginary clock when moving forward. The amount of line being cast and the caster's individual reflex time and style permits some allowances; but at first, try to stay within these guidelines. Make two or three false casts to get the feel and then allow the line and leader to fall to the grass or water. Avoid trying to "throw" the line. Allow the flex of the rod and weight of the line to make it happen.

will throw wiggles in the line and cause the leader to crack like a whip. Wiggles and whip-cracks are both undesirable.

When the line and leader have passed your ear and straightened out behind you, bring the hand forward until it reaches chest level. Allow the line to straighten out and fall to the ground. If you've made all of the motions in a reasonably smooth manner, the line will now be resting right where it was when you started. Repeat the same drill until it feels comfortable. What you're trying for is a fluid, pull-push sequence that forces the rod to bend when pulling the line from the grass and bend again when "pushing" it forward.

Go through this routine many times before you cast back and forth (false casting) more than once, as you may have seen other anglers do. You're not ready for this yet. Do it with the casting hand only; put the other one in your pocket or on your hip.

When you're comfortable with the basic pickup and forward cast routine, take a break and study the casting sequence illustrations. You'll note that the rod is shown as moving through various positions of an imaginary clock. The numbers on the face of a clock are to remind you when to lift and when to come forward. At the outset, the most difficult thing to prevent is to keep the rod from going beyond the 2 o'clock position. The number 2 problem is overcoming a desire to bring the rod forward *before the line straightens out* behind you. One way of being sure this happens is to say to yourself, "line be straight" as the rod passes your ear.

Casting the line back and forth several times is termed "false casting." When dry-fly fishing, false casting is done between completed casts in order to shake the water from the fly so it floats high and dry the next time. It is also done when additional line is being stripped from the reel so a longer cast can be made or when a cast to a different spot is desired.

As the flow of the rod and the tugging sensation of the line moving back and forth is felt,

the mechanics of fly casting begin to unfold. Unlike tossing a lure with a spinning rod and reel or a baitcasting outfit, it's the *weight of the fly line* that makes it all work. With other forms of casting, it's the weight of the lure that pulls the line from the reel. It's not difficult to throw a lure fifty feet or more by hand. A large wet fly can't be thrown half that distance. An air-resistant dry fly can't be hand thrown more than a foot or so, if at all. Try it!

Teaching fly casting to someone who has done some spinning or baitcasting is much more difficult that teaching a rank beginner. It is, because the caster finds it hard to overcome the desire to "throw" the lure to the place he wants it to go. The heavy fly line must be put into motion by the rod in a way that will pull the leader—with fly attached—to the spot you aim for. When you think about it, the entire process is quite amazing. Various laws of physics involving gravity and motion are working against the fly caster at all times yet somehow the fly goes along for the ride.

THE SINGLE HAUL

The simple overhead cast, using no more than twenty feet of line and a leader about the length of the fly rod comprises all the casting know-how needed to reach most trout in streams fifty feet or less in width. Fifty percent of the trout anglers in the world will never find it necessary to cast much farther. (This is the cast you've been practicing.) But as time passes and the casting sequence begins to feel more familiar, you'll probably feel the need to cast a longer line. If you visit wider water, fish lakes, or fall under the spell of saltwater fly fishing, you'll have to cast a greater distance.

The revelation of the *single haul* will come naturally as we begin to pay attention to that tugging sensation on the hand holding the surplus line when the rod is moved backwards. The "drag" or friction between line and grass or water (and the weight of the line itself) plays an important role in allowing the cast to begin. As the rod is set in motion the friction causes it to bend more. At the moment it begins to bend, if the angler pulls the line in the *opposite direction* it will bend even more. The more bend applied, the more forceful the unbending action is, as the rod tries to regain its straight attitude. Forcing the rod to bend is termed "loading." Without pulling the line with the left hand (if you're right-handed) the fly rod cannot deliver its maximum power.

By using the single haul, the velocity of the line as it passes over your shoulder is increased considerably. This additional velocity, in turn, causes the rod to bend more forcefully as the line unfurls behind you. Because the rod bends into a deeper curve, it will propel the line a greater distance in the forward direction.

On grass or water, you'll find that the single haul works better if you pull in a few feet of line before you begin the cast. A downward tug on the line bends the rod, which should be put into

motion at the same instant. If done smoothly, the line will almost leap into the air. By pulling or hauling on the line just before it begins its rearward motion a tighter loop is formed as the line unfurls. A tight loop can only occur when your timing is right. A well-timed cast is self-evident and announces itself. It just feels right.

As a dry fly floats, or a wet or streamer fly is retrieved, slack line will accumulate. When you're casting from a boat, wading in calm water or practicing on the grass, the excess line won't cause trouble if allowed to fall in loose coils. The forward stroke of the next cast will pull it through the guides if too much line doesn't accumulate. There are times when additional care must be taken to avoid tangling. Rocks with irregular edges, sticks, tree limbs, and assorted debris conspire to foul things up. Then it's necessary to hold the surplus line in the non-casting hand, in loose coils, prior to making the next cast. While this sounds simple enough, it does require some practice to do it

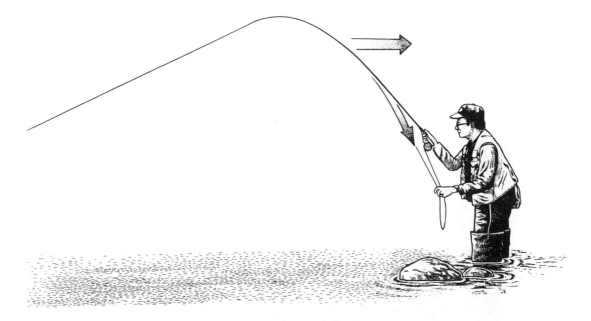

The single haul consists of pulling down on the slack line with the non-casting hand in order to bend the rod tip a little and impart some movement to the line that's on the water or grass. The combined action of pulling or lifting the rod and pulling down on the line helps create line speed necessary for completing the basic overhead cast when longer casts are needed.

automatically. The best place to practice this is on the grass or at a quiet pool or pond. When you're retrieving line, use the index finger of your casting hand as an extra line guide. Allow the line to pass between index finger and rod grip, gathering it in two-foot loops in the non-casting hand. Two or three loops are plenty to handle at first. As the next forward cast is made, release the loops and they will shoot through the guides. As with all segments of the casting sequence, good timing makes it happen.

THE DOUBLE HAUL

I'd bet that a million or more successful fly fishermen have passed through this world without ever learning how to do a double haul. Single-hauling the line and good timing on their backcast served them satisfactorily. Another million or more fly casters on the water today haven't learned how to do either—but they should.

It's extremely difficult to cast beyond sixty feet without using the double haul and almost

The double haul is really two single hauls put together. Begin as shown in the previous illustration. As the line travels past your head, allow the non-casting hand to glide upwards, moving closer to the stripping guide. Just before the unfurling line is about to straighten, pull down on the line in the non-casting hand. This will force the rod to bend even more and impart additional line speed to the forward cast. Put another way, the left hand (for right-handed casters) performs a see-saw action. As this is practiced, it helps to look back over the shoulder to see when the line is about to unfurl. As the line is about to straighten in front of you, lower the rod tip slightly below the 10 o'clock position and release the slack line.

impossible to reach the magic hundred-foot mark. The mighty rods used by European anglers, some measuring sixteen feet or more, are capable of heaving a lot of line, but casting such flagpoles is hard work. Correctly done, the double haul is easier.

The use of the double haul is not restricted to salmon and steelhead rivers, large lakes, or saltwater. Once learned, it will lead to more accurate casting in all fly-fishing situations. It will, because faster line speed delivers the fly to the target area on a straight trajectory. If it seems like I'm trying to make a strong case for the double haul, you're right.

The double haul is two single hauls put together. If you think of it this way instead of a complex procedure that must be done all at once, it will be easier to perform. Begin by pulling down with the line hand as the rod is raised just as you would to make a single haul. Precisely the *same combination* of movements must be done *behind you* when making a double haul. Begin just as you did when learning the single haul: pull 20 feet of line plus leader onto the grass in front of you and hold the line between the first guide and the reel in the non-casting hand. Turn your body 180 degrees. You're now facing the opposite direction with the rod and line extended *behind you* instead of in front. Lift the line by doing exactly what you'd do if the line were in front. Pull down on the line as the rod comes forward. You'll feel that same tugging sensation as the line begins to lift. Continue with the stroke, smooth and strong, until the rod passes your nose. As it does, bring the rod to a smooth stop and allow the line to fall to the grass. You've just accomplished a behind-the-back single haul.

Next, do a forward single haul and let the line fall to the grass again. Repeat this sequence a few times and the mysteries of the double-haul will start to clear up. The final step is to combine the forward haul and the rearward haul into one complete cycle, and you've got it!

SHOOTING LINE

The primary purpose of the double haul is to send fly line, leader, and fly to a spot not reachable with the basic overhand cast. Keeping more than fifty feet of line in the air as false casting (using a double haul) is continued for more than two or three cycles is tiring and counterproductive. No matter how good you are, sooner or later a vagrant breeze, momentary lapse of concentration, muscle spasm, or something else will interfere. As more line is carried in the air, timing becomes more critical. Even champion casters cannot keep seventy feet of line going back and forth forever. The law of gravity eventually takes over and everything comes crashing to earth.

Every fly caster should learn how to "shoot" line. This is accomplished by having surplus line on the grass beside you when the first haul is made. Start with about 12 feet or so. Make one forward haul, allow the line in the air to straighten out behind you and make a back haul. As the line passes your cheek on the forward stroke and the tug on the line hand begins to build, let go of the surplus line and it will shoot through the guides. If you stop the rod's forward progress at about the 9:30 position on that imaginary clock, all of the line at your feet should now be lying straight out in front of the rod tip. If it isn't, try again.

As line shooting begins to feel manageable, increase the amount of line to be sent forward. You'll discover that there is a limit to how much can be shot in combination with the length of line being carried in the air. More line weight moving at high speed will pull more line through the guides. Well, up to point. Too much line in the air allows gravity to take over—and that's that.

THE ROLL CAST

Many trout streams are lined with brush, trees, high banks, and other obstacles that prevent

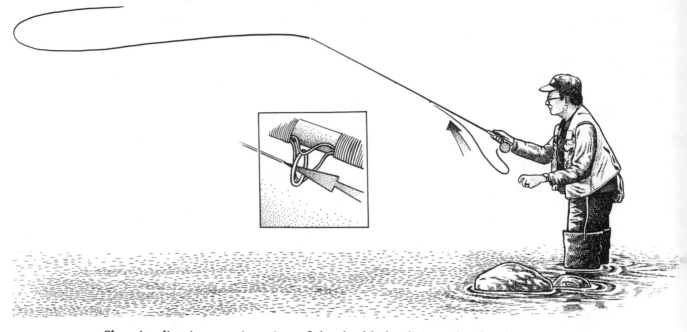

Shooting line is a continuation of the double haul. Line that has been stripped in and allowed to hang free or coiled in the hand will shoot through the guides with ease if the double haul is correctly timed. If the rod tip is held too high as the line is released, its forward progress will be hampered due to friction between the rod tip-top and the line.

making a conventional, over-the-shoulder cast. There isn't enough open space to allow the backcast to straighten out without snagging on something. Executing a roll cast will solve the problem. A roll cast is also useful at other times, especially when a cautious trout is likely to take flight if too many false casts are made over it before the fly is delivered. It's also the best way to make an instant second cast to a fish that has followed the fly but not taken it. Knowing how to make a roll cast is not only important, it's imperative!

Unlike practicing other casting skills, learning the roll cast must be done on water. Since it's surface tension between water and line that makes the roll cast work, it can't be managed well on grass. A helper can place a foot on the leader and make it work— sort of—but the line will seldom unfurl correctly. A parking lot after a rain can be put into service if there is a

twenty-foot puddle more than a half-inch deep.

Begin by making an overhead cast of about twenty-five feet. Lower the rod tip until it is parallel with the surface of the water. Lift the rod smoothly—not too fast—until it passes your ear. When done correctly there should be a pronounced sag in the line between tip and the water. The rod should be positioned just past vertical. Bring the rod hand forward in a chopping motion, just as you would if you were striking down with a hammer or hatchet. The forward stroke should be brisk, not violent. If all of these moves are made correctly, the line, followed by the leader and fly, will roll up and over the rod in a near perfect circle, shooting the fly in the direction the rod tip is pointed. It works best if the final position of the rod tip is near horizontal.

It's amazing how much line can be put in motion though use of a roll cast. With a dou-

Before trying the roll cast, check the text for a more complete understanding of this seemingly mechanical marvel. It cannot be practiced on the grass because this cast depends on surface tension. Begin with about twenty-five feet of line and leader on the water following a forward cast. Lift the rod slowly to the vertical position, which will cause the line on the water to slide towards you. At the moment the line passes the rod just behind the ear snap the rod down and slightly forward with a chopping motion. Stop it at the 10 o'clock mark. It's important that the change of direction moving the rod backwards and then smartly forward be a smooth transition. If a pause is allowed, the halt in line speed will nullify the action. The line and leader will roll upwards and outwards in a near perfect circle.

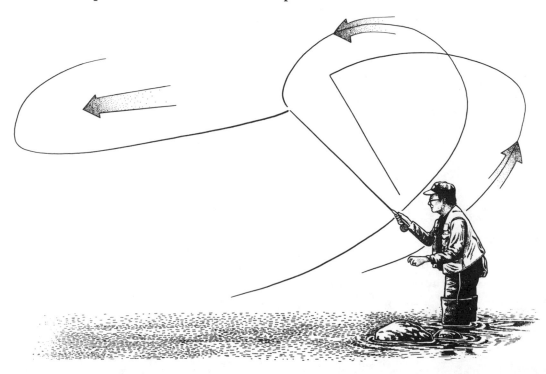

ble-taper line, well matched to the rod, and a leader that is behaving well, 40-foot roll casts are possible.

CHANGING DIRECTION

If you've made a cast slightly upstream and the current has carried your fly downstream or below you, one roll cast isn't enough to send it back for another try. Assuming that an overhead cast can't be made, you've got to make more than one roll to present the fly again. By moving the rod a few feet upstream between each roll you can "walk" the fly back to its previous destination. A roll cast won't move sideways all by itself. The line will want to go where the tip is pointed but it won't go there all in one stroke. Take your time and roll as many times as you must to get it there.

Roll casts can be made with the rod slightly turned to one side or the other, and they can also be tucked beneath overhanging branches on the far side of a pool. By experimenting, you'll discover how much of a side-roll you're capable of making. Such a cast is a little tricky, because when the rod is laid to one side there will be more line on the water, thus increasing the surface tension. A bit more snap is needed to make it unfurl. "Tucking" is another variation of the roll cast that comes in handy. Just as the final three feet of the leader is unbending from its curving arc, a sudden lowering of the rod tip will pull it down and cause the fly to assume a lower trajectory. When it works right the fly will pop beneath those low-hanging branches.

THE ROLL-OVERHEAD COMBINATION

Many times during a day of fly fishing you'll find the fly in a downstream position that prevents making an overhead pick-up. Even without the handicap of background limbs, pulling the fly from the water will result in an annoying slurp that could spook a nervous fish. By pulling a few feet of line through the first guide and executing a roll cast, you can immediately slide into a conventional overhead cast. By doing so, you can change direction quickly. The trick is to begin the backcast while the fly is still in the air in front of you. While this may sound complicated it's not. Once you've mastered the basic roll cast, mixing it with other moves will come easily.

THROWING A CURVE

When a wind is present, we sometimes make the best curve casts possible. If an upstream curve is desired and the wind is blowing in that direction, it may just happen and we accept our good luck. But we can't always depend on luck. Purposeful curve casts are immensely helpful when a spooky fish isn't interested in a fly that drags over its position due to conflicting currents. When there's no wind to help and a longer drag-free drift is desired, we've got to throw a curve into the line or leader, or both.

It's much easier to introduce a curve into the line if the rod is cocked a bit to one side as it moves forward. Put the same amount of force into the backcast, but as the line unfurls on its forward trip, reduce the power in a way that forces the line and leader to slow down. This can also be described as a soft forward cast. As the fly is drifting slowly forward through the air, scribe a half circle with the rod tip in the direction you wish the curve to appear. If this motion is timed correctly, a pretty half-loop will fall to the water. Oh yes, this move also requires practice and quite a lot of it.

MENDING THE LOOP

After the fly has made contact with the water, it's still possible to toss some curve into the line by "mending" it. Raise the rod tip a couple of

To throw a curve into the fly, roll the wrist slightly to one side as the forward cast is falling towards the water. A soft snap, one way or the other, is the best way to describe it. The motion is slightly up and to one side while the fly is still in the air.

Current

Mending the line, after line, leader and fly are on the water, is basically a sort of half-roll cast. Lift the rod a couple feet above horizontal and snap it slightly up and forward in the direction you want the line to go. Mending is useful when the current between rod and fly is faster than it is where the fly is and you want to prevent the fly from dragging . This maneuver must be practiced on the water.

feet from horizontal and make a snappy "half-roll cast" with a combination forward and side movement. This will cause a few feet of the line to roll left or right, depending on which way the rod is directed.

Watching experienced anglers mend a drifting fly line appears to be a combination of magic and luck. As with a number of fly fishing maneuvers, no two rod handlers do it exactly the same. Some appear merely to make a quick sideways switch with the rod tip and lo, the line leaps off the water and moves one way or the other. Others raise the rod tip a foot or so and seem to make an abbreviated rollcast. Combinations of both styles are also common. What must be understood when mending line is that the rod tip first moves in

the *opposite direction* from that of the movement applied to the rod grip.

When the rod hand snaps the grip toward the water the tip first reacts by moving away from the water. It does because the rod flexes. A broomstick will not do this, but a thin, resilient fly rod does. Snap the rod hand down and then lift it and a few feet of line will pop into the air. At that instant, roll the rod in the direction you want the line to go. Mending line cannot be practiced with any degree of satisfaction on the grass. As for the rollcast, there must be some surface tension from the water in order to make it work. In my opinion, mending line is one of the most difficult fly fishing skills to master.

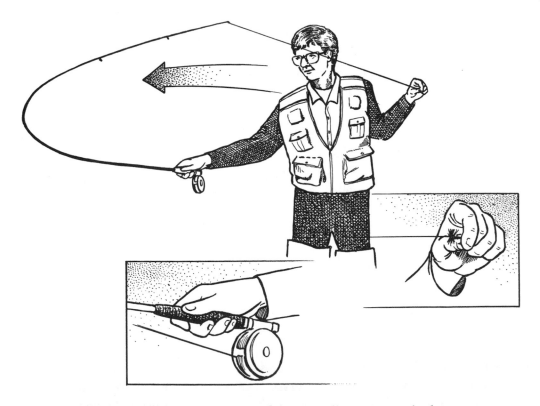

The bow-and-arrow cast is useful on small streams and where an overhead cast may cause problems due to overhanging brush. Hold the fly hook between thumb and forefinger and bend the rod as if to shoot an arrow. Aim the rod tip at the desired target and release the fly.

BOW-AND-ARROW CAST

On small brooks and occasionally on larger streams there are spots that just can't be reached by using the conventional overhead cast or even by the best tucked roll cast ever made. Overhanging brush, logs, or other debris won't permit it. The bow-and-arrow cast is the answer.

The only drawback to the bow-and-arrow cast is that it's impossible to shoot much more that a rod's length of line and leader. Even so, I can't count the times the trick has added trout to the daily tally. It's done by bending the rod in archery fashion, aiming the fly at the desired spot and letting it go. Zip! Like a catapult, the fly zooms straight to the target.

Hold the fly by the bend of the hook between the nails of thumb and forefinger. Pull the fly to a point about eight inches from your sighting eye while bending the rod upwards or sideways. (The bow-and-arrow cast seldom works if the rod is bent towards the water.) Aim the fly by lining it up with the tip of the rod and the target spot. You'll be surprised how speedily it travels. As with all casts, the fly, leader, and line usually travel to or near the spot the rod tip is pointed.

SLACK-LINE CAST

Slack-line, S-cast, check, parachute, and several other labels are used to identify this cast. It's worth is well known among those anglers with a lot of dry-fly experience behind them. It's one the easiest and most productive ways of fooling cautious fish, because the dry fly will float over them with little or no drag. This is good place to insert yet another reminder that drag—the effect of seen and unseen currents—is the major reason trout shy away from dry flies.

The check cast can be done in any direction, but its most obvious application occurs when a rising fish is downstream from the angler. Let's say you've been casting across or upstream when

a sizable ring on the water appears twenty feet away on your downstream side. To wade towards it or move to a spot below it may send it running. This is a perfect setup for a check cast (see page 71)..

First, false cast once or twice to one side of the fish's location (don't pass the fly over its head). Watch the forward progress of the fly and allow a little extra line to slip from the line hand. Once you're sure you'd overshoot the fish by about five or six feet, you're ready to make your move? Allow the final forward cast to drive the fly to a point directly above the fish, stop the cast at about the 10 o'clock position, and then quickly raise the rod tip to 12 o'clock. The fly will be pulled toward you (still in the air) and flutter softly to the water a few feet in front of the target. This checking of the cast will cause the line and leader to fall in loose curves and allow the fly to float toward the fish in a drag-free attitude. Another way to achieve the same result is by wiggling the rod tip from side to side as the as the fly drops to the surface (see page 71).

Tip: When a fish takes the fly you'll stand a much better chance of hooking it if you pull the rod to the left or right instead of straight up. Pull in some of the slack line and leader with the line hand, catching it under the forefinger of the rod hand while pulling the rod the to the left or right. By doing this, the hook point will be driven into the corner of the fish's jaw instead of into the tip of the snout. When fish are directly downstream, they are very difficult to hook if the rod is moved straight up.

Slack-line casts can be delivered upstream, downstream, or across with equally good results when conflicting currents require it. It's done just as it would be in a downstream situation. Aim beyond the fish, to that imaginary spot above its head, check the cast, and pull back on the rod at the moment the fly begins to drop. When a long leader, one of 12 feet or more, is used and its front half is constructed of limp monofilament, the extra feet of drag-free float obtained is amazing.

The slow, soft descent of the fly itself when cast this way is tantalizing to many trout. It's not unlike the landings made by real insects, particularly mayflies. When you can arrange to have your artificial meet the water as gently as a butterfly's kiss, more than half the battle has been won.

GENERAL CASTING TIPS

It can't be emphasized enough that all fly casting is easier if the fly line is periodically cleaned. I'm as guilty as the next guy about not doing it as often as I should. I keep promising myself to do it more regularly, but in the excitement of getting into the action we all tend to overlook the details that are so important. Some line makers include a tin of cleaner with each line, and it really helps. Fly tackle shops sell line floatants, but most dry-fly preparations work equally well.

Before applying anything it's best to wipe the line with a soft cloth soaked with water and a dab of mild soap. Following the soapy water treatment, wipe the line dry with another cloth or paper towel and coat it with floatant according to directions. Dirty line does not shoot well through the guides.

Speaking of guides, check all rod guides a couple times each season, or more frequently, for nicks and rough spots. The tip-top and stripping guides are most prone to damage. If there are problems, smooth the scratchy spots with fine emery paper. If the nicks are really serious, replacing the worn guides is the only solution. The same applies to reels. If the side of the reel frame—the spot the line rides over as you pull line from the spool—is rough, it too will need some smoothing. The coating on modern fly lines is tough but no match for rough metal.

If a lot of long-distance casting is anticipated, coating the shooting portion of the line with a lubricating solution containing silicone can help. Armor-All is recommended by many experienced casters, and there are several others. Do not use petroleum-based oils.

The mechanics of fly casting are not difficult to master, but attaining proficiency requires time on the water. Until you've spent more than a hundred hours or so at the game, keep these few basics in mind.

1. Do not allow the rod to travel too far beyond your ear on the backcast. As your timing becomes better and it's no longer necessary to look over your shoulder, you'll be able to allow the rod and line to travel back farther, for longer casts.

2. Unless the line is fully extended—in front or in back— the next move can't be made without something bad happening. When this happens (and it happens to the best casters in the world at times) shorten up, reel in some line, and begin again.

3. Keep the thumb or forefinger on top of the rod grip pointed directly where you want the line to go. Don't allow it to slip to one side of the grip. Keep the wrist and forearm flexed, but not absolutely rigid. A death-grip is fatiguing and accomplishes nothing.

4. Try for smoothness in the transition from backcast to forward cast. A sudden *stop* as the rod passes the ear and another *stop* as the fly line reaches the end of its journey in front will throw waves and wiggles into the line. Make an effort to avoid these by stopping the rod with a *smooth* pause instead of jamming on the brakes. Ease into the change of direction and your casts will be better.

5. Concentrate on making accurate casts at first and go for distance later. Long, beautifully executed double hauls are fun to watch and satisfying to perform. Yes, there are times and places where long-range casting is vital, but season in and season out, far more fish will be hooked as a result of well-placed, 20- to 50-foot casts.

4

Flies for Trout

Assuming that you now understand the rudiments of fly casting and own a suitable 8- or 8½-foot fly rod properly loaded with reel, line, and leader, it's time to talk about flies. Selecting flies is at once fun and frustrating. It's not unlike Abraham Lincoln's observation on being President: "You can fool some of the people all of the time and all of the people some of the time but not all of the people all of the time." Substitute the word *fish* for *people* and Abe's quote covers the fly selecting conundrum perfectly.

Every fly fisherman with a few years of experience behind him has enjoyed days when nearly any pattern—reasonably well presented—caught fish. He has also cataloged days when a single pattern, in the exact size, had to be perfectly laid on the water in order to interest even the smallest of trout. The immense variety of situations that confront the fly angler is what keeps us coming back for more. If fly fishing were a simple matter of tying a fly, any fly, on our leader, and catching all the fish we want to catch, trout fishing would hold little sporting appeal. On the other hand, not catching fish isn't much fun either. What do we put into our fly boxes?

References to various forms of life that fish feed on will appear many times in this book. So about now is an excellent time to conduct an examination of what it is we're trying to suggest with our fly patterns. Mayflies, caddisflies, stoneflies, beetles, ants, minnows, crayfish, grasshoppers, crickets, scuds, slugs, and assorted small reptiles and amphibians are all natural models for fly patterns. Depending on where and what time of year you are fishing, you may find any and all imitations of these creatures to be useful. Mayflies are the most abundant insects on trout streams and the patterns that suggest them are therefore the most popular.

In the next chapter I'll discuss fishing with the dry fly, so let's stay in sequence. We're going to be dealing here with patterns suitable for trout, because 95 percent of the dry flies sold in the world are designed for and destined to be cast at trout. Fishing for most other species is more an attractor game instead of an imitative one, and the flies are generally larger and more colorful. Of course trout will strike brightly colored attractor-type flies on many occasions, but most of the time better results will come from flies that look like creatures they eat regularly.

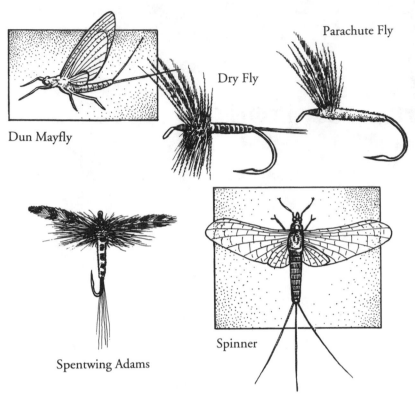

Dun Mayfly

Dry Fly

Parachute Fly

Spinner

Spentwing Adams

The dun form of the mayfly usually floats along with wings upright and tails slightly arched above the surface. After mating, fly is called a spinner, and its wings lay flat, or "spent," on the surface. Colors are also less intense on the spinner and the wings are nearly transparent. A number of popular dry fly patterns, such as the Adams, are tied in both silhouette styles.

MAYFLIES

Mayflies belong to the order of insects known as *Ephemeridae*. They have an overall graceful silhouette with large, upright wings and long, flowing tails. Some mayflies have three tail shafts and some have two; otherwise most mayflies are quite similar except for color and size. Color and size, however, are what keep fly tiers busy and fly fishermen thinking about what to cast to the fish. Since there are hundreds of species and subspecies of mayflies, the combinations of colors and sizes are almost unlimited. Is it necessary to carry a suggestion of all the mayflies in our fly boxes? No, it isn't, because many fly patterns overlap in purpose. At the outset, it's important to keep in mind that a well-fished fly that isn't precisely like the natural will fool more fish than a perfect imitation that is not well fished. Put another way, presentation of the fly is always more important than the fly itself. In an apparent contradiction

of that statement, we still need *some* variety of size and color if we are to be successful during an entire angling season.

In this chapter I'll suggest basic dry flies, wet flies, nymphs, and streamers. The first three are tied to suggest insects in specific stages of their life cycle. Streamers are tied to suggest minnows and other small fish. To understand why three types of flies are needed, we must first understand the life cycles of the insects that they imitate.

The Mayfly's Year

The mayfly fluttering about in the air or seemingly erupting from the surface of the water has just hatched. It is an adult dun or *subimago*. Regardless of size or color its wings and body will be opaque or somewhat cloudy. Depending on species, some duns may hatch quickly and seem almost to leap from the surface, while oth-

A typical mayfly, the winged insect suggested by the majority of dry-fly patterns. The naturals come in many sizes and colors. Some are two or more inches long while others are no larger than a single letter on this page.

ers flop about as they unfold their wings and flex them a few times before attempting to fly. This flopping about is usually more than a hungry fish can bear watching, and if the mayfly isn't pretty quick about it, it's eaten before take-off time.

If the dun mayflies hatch perfectly (many don't form correctly as they hatch and are quickly eaten) and escape fish and birds, which also eat them with relish, they fly to a tree, bush, rock ledge, or some other protected spot. There they remain (usually in a shady spot) for a few hours to a day or so while they molt.

The molting process consists of a transformation from the opaque state to one of near transparency. The wings become clear and glossy with the veination lines showing distinctly and sexual parts undergoing final development. At this stage, the mayfly is called a spinner or *imago*.

When molting is completed the spinners return to the water for mating and egg-laying duties. Where some duns may emerge sporadically, spinners usually appear in great numbers to find a mate. Spinners are most abundant during the evening hours, and on some waters the air over riffles can be full of dancing mayflies. Indeed, they do appear to dance as they methodically hover up and down in a kind of waltz-time undulation. Males eventually find females and grasp them with tiny tentacles to fulfill their sexual obligation in midair. The egg mass, attached to the end of the abdomen, is fertilized and the females then dip to touch the surface of the water and drop them.

After fertilization and egg-laying the spinners die. Since they have no mouth parts, they are incapable of feeding and the mating process totally exhausts them. In their death-

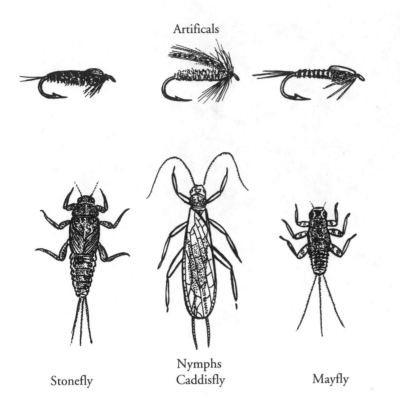

Artificals

Nymphal (underwater or wet) forms of the three most common aquatic insects and their artificial counterparts.

Nymphs

Stonefly   Caddisfly   Mayfly

throes, the spinners are easy prey for fish as they drift along helplessly. It is important for the fly fisherman to know that the spinner form is unlike the dun in that its wings are extended in a flat or "spent" attitude on the surface instead of being in the former upright position. There may be duns and spinners on the water at the same time and the fish may show a preference for one over the other.

The eggs fall to the streambed where they hatch into the nymphal stage within one to three weeks. The nymphs will remain on the stream bottom for a full year before they see daylight again or breathe air. Feeding on microscopic organisms, the nymphs grow by shedding a series of coverings or skins, much like crayfish do. At the appropriate time, just before they are a year old, the fully grown nymphs swim to the surface to begin the cycle once more. Because mayflies go through but three stages of growth and development—egg, nymph, and adult—their lives are termed an incomplete metamorphosis.

CADDISFLIES

Caddisflies are of the order *Trichoptera* and are totally different from mayflies in that they undergo four stages of development. Theirs is a complete metamorphosis, consisting of egg, pupa, larva, and adult. Another significant difference between caddisflies and mayflies is that the caddis pupa either builds a case to protect itself or constructs a small net that actually captures minute food particles. The various species that construct cases do so with amazing dexterity and sameness of design, some using tiny stones with others selecting bits of wood and vegetable matter. Within their bodies they secrete an adhesive that binds all together. Most caddisflies are case builders.

Ten days or so before becoming adults, the caddis pupa leaves its protective case and moves about, underwater, in another casing or membrane. It is now in the larval stage. Some species are quite active at this point. Fish love them. When the spirit moves them, the swimming larvae travel to the surface and, like the mayflies, hatch as quickly as they can fracture the protective membrane. Some species fairly jump into the air. Not all caddis are expert fliers, however, and may make several false starts and return to the surface and flop about before finally making a good job of it. More good fish and bird food!

Unlike mayflies, caddis fly about the water for several days or even a week before dying, thus giving the fish some additional time for dining. When they emerge, caddis adults are capable of mating immediately and may do so several times before finally expiring. Mating is done in midair and eggs may be dropped on the surface or directly on the bottom of the stream; some species actually dive to the bottom and attach their eggs to logs and stones.

As with mayflies, there are hundreds of species and subspecies of caddis, but all are shaped similarly. The two sets of wings fold over the body when the insect is at rest and are much larger than the body itself. A general oval shape best describes the silhouette. Caddis of nearly all colors exist, but the vast majority of them are tan, gray, or olive. When flying, the caddis appears to have no specific direction and flutters about more or less aimlessly, touching down on the water from time to time.

STONEFLIES

Unlike the mayfly and caddis juveniles, stonefly nymphs look much like the adults without wings. The nymphs resemble mayfly nymphs in many ways, but the bodies are generally longer and they have but two tails that extend from the sides of the extended abdomen instead of the center. The abbreviated twin pairs of what will become wings on the adults are visible. Stonefly nymphs eat both plant and small animal life.

When the nymphs are transformed into flying adults, they split the nymphal shuck much like other aquatic insects do. By studying the remains of these cases, found at streamside fol-

lowing a hatch of stoneflies, the angler will have a good idea of what the nymphs and adults look like. The wings are large and make the insects look even bigger when in flight. They are not expert fliers and their clumsiness makes them easy prey for the fish.

The so-called salmon fly of the western states is really a large stonefly and many specimens have bodies that are a full two inches long. The nymphs of the larger stoneflies are known as hellgrammites and are regularly gathered by bait fishermen, especially for smallmouth bass. But all freshwater species seem to love stonefly nymphs and the adults as well.

Stoneflies belong to the order Plecoptera. They are crawlers instead of swimming nymphs, but they can move slowly near the bottom by wiggling their legs and flexing the abdomen. Knowing this, the angler should fish his stonefly nymph imitations on or near the bottom. While there are a few exceptions, most stoneflies are black, brown, or gray.

Trout are amazingly democratic about what they eat and highly opportunistic. If this is so, the neophyte may ask, why can trout be so annoyingly selective at times? It's probably not because of superior intellect, since even a big trout's brain isn't much larger than a pea. My guess is that it's a case of availability. If there's a sizable quantity of one particular insect drifting over their heads they get locked onto that size, shape, and color and won't be easily coaxed into sampling anything else. It's like the famous potato chip TV commercial: "Bet you can't eat just one!"

Trout can be highly selective, but fortunately there are some dry-fly patterns that have proven to be universal fish getters. They do a reasonably good job of suggesting a wide variety of insect life and constitute a good group to start with. The list of basic dry flies which appeared in my *Trout and Salmon Fisherman's Bible* (Doubleday, 1991) remains appropriate, with the addition of a caddis pattern or two.

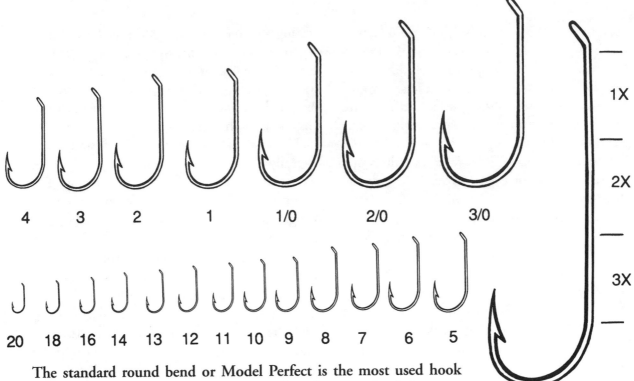

4   3   2   1   1/0   2/0   3/0

20   18   16   14   13   12   11   10   9   8   7   6   5

1X

2X

3X

The standard round bend or Model Perfect is the most used hook style for flies. When the letter "X" is used to describe a hook it means a multiplication of 1. For example, 1X stout or heavy, indicates the wire used is one times heavier than normal. 3X long, signifies that the hook shank is three times longer than usual, etc.

DRY FLIES TO START WITH

Adams. This is the most widely used dry fly in the United States and has nearly as many admirers in other countries where trout are found. It is a fly that will catch some fish on every trout stream on any day that fish are rising. It is basically a brownish-gray fly with black and white wings. These are the colors of most insects and as an all-purpose dry fly it has no equal.

The Adams can be tied in slightly different ways—longer wings tied upright instead of spent like tiny airplane wings, more or less hackle, thick or thin body, to offer a varied silhouette. The shades of all the materials can be changed considerably and you still have an Adams. No two tiers make it exactly alike; all of them will catch fish. If there is one essential dry fly in your box this is it. Carry it in sizes 10, 12, 14, 16, and 18.

Spentwing Adams is North America's favorite dry fly and arguably the best one. It has caught trout worldwide. It should be in every fly box in an assortment of sizes from 10 to 18.

Many popular and effective patterns, such as the Light Cahill, Quill Gordon, and Olive Dun are tied "parachute" style. The winding of the hackle around the base of the upright wing allows the fly to float in the surface film. The wing is easy to see on the water.

Light Cahill. This pale tan fly is a favorite pattern of thousands of anglers from the middle of May until the end of June on eastern waters and is equally useful in the West during the late summer and early fall. Not only does the Light Cahill suggest pale-toned mayflies, it does an equally good job when tan caddisflies are on the water. Carry in the same range of sizes as suggested for the Adams.

Gordon Quill. Since so many natural insects are a bluish-gray shade, we need a fly or two in this color range. The Gordon Quill, Dark Hendrickson, and several others are this color, and while either one would be a good choice, the Gordon Quill gets my vote. Flies of this shade are not easy to see on the water during the evening hours but we must have them. Some anglers solve this visibility problem by tying or buying Gordon Quills with upright wings of white calf tail or some other kind of hair. A small measure of effectiveness may be sacrificed by doing this—but not much. It's worth trying. Same sizes as above.

Grey Hackle Peacock. This extremely simple fly consists of nothing more than a hackle and tail of barred black and white (often called grizzly or barred rock), and a body of peacock herl. It's another wonderful all-purpose fly that suggests a multitude of insects. The neutral colors in the hackle and the iridescent "bugginess" of the peacock herl is the secret. It looks like a lot of insects in general but not like anything specifically. This may be the reason a Grey Hackle dry fly doesn't work as well in large sizes as it does in sizes 14, 16, 18, and 20. When fish are rising for something that can't be easily seen on the water, a Grey Hackle in size 18 or 20 is often an excellent choice.

Royal Wulff. This dry fly goes beyond the Grey Hackle in not imitating anything in this world. Yet, it has been highly popular ever since Lee Wulff first introduced it fifty years ago. The Royal Wulff is an "attractor" pattern, one to tie on when no natural insects appear to be present. It has an uncanny way of exciting trout, sometimes very large trout, to take a whack at it when they can't be coaxed into rising for more somber offerings. But this doesn't mean that the

Royal Wulff is a classic among dry flies and, like the Adams, has caught fish everywhere it's been used. It is a wonderful "searching" pattern.

Royal Wulff won't work when natural flies are plentiful. It can be especially effective late in the evening when drab colored patterns can't be seen. The upright white wings stand out like twin beacons. Carry it in sizes 10, 12, and 14.

Olive Dun (or Blue-Winged Olive). There are many small bluish-gray mayflies that also have bodies of varying shades of olive. Curiously, trout are often more selective about tiny flies than they are about large ones when the naturals are on the water in abundance. The reason may be that large, fluffy dry flies coast down to the surface in a more graceful and lifelike manner. Small, less wind-resistant artificials do not. That aside, we still need a small, olive-bodied dry fly and the Blue-wing Olive pattern is the best there is. Sizes 14, 16, 18, and 20.

Badger Bivisible. This is another very simple fly that is all hackle and tail—no body. It's valuable as a "searching" fly when fishing fast or rippling water. Bivisibles of other colors such as gray, grizzly, black or brown are also useful, but the mixed cream and black of badger hackle has a particularly buggy look. Sizes 10, 12, and 14.

Black Beetle. At any time of the year, few fish will refuse a well-cast black beetle of some sort. This fly is really a generic pattern since few fly tiers make black beetles that look exactly alike. What's needed is a basic black, oval-shaped silhouette with several short legs. Most of the time such a beetle should float, but it won't matter if it sinks once in a while—the fish will still be interested. Sizes 10, 12, 14, and 16.

Brown Ant. As with the beetles, ant patterns are really a type of fly featuring a pinched waist with a bump on either end. It's the antlike silhouette we're after. Trout like ants and eat them whenever they fall into the water. Black and brown are equally effective but a brown one is easier to see on the water. Sizes 14, 16, 18, and 20.

Caddisflies. Caddis patterns vary greatly in color from region to region, but the general shape and style remain. Wings should lie along the top of the body instead of upright with enough hackle wound on to make the fly float well for "skittering." The natural caddisflies fly about erratically and do a lot of skittering and scooting across the surface. The Henryville Special, Elk Hair Caddis, and the conventional Adams when tied with wings extending to the bend of the hook are all good choices. Sizes 12, 14, 16, and 18.

Grasshoppers. Pick a grasshopper pattern that suggests the local hopper size and coloration. There are dozens of variations and most of them work at one time (or place) or another. If you're in doubt, start with a Letort Hopper. Sizes 10, 12, and 14.

Spiders. A spider fly is nothing more than an oversized hackle and extra-long tail on a light-wire hook. Such flies flutter gracefully to the surface and this soft landing often attracts a watching trout. These are wonderful flies to cast onto fast water when it's necessary to get the fish's attention in a hurry. They float like a cork and when pulled across the surface in short hops will often bring a strike when nothing else

Deer-hair grasshopper in the right size is very effective on streams that flow through pastures and meadows. Try to match the shape and color of the hoppers that are most numerous. The same fly form in black is also a good cricket suggestion.

Spiders and bivisibles, flies consisting of mostly hackle and tail, are often all that's needed. Particularly good on fast or rippled water when a high float and good visibility are required.

will. White, black, and badger are the best colors. Sizes 12, 14, and 16.

This list is by no means the only fly selection that will catch trout and may not be the *best* list for the waters you fish most regularly. Every locale has its favorite flies and special times to use them. Spend some time talking to tackle-shop clerks and local anglers. If the fly that's working well for the local talent happens to be a size 16 Light Cahill, the angler who insists on using a size 10 Adams is not likely to catch many fish. This list has, however, done well on trout streams across the nation and in several foreign countries.

If you don't receive some input from a local source, try to capture one of the insects that happens to be on the water. Pick a fly from your box that appears to be most like it in size and color. Happily, this method of choosing a fly works much of the time and no further scientific experimentation is required.

The Progression of Color

There is a progression of insect color or shades of color that follows a natural "script." The first flies seen in the early spring are darker and gen-

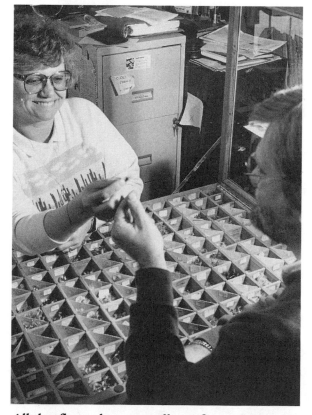

All dry-fly anglers, regardless of experience, are well advised to listen to the local tackle shop clerks when choosing flies for new waters. They know what the "hot" patterns are and want you as a regular customer.

erally smaller than those that follow. Very dark gray, bluish-dun shades and dark browns are the colors seen as the spring leaves begin to take form. Then come the pale browns, light grays, and mottled tones. As summer approaches the flies tend to be larger and mostly very pale shades of cream, some true yellows, and a light green one or two. During late summer and early fall the more prevalent insects switch back to dark grays, olive, and brown. More details on selecting flies will be found in the chapter titled "Fishing the Dry Fly."

WET FLIES

Most wet flies are designed to suggest nymphal forms of insects or near-adults that are struggling to reach the surface in order to emerge as adults. Recently, these about-to-hatch insects have been tagged as "emergers" and the label is highly appropriate. A few suggest tiny minnows whereas a large number are fanciful attractors and imitate nothing in particular. All types are useful and some of each should be in everyone's fly box.

Wet Flies to Start With

My favorite list of seven wet flies hasn't changed much over the years. These Lucky 7 coax trout (and panfish as well) with great consistency. As much as I love to experiment with new creations and colors, these old favorites are invariably turned to before a fishing day is over. They just keep on working.

Gold-ribbed Hare's Ear. This is the best wet fly ever created. It seldom fails to make anyone's wet fly list. Its scruffy, scraggly, chewed-on appearance suggests many aquatic creatures. *If I could have but one wet fly this would be it.*

Leadwing Coachman. Certainly the No. 2 wet fly in U.S. popularity contests. I like it best when a tiny tag of gold wire is tied near the bend of the hook.

Gordon Quill. Another traditional pattern that covers those dark gray/blue insects during early spring and late fall months.

Light Cahill. A wonderful pale-cream fly that suggests a wide range of late-spring insects. Tie or buy this pattern with creamish or very light tan hackles. Many of the commercial versions are too brownish.

Professor. This is an attractor pattern that resembles nothing in the real world. It will often interest trout when the dull colors won't. A great rainbow trout producer.

Royal Coachman. This ancient pattern is an attractor too and it's probably the best-known fly in the world. A wonderful brook trout fly, but all species have been lured by the RC.

Black Gnat. There must be a black fly in every box and this pattern is as good as any.

The most useful sizes for all of the above wet flies are 16, 14, 12, and 10. For special situations, a few 18s should be carried and, if you try fishing after dark, sizes 6, 4, and 2 can perform wonders. We'll get into that area of excitement in the chapter on fishing wet flies.

Gold-ribbed Hare's Ear may be the best wet-fly pattern ever designed. Like the Adams dry fly, it should be in every fly box in a wide range of sizes.

NYMPHS

It's easy to walk into any well-equipped fly fishing shop and find the traditional dry and wet fly patterns. Coast to coast and nation to nation, the Adams, Royal Coachman, and Hare's Ear are recognizable. It's different with nymphs. The standardization of nymph patterns has yet to occur and it probably won't. With so many outstanding fly tiers concentrating on these underwater creatures—and each of them taking a different approach in the tying—beginners find it difficult to identify nymph patterns. As we check fly catalogs and tackle shop display boxes we discover that Whitlock's Scud is totally different from Arbona's Scud. The addition of the surname is about as close as we can come to standardization. The natural and artificial nymphs vary so in size, color, and materials that to make a blanket statement about one of them is nearly impossible.

A good way to stock a nymph box is to spend some time studying catalogs to discover which patterns look more like the naturals in the waters you fish. Several of the mail-order houses offer nymph assortments designed for particular areas. For the most part, these assortments represent input from a number of anglers familiar with the streams of the region. You can't go far wrong with them.

The easiest and perhaps best way for a beginning nymph fisherman to stock his box is to ask the clerk in the local tackle emporium to help. He'll want you to come back as a satisfied customer so he's not likely to load you up with unusable junk.

Nymphs to Start With

Hare's Ear Nymph. Yes, here's the Hare's Ear again with stubby wings. It's a winner tied as a nymph too. Sizes 10, 12, 14, 16, 18.

Caddis Pupa. In various shades of olive, brown, gray, and dirty/cream this stage of the caddisfly is a highly effective fish-catcher. Best versions have bit of "sparkle" in the body. Same sizes as above.

Freshwater Scud. There are scads of scud imitations about, and while appearing very uncomplicated, they catch fish everywhere in the world. Scuds look like tiny shrimp and are, in fact, crustaceans. Pink, tan, yellow, and brown are favorite colors. Sizes 14, 16, 18, and 20.

Hendrickson. From fly shop to fly shop you'll find dozens of variations of this popular nymph. While Hendrickson does refer to a specific mayfly, it's become a generic term. Nearly all versions work well as a suggestion of many nymphs of about the same size. Sizes 10, 12, 14, 16, 18.

Green Drake Nymph. The nymph of this large mayfly is best tied on a size 8, long-shank hook. Not many other nymphs are as large but the style and materials are useful for other sizes. If you tie your own or have others tie flies for you, simply scale down the size and many other mayfly nymphs can be imitated. Sizes 8, 10, 12, 14.

Zug Bug. This is a nymph pattern that a lot

A thorax-style nymph that covers a wide variety of insects. While some nymphs have one tail instead of two, it's not important. Trout can't count. General shape, color, and presentation are far more important than minute details when nymphing.

of anglers use. Like the Hare's Ear, it imitates nothing in particular but everything in general. I wouldn't be without a Zug Bug or three. The sparkly peacock herl on the body is the magic ingredient. Sizes 10, 12, 14, 16.

San Juan Worm. For lack of a better category, this remarkable fly fishing lure (how can it be termed a fly?) is the western trout stream wonder. Don't go west without it. Works in the east too. Orange, red, and hot pink are the right colors. Sizes 10, 12, 14, 16.

STREAMERS

All of the comments about nymphs and the wisdom of paying attention to the local favorites applies to streamer flies. Since streamers are predominantly tied to suggest minnows, the best of them are those that look something like the tiny fish in the water at hand. As with wet flies, some highly popular streamer patterns also fall into the attractor category; they are simply flashy, colorful flies designed to get the fish's attention.

Included in the core group of attractors and imitative styles anglers will find useful are a few newcomers that have made a firm bid towards becoming standards. The following list of streamer patterns (or patterns very close to them) should be represented in every trout fisherman's vest.

Streamers to Start With

Muddler Minnow. It's safe to say that this pattern has caught more trout (and other species as well) than any other streamer pattern. Originally designed by Don Gapen as a suggestion of the sculpin minnow, this rather dull brown fly works everywhere. Sizes 4, 6, 8, 10, 12, 14.

Mickey Finn. Created by master angler John Alden Knight at least seventy-five years ago, The Mickey Finn, with its silver body and red and yellow wing, doesn't resemble any minnow

Muddler Minnow is the first-place winner among streamer patterns. Another "must-have" pattern in sizes 10, 8, and 6 on all trout streams. A great all-purpose fly that suggests minnows, crayfish, grasshoppers, and large nymphs.

Mickey Finn is remembered as much for its name as its effectiveness. As an attractor pattern it's a dandy. It works even better when tied with painted eyes.

ever seen. Millions of trout have fallen for it along with dozens of other species. Same sizes as above.

Black Ghost. Another well-known, highly popular streamer pattern that's been around for many decades. Basically a plain black and white fly, it

Black Ghost is another traditional streamer pattern that has proven its worth on all trout waters. This one is tied correctly, with the wings extending slightly beyond the hook end. A painted eye improves this pattern too.

looks very minnow-like when wet. Same sizes.

Grey Ghost. A creation of Maine fly tier Carrie Stevens, the Grey Ghost is supposed to suggest a freshwater smelt and was first used on landlocked salmon. It works equally well on trout and is found in fly shops around the world. Same sizes.

Other Streamer Suggestions

Streamer flies come in myriad shapes and colors as there are hundreds of regional favorites. It would be confusing to list them by their local names but certain styles of streamers have become identifiable. Dave Whitlock's Sculpin series of streamers are well proven as are Keith Fulsher's Thunder Creek flies. The Matuka streamer type, which originated in New Zealand, is another excellent producer. The Woolly Buggers, the Maribous, Rabbit-fur Zonkers, and Leeches are more or less generic and it seems that every major trout stream has spawned a version of each. Here again, watch, listen, and pay attention to what the local talent recommends.

THE "RIGHT" FLY

Involved discussions, lengthy articles by the thousands, and many books have belabored the question of pattern vs. presentation since fly fishing began. I won't solve it here, nor can anyone because the issue is the essence of the sport. In two sentences the argument comes down to: (1) If the fly presented is a reasonable facsimile of some creature a fish chooses to eat, you'll probably hook the fish. (2) The fly selected is not terribly important if it's well presented.

Depending on who's doing the explaining or expounding, other qualifications will be added to these dogmatic schools of thought. The beginning fly fisherman will be confronted by these two avenues of angling philosophy before his first season ends. He may decide to embrace one or the other in short order but will probably switch back and forth several times during his angling career. Most of us have because fish don't always act or react as humans would like them to.

We will come to know anglers, very good anglers, who fish an entire season with a half dozen patterns or less and appear to catch as many fish as the rest of us. We'll also come in contact with the dedicated "match-the-hatch" insect watchers who wouldn't dream of casting a fly that wasn't a near duplicate of the prevailing natural. Some in this group will also rack up impressive annual trout tallies.

The intelligent compromise is to select a fly that's pretty close to what the trout are eating in size, color, and silhouette and then present it as well as possible. The one-fly angler who knows his water well is always going to catch some fish because he casts to the productive spots. The hatch-matcher will catch some too because he's got the right fly on. See what I mean, the argument is not really an argument at all and will remain unresolvable. Be flexible in accepting new ideas while never forsaking the traditional approaches that have so well served other generations of fly anglers.

5

Fishing the Dry Fly

Many veteran fly fishermen argue that fishing with the dry fly is more fun than fishing with flies that swim beneath the surface. For that reason, even when the trout could be more easily fooled by subsurface methods, some anglers elect to use the dry fly. Beginners like dry flies too because they can see the fly and have a better grasp of what's going on. Watching the fly vanish in an eruption of water or gently sucked under by a feeding trout is high excitement. Faulty presentations are also obvious and how to make the necessary corrections are more evident. The trout itself is sometimes seen just before it takes or rejects the dry fly, which adds still more heady anticipation.

THE PERFECT SETUP

Let's accompany an imaginary angler onto the stream and watch him fish a dry fly. Let's say his name is Bill.

As Bill nears the water's edge the sight and sounds of fish rising to gulp floating insects tell him that a hatch is in progress. Flies are in the air and also on the water as they struggle to shuck their nymphal cases. The fish are eagerly eating the flies, and they are large enough to see easily. Bill can't wait to make the first cast. But he pauses. He won't tie on any old fly. He snatches one of the insects from the air to check size, color, and overall silhouette for comparison with what's in his fly box.

A size 12 Adams looks a lot like the mottled-tan mayflies coming off the water. The flies are actually March Browns, and the Adams is about the right color. There's a heavy splash over there beside that big rock. Bill glances up from tying on his fly in time to see the tip of the fish's tail as it completes a classic head-and-tail rise. A sure sign of an active feeder. He makes three cautious steps into the water a few feet below and across from the target. He's going to cast up and across the stream. He begins to strip a few feet of line from the reel with each false cast, measuring the travel of the fly through the air. He's making the false casts to one side of the fish in order not to spook it. Now he's got the right amount of line and leader in the air. The rod comes forward and—splat! Uh-oh. A little too short and a landing that's a tad too forceful.

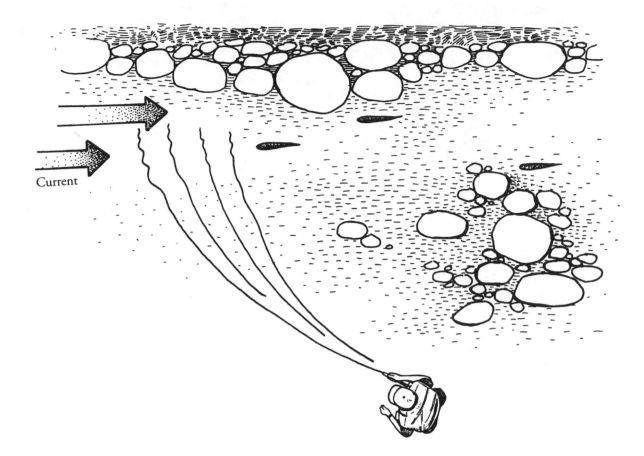

Current

Casting up and across is the standard dry fly approach. If you see a fish rise before you cast, try to place the fly four or five feet upstream from its position. If you're not sure exactly where fish might be, begin casting at the tail end of the pool and methodically work your way upstream.

But the fish rises again. It wasn't frightened. Bill's being careful. He's not picking up the fly too soon. A noisy pick-up might scare the fish. He waits until the fly floats well past the feeding position. He makes two more false casts while stripping out a few more feet of line. The rod is checked at about the 10 o'clock position and the fly pauses in midair. It floats down softly and lands about four feet in front of the fourteen-inch brown trout. The leader falls in a loose series of S-shaped wiggles and the fly is floating, drag-free, towards the hotspot. The trout sees the fly. Here it comes. With a curving twist of the body, the trout tips its head through the surface film and takes the fly.

Pulling the slack line tight with one hand and raising the rod with the other, Bill brings the fly hook perfectly into the corner of the trout's jaw. The fish is solidly hooked. Bill pinches the line against the rod grip and reels up the slack line. Not a monster trout—but a nice one. Bill wants to get the trout on the reel in case it makes a run.

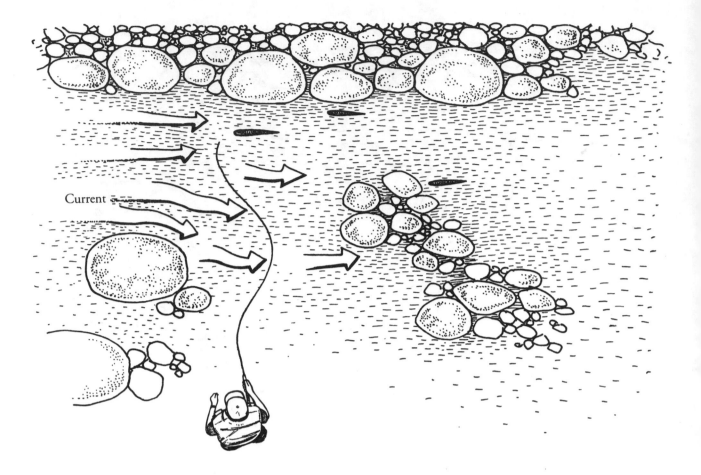

Current

Conflicting currents, seen and unseen, often disrupt an otherwise perfect cast, causing the dry fly to "drag" unnaturally. Casting curves and wiggles may solve the problem. If this doesn't work with an upstream cast, it may be necessary to move to a position upstream of the rising trout for a different casting angle.

It does. He releases the line between fingertips and rod grip and allows the trout to run against the drag of the reel. There's another run and some splashing on the surface. Bill's playing the fish correctly by allowing the fish to fight against the reel. And he's also keeping the rod tip just above the horizontal in order to bring the rod's resistance into the fray. Nicely done, so far.

Now the fish is tiring and it's showing a flash of white belly. Bill reels in some line—slowly now—no herky-jerky movements. He wades a step forward to keep the fish out of the silt that

forms in the shallows. Bill will release this fish and he doesn't want it to breath in too much of that muddy silt. He's sliding his hand down the leader and finds the hook. A quick twist between thumb and forefinger and the fish is free. This time he didn't have to net it or hold it. Good show. The fish remains motionless for a second or so, then it regains its equilibrium and fans away quickly to seek the cover of deeper water. Fine job, Bill!

In the foregoing situation, where a sizable quantity of naturals are present, the trout are

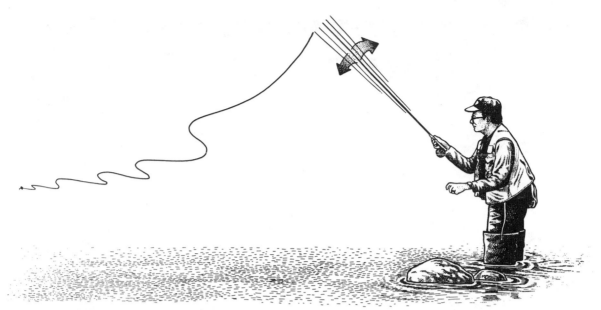

An "S" cast introduces wiggles into the line and leader by moving the rod from side to side as the fly drops to the surface. The timing is not difficult to master if you keep your eye on the fly and wiggle the rod when the leader is five or six feet from the water.

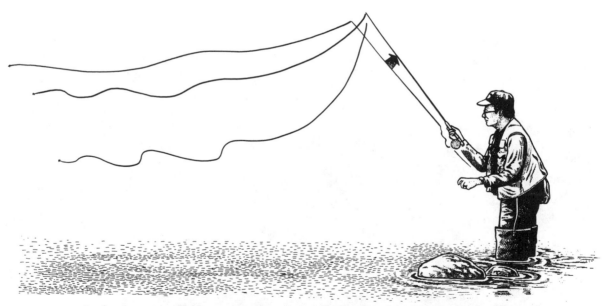

A check cast will also put curves into the leader almost automatically. False cast a few times to be sure enough line and leader are extended. Cast as if to put the fly beyond the fish. As the forward cast reaches maximum distance, pull back smartly on the rod tip. The fly will stop in midair and several "S" turns will form in the leader. Note: This technique will work much better if the tippet section of the leader is at least 30 inches long.

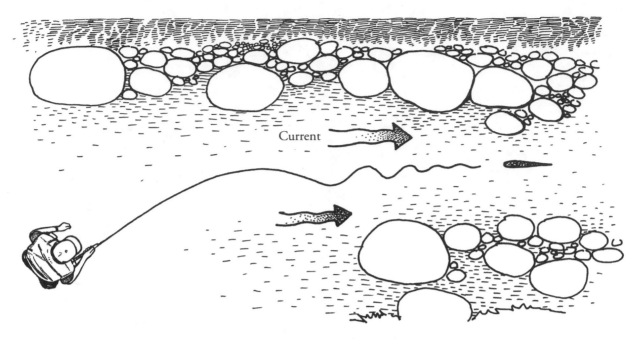

Current

Here's a common trout fishing situation where the rocks on both sides of a rising fish prevent an up-and-across cast. A check cast is the best way to handle it.

Three or four-inch movement of the wrist is enough to set a small hook in trout's jaw—if the slack line has been stripped in as the fly floats downstream. More leader tippets are broken at the strike than at any other moment in the struggle.

When a fish is hooked, reel up the slack line as quickly as possible while maintaining tension with the fingers of the rod hand.

quite confident and not nearly so likely to be put down by a misdirected cast or loud, splashy wading. The Adams did a good job of suggesting the natural March Brown and Bill remembered to execute the check cast. Don't be overcome by the seemingly large number of details a fly caster has to keep in mind. As your time on the water increases, they'll all come together.

A CADDISFLY HATCH

This time, the rises seen are not the head-and-tail movements that result in perfect circles etched on the water's surface. Instead, they are splashes caused by leaping and lunging trout. It appears that the trout have gone bonkers and such activity will speed up the angler's pulse rate as well. This kind of action usually means caddisflies are hatching.

Bill's back on the water. Some of the fish are actually leaping into the air to grab an escaping insect. Seeing the insects is not difficult; their flight is erratic—up, down, and sideways. Some of them didn't hatch into perfect specimens, and they buzz, jump, and scoot crazily across the surface. The trout are feeding on them greedily. Bill has decided they're a pale grayish

color and that a size 16 fly is about right. He chooses a Henryville Special.

The first cast is sent to land about four feet upstream of the nearest rise. A perfect float over the chosen spot brings no action. A second cast, a third, fourth, and several more—with the same result. Maybe he spooked that fish. Splash! The fish rises again. Well now, it wasn't spooked. What's going on here? We can see Bill's brow wrinkle. He's puzzled. Good cast, good float, the fly looks darned near like the naturals. It's hitting him now. The naturals are *moving*. He's got to give his fly some *action*.

At the moment his next cast sends the fly to a likely spot he moves the rod tip to one side in a series of three quick jerks. The fly ducks under the surface on the third but a trout grabs it as it does. Bill strikes. No hook-up.

Bill reaches out and pulls in his line, hand over hand. He examines the fly. Hook intact. But it's not floating well. He applies a dab of dry-fly floatant and false casts the fly four or five times to shake off the surplus. Out it goes, and he tries the jerk-jerk-jerk routine again. This time the fly scoots across the surface much like some of the naturals are doing—and there's a strike. It comes so fast Bill nearly breaks his leader tippet with his equally fast reaction. He's hooked up with a foot-long trout that makes two lightning-fast leaps. The hook pops loose on the second jump. That's okay, Bill, you did it right and there are more trout rising. You'll have plenty of chances before the morning's over.

The three-jerk technique Bill brought into play is but one way of giving the fly a life-like action. Longer or shorter jerks, changing directions, long sweeping pulls and repeated roll casts to give the trout a different look at your fly are all useful tricks. The idea is to imitate the actions of the caddis through rod and line manipulation.

FISHING TINY FLIES

Trout being opportunists, they'll feed on what's available. During many weeks of the trout season, very small insects are the most abundant food in a stream. Many mayflies, especially those of the genus *Paraleptophlebia* in the East and the *Baetis* in the West, are usually size 20 or smaller. Various gnats, midges, ants, and other terrestrial insects also fall into the group of "invisibilia" that anglers are so often faced with.

When insects must be suggested by hooks of size 18 or smaller, we've got to alter our techniques and terminal tackle to some degree. There are different ways of coping with these nearly unseeable creatures, but one constant remains: the dead-drift or drag-free float is almost mandatory.

While the best and most exciting places to use tiny dry flies are placid pools or still ponds, small to medium sized trout will often be found feeding on midges in fast water. Believe it not, catching such fish is the easiest kind of small-fly fishing. It's nearly impossible to follow a size 18 fly on broken or ripply water, but if you watch the touch-down of line and leader you'll know about where the fly is drifting. If you see the slightest surface disturbance or the flash of a fish's side or belly, raise the rod tip and the leader. You'll be surprised how often the line will come up tight.

An effective method of fishing tiny flies is to tie a small piece of colored yarn above a leader knot as a strike indicator. If the tippet section is about 30 inches long, that's a good place to attach it. Any kind of yarn will work, but if it's wool it'll have to be soaked with dry-fly floatant

In fast and ripply water or when using tiny flies or hard-to-see colors, a strike indicator may help. A small sphere or cube of cork, balsa wood, or plastic foam will do the job. Cut a slit into the float with a razor blade or sharp knife and press in the leader. Paint the float with florescent fingernail polish for better visibility.

every ten minutes or so. Some synthetic yarns will float all day without any treatment. A small chunk of plastic foam, like the little white "peanuts" used as packing filler, work perfectly. A chunk about the size of a pea is just right. Cut a slit with a razor blade and slip it onto the leader. Have some extra "floats" pre-cut so another one can be snapped into place when needed. It will be.

In moving water, under bad light conditions or as an aid for less than hawk-like eyes, the yarn or plastic indicator is a boon with tiny flies. When several fish are in your target area and the rises are little more than dimples on the surface, the slightest wobble of the indicator is the signal to *pull* with the rod tip.

Note the word *pull* instead of strike. The hooks on tiny flies have very small gaps between shank and hook point which reduces the likelihood of the hook point finding a place to stick. Hook-setting with size 18s or smaller is a knack that must be developed. Fortunately, the character of the usual rise to a tiny fly helps in that fish take the little naturals slowly and positively. Much of the time the fish which is about to take your fly will be seen a second or longer before it actually does. Granted, it can be more than a trifle unnerving to see a sizable trout fanning towards your fly and not pull too quickly; steel yourself. Wait until you see the jaws close or the fly totally disappear before moving the rod tip or pulling on the slack line. Once the timing sequence is solved, solid hook-ups will take place with astonishing regularity.

Because tiny hooks have proportionately small eyes, thick leader material won't pass through them. Even if it did trout wouldn't take the fly because it wouldn't drift along in a natural manner. Longer, smaller-diameter leaders must be used with tiny flies for more delicate presentation and for longer drag-free floats. An easy way to modify one of the leaders described earlier in this book is to lengthen the last two sections by a foot to 14 inches. The tippet section should be at least

30 to 40 inches long. Such a long tippet is somewhat more difficult to cast accurately, but the tiny fly doesn't offer much air resistance, and after a dozen casts or so, you'll get the "feel" of it. A bit more power applied on the forward cast will help. Don't fret if the leader doesn't straighten out nicely as you might want it to in other situations. Extra curves and wiggles in the long, fine tippet is exactly what you're trying for. The curves deliver a longer drag-free float and that's the key to fishing tiny flies. Those last two leader sections should be of .006 and .004 or .003. The last diameter listed will test about one pound. Yes, that's pretty fine and not all fish will be subdued by it, but you'll enjoy a lot more hook-ups.

Several of the fly patterns in the basic dry-fly list are effective in sizes 18 and smaller. The Adams, Light Cahill, Gordon Quill, and Grey Hackle Peacock are excellent producers when tied that small and even smaller. The Brown Ant is a universal fish taker and will often work as a suggestion of other insect forms.

Remember, we're talking about small flies here. While it's true that the trout sees these tiny morsels at close range, they're still *small*. Details of construction are not as important as with larger flies. This is particularly true of insects with prominent wings. Wings on flies of size 16 and larger are, to many experienced anglers, important to success. On flies of size 18 and smaller, wings are sometimes of no consequence. However, a few of the tiny mayflies (the *Baetis* group, for example) have wings that are quite large in comparison to the rest of their anatomy. It's best to have some winged and wingless styles.

The style of dry fly now known as paradun has become a great favorite of anglers when trout are rising to the small stuff. Paraduns are tied with what's known as "parachute" hackles. The hackle is wound around the base of the wing instead of around the hook shank. This causes it to lay flat on the water instead of perching the fly on hackle tips. The wings of a

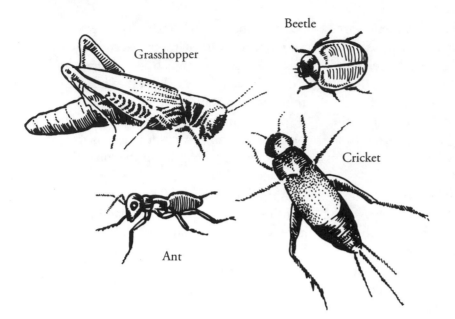

Grasshopper

Beetle

Cricket

Ant

Crickets, ants, grasshoppers and beetles of many kinds are common on many trout streams. These creatures usually float when in the water, thus requiring a surface imitation. If a dead drift doesn't produce a strike try working a terrestrial by imparting some jiggles and jerks.

paradun consist of hair, feather barbules, or synthetic material tied in a clump.

TERRESTRIALS

The land-born creatures that find their way to the water, on purpose or by accident, are more varied in size, shape, and color than are aquatic insects. All of them may be eaten by fish at times while several are regular menu items.

Grasshoppers, crickets, ants, Japanese beetles, ladybugs, leaf hoppers, locusts, measuring worms, and caterpillars are terrestrials, and there are many more that have some importance as trout food. How often trout eat them depends on what sort of environment a stream flows through. For example, expect to find more grasshoppers near streams adjacent to fields and cropland, crickets where there are plenty of flat stones along the bank, and measuring worms and caterpillars where a forested landscape predominates.

Most of the common terrestrials have inspired an artificial counterpart. Some of them, like the grasshoppers and crickets, have several, the size and color depending on the local variety of the natural. Here again, check as many fly catalogs as possible. The good ones show several terrestrial patterns as well as the old favorites, and even the experienced fly fisherman who thinks he's seen everything may be surprised.

How an angler knows when to fish a particular terrestrial imitation can come about through direct observation, an educated guess, or a total accident. The best clue comes from actually seeing a fish rise to eat a specific insect. Tie something like it on your leader and go to it. A good guess might be made if you see some small rise forms, nothing more than dimples really, and play a hunch that the fish are working on ants. If a brown ant in size 18 or 20 catches fish, congratulate yourself.

FISHING BLIND

The most rewarding dry-fly fishing comes from seeing the fish rise before you cast, then selecting a fly and seducing the fish with it. To some anglers, casting to rising fish is the only acceptable way. It's difficult to argue with the satisfaction level of this approach, but we must be realistic. Trout don't rise precisely when and where we'd like them to at all times. Nor can all of us fish as often as we'd like. We've got to take the

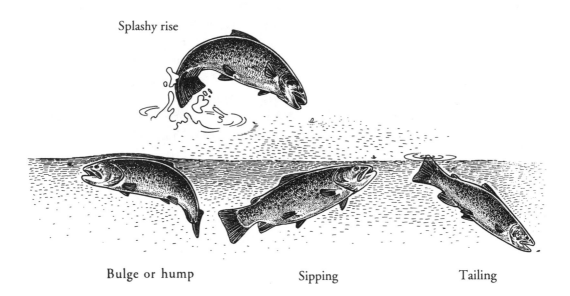

Splashy rise

Bulge or hump   Sipping   Tailing

To determine the kind of fly to try first, observe the "rise form" on the water. From left to right: a bulge or hump on the water usually indicates the trout are feeding on nymphs that are barely under the surface. A splashy rise, with the trout coming completely out of the water, is a sure sign of flying or drifting insects. A sipping rise is the clue to use a very tiny dry fly. The tailing rise (often difficult to determine) tells the angler that the trout are grubbing on or near the bottom for nymphs, caddis cases or crayfish.

fishing days and situations as they come. "Fishing blind" or "fishing the water" without the advantage of seeing the rise is what anglers face more often than not. Happily, trout can be caught regularly without a horde of mayflies in the air. We just have to find them.

As mentioned earlier, a black beetle or black cricket is usually my first choice as a dry fly when there doesn't appear to be much surface activity. This is an especially good beginning strategy on calm or slowly moving water. Float it through the pools in a dead-drift manner for several casts and then try a slight twitching technique (as we did with the caddis imitations). If you spot a fish moving toward the fly that turns away at the last second, try a smaller version of the same fly. Switching to a smaller fly is, by the way, a good move any time you see that kind of rejection.

When fishing faster or ripply water, an excellent searching fly is the Badger Bivisible. It's a simple, high-riding fly that's nothing more than two hackles wound around a hook with a tail of the same color. Badger hackle is cream colored with a dark-brown or black center. It looks buggy, floats well, and is easy to see on broken water. The most famous fly pattern in North America for blind or search casting is the Royal Wulff. Its divided, upright white wings stand out like a beacon on all water surfaces. Like the bivisible, it floats well and trout seem able to see it at great distances and from great depths.

The Royal Wulff is the among the best of fly patterns for performing a dry fly trick known as "creating a hatch." This stunt calls for directing cast after cast over a likely-looking spot, in an attempt to make the trout think an actual hatch is taking place. To do this successfully requires that each cast be a near duplicate of the last one, causing the fly to float through a specific area in precisely the same way. It's challenging to be sure, but when not much else is happening it's great casting practice so the time is not wasted. Surprisingly, this repetitive casting produces a rise often enough to make it worthwhile. The best dry-fly angler I ever knew, Robert N. Pinney, of Coudersport, Pennsylvania, often used the technique to perfection. I was an early teenager when Pinney first showed me how it was done. This was before the Royal Wulff was widely known, so Pinney usually used an Adams or a Light Cahill in size 12 or 14. My mentor's demonstration was a thing of beauty.

6

Fishing the Wet Fly

In the broad sense, any fly type that is not designed to float on the surface of the water can be considered a "wet" fly. This includes nymphs, streamers, and the traditional wet fly itself. Most early wet flies were created as imitations of winged insects, and the patterns used over 400 years ago look amazingly like modern versions. With the exception of the eyed hook, they were made with the same basic materials—fur, feathers, and thread. Bending the hook steel to form an eye didn't occur to hook makers or anglers until the late 1800s. Loops made of twisted gut or short pieces of gut known as snells were used to connect the fly with the leader. Even after eyed hooks were commonplace, many anglers clung to the snells and gut loops, believing them to impart a more lifelike presentation to the fly. They didn't, in fact, but in fly fishing, as in most human activities, old ideas die hard. Conversely, it's lucky for fly fishermen that some old ideas continue to hang around. A few, like the centuries-proven fishing tactics of long ago, still form the basis of how best to use wet flies on today's waters.

The wet fly in its simplest and most common form consists of a tail, body, wing, and hackle or throat. All of the materials used for these components can be switched around to

The Royal Coachman (top) and March Brown are representative of standard wet-fly style. If a more nymph-like profile is wanted, simply trim the wings with fingernail clippers to the desired length.

create an unlimited number of patterns.

In Chapter 4 we offered a list of seven wet flies that can be counted on and some comments about each. To save you the trouble of checking back, here they are again: Gold-ribbed Hare's Ear, Leadwing Coachman, Gordon Quill, Light Cahill, Professor, Royal Coachman, and Black Gnat. These patterns are essential. That doesn't mean that other patterns are not useful and in some cases as good or better. Certain locally designed patterns will indeed perform better on some waters, but with the above flies anglers can fish for trout anywhere in the world and expect to catch fish. In addition, these flies are generally available in fly shops around the world.

ACROSS-AND-DOWNSTREAM METHOD

Casting across and slightly downstream has been, is, and will continue to be the foundation of all wet-fly fishing.

As the flies (most anglers fish two or three at a time) meet the water they sink, and as the current carries them to the full length of line and leader they rise and begin to travel back to the surface. This combination of sinking and rising provides enough action to interest many feeding trout. In addition, as the line and leader near the end of their drifting and sinking time, the current takes over and causes the flies to move

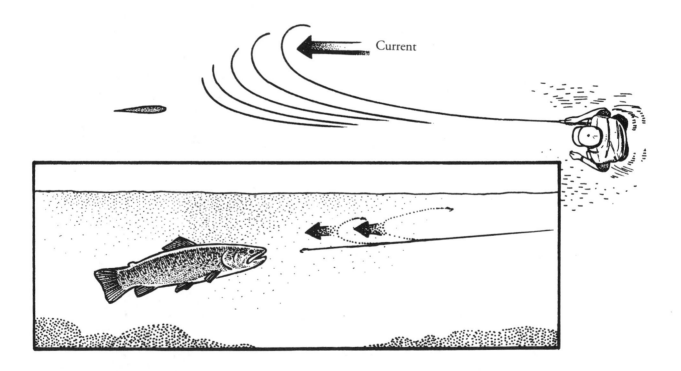

Current

The standard wet-fly approach is to cast down and slightly across the current. The fly (flies) can be allowed to drift freely, stripped or retrieved by the hand-twist method. Without any assistance from the angler, wet flies will "buttonhook," or turn, as they reach the end of their drift. This action alone will often produce a strike.

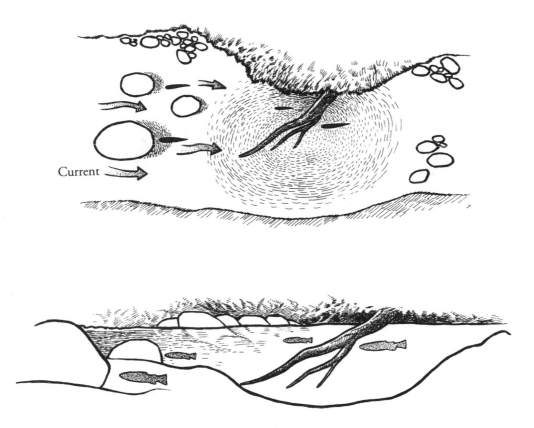

Here's a typical trout pool with rocks, a grassy bank, and a half-submerged log. Trout like cover and overhanging protection. Fish such places thoroughly beginning with short casts. Wade carefully and fish with the sun in your face when possible.

faster. Just before the leader is fully extended in a straight downstream attitude, the flies do a quick "buttonhook" or "curl" maneuver. The change of drifting speed, the buttonhook move, and the rising of the flies is a near perfect rendition of how a nymph acts when it's swimming to the surface to hatch into an adult winged fly. By doing little more than following the progress of his line, watching for the telltale "winks" under the water and being alert for a stout pull on the fly, a novice angler will catch a fair number of trout.

The novice is probably shaking his head in amazement at this apparently simple method of fishing the wet fly. Well, it is simple and the

dead downstream drift described is the correct way to begin any session of wet-fly fishing. If it doesn't bring a strike after a dozen casts, some variations must be added. The introduction of some jiggles and jerks should be tried next. Keeping the rod at about a 35-degree angle above the water, raise the rod in three-inch jerks, lifting and pumping as the flies drift downstream. Many aquatic insects dart about swiftly just before they hatch and that's precisely what you're trying to suggest with the pumping and jerking. Don't be violent about this at first—move the rod only a few inches so that the flies move no more than three or four inches with each jerk. Continue doing this for four or

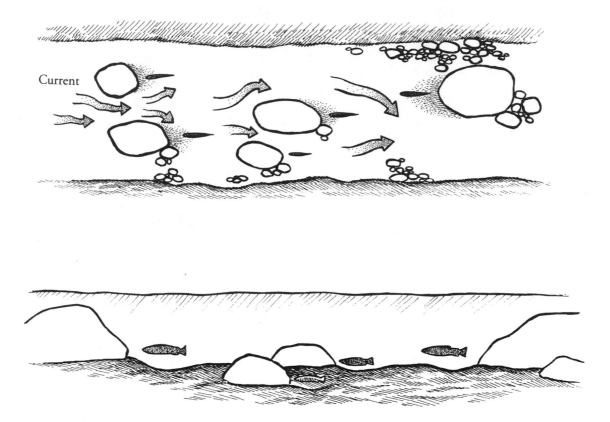

When fishing wet flies in a rock-strewn pool such as this one, expect to find fish in the slight eddies behind and in front of the rocks. If the current is moving rapidly, retrieve the flies at a speed that is just slightly faster than the water is moving. If the water is deeper, say three feet or more, move all sunken flies at a slower and more deliberate pace. Before giving up on a particularly fishy looking spot, be sure to vary the action of the flies and the speed of retrieve.

five strokes even after the flies have hit the maximum downstream position and have risen to the surface. Many times a trout can be coaxed into taking the dancing fly on the surface which appears about to take wing.

Within this jiggle-and-jerk tactic, a wide range of action can be given the flies. The jerks can be made smoothly in such a way that the fly sort of glides in an undulating manner. They can be done faster and the cadence altered. An old-timer I once fished with jiggled his wet flies in nearly perfect waltz time—one-two-three-pause-one-two-three-pause. If trout were interested in wet flies at all, this veteran never got skunked.

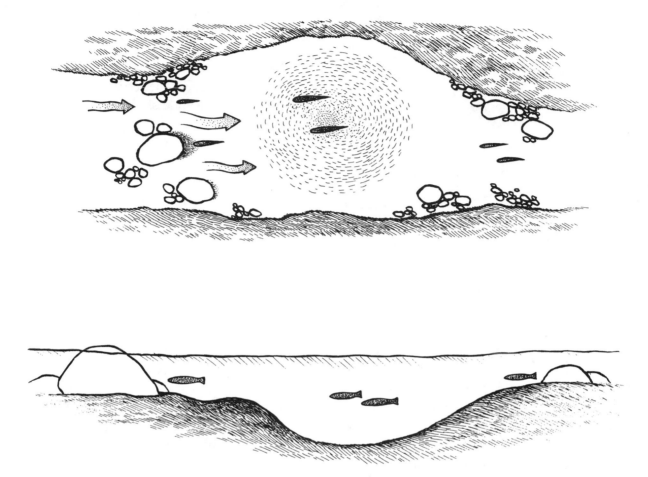

In a pool such as this one where some fish may be at the shallow ends, it's a safe bet that the larger ones will be in the deeper water near the center. Try a fast retrieving speed at the ends and a slower rate in the middle. Wait a few seconds before beginning the retrieve when working the deeper water in order to give any sort of sunken fly more time to reach the productive area.

The important lesson here is that by adding some lifelike movement through use of the rod hand alone, dozens of subtle variations can be tried. When a particular move brings a strike you may have discovered the secret of the day. It's what the bass anglers refer to as finding the pattern.

STRIPPING RETRIEVE

When casting wet flies across and downstream in moving water, the current itself often provides enough action and movement to attract fish. Moving the rod in various ways contributes still more movement, but there are

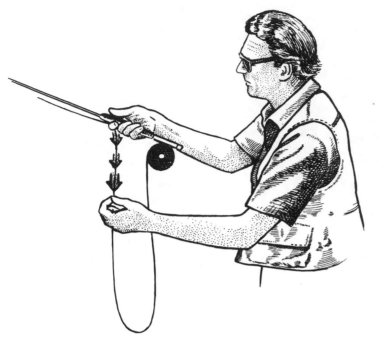

Stripping line when retrieving sunken flies is done by allowing the line to pass between rod grip and finger(s) as it is pulled with the non-casting hand. The flies can be moved fast, slow or at any speed or combination the angler chooses. Varying the retrieve speed can often work wonders!

times when a faster swimming pace is required. Following a very short cast, some anglers move the rod up or to one side in a series of progressive jerks, but this technique has a serious drawback. If the rod is raised too far up or too far to one side, it is in a poor position for striking. In fact, striking hard with the rod at a near vertical attitude can easily break the tip section. This is precisely why so many vintage fly rods feature short tips. A far better way of accomplishing this is by stripping line with the non-casting hand. After the cast is completed, get the line under the index finger of the casting hand and use it as an extra guide. By pulling the line through the hooked finger and pinching it slightly after each pull, you can impart longer jerks or a kind of gliding action to the fly.

As each pull is made, allow the line to fall in loose coils at your feet. Some care must be taken to prevent the line from winding about your feet, or around rocks or other obstacles, but most of the time it won't. The thickness of the fly line helps in preventing tangles. Of course, it's necessary to make a couple of false casts to

extend the line for the next cast. If a fish is hooked, pinch the line between finger and rod grip and reel up the slack. This is very important, for while you're engaged in fighting the fish, a step in the wrong direction may wrap the line around your ankles.

HAND-TWIST RETRIEVE

When fish are feeding with considerable abandon, anglers who can walk and chew gum at the same time will catch some fish no matter how the fly is retrieved. At other times, even when plenty of fish seem to be active, it may be impossible to beg a strike. This is often the case in calm or nearly calm water. Here is where the *hand-twist retrieve* may come to the rescue.

After you cast, grasp the line dropping from the stripping guide and hold it between thumb and forefinger of your non-casting hand. By twisting the wrist, a half-circle of line will be formed. Bend the other fingers in such a way that the half-circle is folded into the palm. Holding the line lightly with the fingers, twist

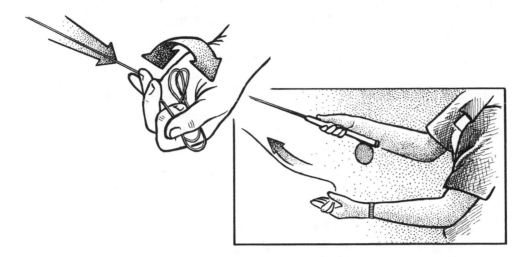

The hand-twist retrieve consists of coiling the line in the non-casting hand through a kind of rolling motion. It can be learned easily with ten minutes of practice. Wet flies can be made to move in an undulating, lifelike manner by hand-twisting and bobbing the rod tip up and down. Mixing the retrieve styles and speeds is the key to successful wet-fly angling.

the wrist again and another half circle will form. Lightly grasp that one and keep on twisting. If you do it right, the line will slide out the hand like a soft spring on the next cast. For some anglers this is the most difficult wet-fly maneuver to perform, but like a number of other exercises, this too will become second nature with practice. The hand-twist retrieve is not easy to explain in print, so study the illustrations.

As with the stripping retrieve, speed and cadence can be mixed through use of the hand-twist to create all sorts of fly action. In calm water where lack of current doesn't add much to fly movement, the hand-twist, done at a slow, steady pace can work wonders. Trout usually feed in a more leisurely manner in still water. Because the food is not about to be swept away by the current, they take their time in deciding which morsel they'll eat next. When mayfly, caddisfly, and stonefly nymphs are swimming

toward the surface they too seem to move at a relaxed pace in slow-moving water. A retrieve cadence that often works well in such situations can best be described as "twist—pause-pause-pause—twist—pause-pause-pause."

FISHING MORE THAN ONE

It's important to remember that wet flies need not always be fished completely beneath the water's surface. Long before dry flies were popular, wet flies were often retrieved rapidly in a deliberate attempt to keep them on the surface. The idea was to imitate the fluttering caddisflies and hatching mayflies that sometimes flop about for a few seconds before taking wing. And don't sell that old technique short. No seasons pass without seeing several days when wet flies moved rapidly across the surface catch trout like crazy. For such fishing, nothing beats a pair or even a trio of wet flies on the same leader. And that brings us to one of the few dogmatic opinions you'll find in this book: Downstream wet-fly fishing is more productive when two or three wet flies are fished on the same leader.

It's not unheard of to fish four or more flies at once; trout anglers in Scotland, for example, once fished entire fleets of a dozen or so. Most wet-fly fanciers stop at three. I do, because I believe that three is a magic number for attracting trout. Besides, three is about all most anglers can cast comfortably.

During the first half of the century, wet flies were tied with short leaders, or "snells," attached. The 6-inch snell had a loop on one end and this loop was interlocked with a corre-sponding loop on the standard wet-fly leader. Such leaders were sold everywhere fly tackle was displayed, and the usual style featured a loop on each end and two additional loops spaced evenly between the end loops. Most of these were 6 feet long. While this arrangement sounds primitive to today's fly anglers, the four-loop leader with snelled flies probably accounted for more trout than those alive today in any three states. Three wet flies similarly strung on a modern monofilament leader are capable of outfishing all other fly fishing meth-ods during a full season. For my money, the old-fashioned wet flies remain the most consis-tently productive trout-getters an angler can attach to his leader.

The right leader for fishing three flies is the

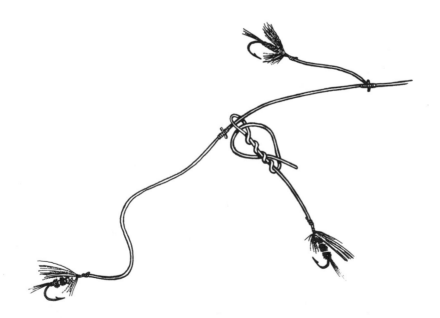

At the outset, one fly may seem enough to be concerned with but two or three wet flies fished simultaneously will bring more strikes most of the time. The logic is simple: three different patterns, at three depths, and three different movements increase chances for success. Droppers can be extensions of a blood knot or attached with an improved clinch knot.

same one used for dry flies with one exception: it has "droppers" to accommodate the extra flies. An easy way to make a dropper is to extend one of the blood knots that connect different diameters of monofilament as the tapered leader is being constructed (see drawing). Plan the leader in such a way that the droppers are at least 20 inches apart. Any closer than that and tangling may occur when false casting. They can be spaced as much as 3 feet if you decide to use only two flies. Be sure to extend the thickest part of the leader material as the dropper, the section closest to the rod tip. It's less likely to wrap around the body of the leader itself.

Another way to attach droppers is by using a short piece of mono, no lighter than 3X, as a snell. Tie a 12-inch section of mono to the body of the leader using an improved clinch knot. Slide the clinch knot towards the next blood knot on the leader and pull it snug. Use monofilament of the same diameter as that of the section you're tying to. Attach the fly in such a way that the dropper snell is no longer than 7 inches. Then tie on a dropper for the "hand" fly, the one closest to the rod tip or the angler's hand, 20 inches above this one. If longer, it's more likely to wrap around the leader when casting. If different size flies are used on a multi-fly leader, be sure the heaviest or largest fly is at the end of the leader and the smaller ones on the droppers. Here again, they'll cast better with the heavy fly leading the way.

An advantage of using snells tied to the leader with a clinch knot is the ease of removal. Should you decide to switch to dry flies, simply clip off the snell and you're back to a conventional tapered leader.

The advantage of the three-fly arrangement is that it can offer the fish a choice of *three patterns, three sizes, and three different presentations* on the same cast. The point fly will sink faster than the middle dropper and hand flies as they begin their downstream drift. Right away, you're offering the fish flies at different depths. The current will press against the middle of the leader with extra force, which causes the point fly to begin its curling swing before the other two. This moves each fly at a different speed. Any added action, such as jiggling the rod tip, or retrieving by hand-twist or stripping, moves each of the three flies at a *different* cadence because the action imparted will affect the fly closest to the rod tip a micro-second before the other two.

The most amazing result of this technique is that a lot of trout take flies presented this way and hook themselves. The angler helps his cause by casting to the right place and performing some enticing rod movements, but the fish are usually less wary about taking wet flies than the floating ones.

The angler is in charge of the flies he chooses and this process is also enhanced by the three-fly cast. If you begin by selecting three different patterns and discover that one of the flies is receiving all of the strikes, it's not a bad idea to add another of the same pattern. You may end up with three flies of the same pattern on the leader and have a spectacular day. It may also happen that the hand fly, the one that's tickling the surface as it swings or is being retrieved, is the best producer. When this happens it may not be a matter of pattern—it's a case of fly action instead of size or color. Pay attention and become a fly-fishing detective.

My admiration for the traditional wet fly is strong, I'll admit, but don't be lulled into being a one-style angler. When fish are obviously rising to surface food, not to fish a dry fly would be foolish. If a full hour of casting wet flies doesn't produce a strike from water you know contains trout, it's wise to try something else.

7

Fishing the Nymph

For angling purposes, *nymph* refers to an aquatic creature that may or may not eventually become a winged insect. Ambiguity is necessary here because many nymphlike life forms that inhabit lakes and streams, such as scuds, creepers, cress bugs, leeches, and snails, never grow wings. All of these are basically underwater dwellers and are suggested and imitated by using flies that are fished as nymphs. We're forced to use the word *imitate* here because in no other quarter of the fly-tying art has such near duplication taken place. By combining man-made materials with natural furs, feathers, and fibers, eye-fooling realism is possible.

For convenience, it's best to separate nymphs into two general categories: the realistic and the suggestive, just as we do with other flies. With nymphs, however, both categories tend to look more like the real thing than standard dry and wet flies. They have to since they are usually fished deeper and slower—right down there in the fish's living room where they can be closely examined.

The Latin names for insects are used occasionally in this book and many serious nymph fishermen are familiar with them. If learning the names pleases you, by all means go ahead and do it. Being a good streamside observer is important in fly fishing, and nymphing is no exception. What's more important, however, is the ability to distinguish the differences between the various families of nymphs. It's not vital to learn the names but knowing that the prevalent nymphs in this stream look different from those in another stream can play a big part in your angling success. If you know that large stonefly nymphs are not common in the stream you're fishing but medium-sized mayfly nymphs are, you can choose a pattern with more confidence. Check the illustration of the basic differences between stonefly and mayfly nymphs and you'll see why this is so. Caddisflies, in their cased and larval forms, are also present in many streams. The nymph angler should examine the underside of stones sifting through stream bottom silt for these latent insects.

While the beginner will find dry-fly fishing more exciting and downstream wet-fly fishing more productive, the odds are good that trout eat more bottom-dwelling nymphs than anything

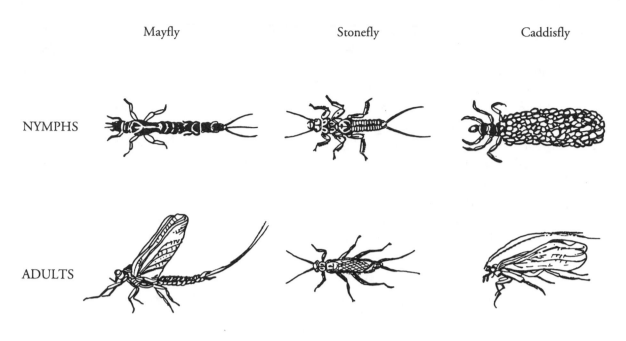

In some waters nymphs make up more than 75 percent of the trouts' diet. The angler can't always be on the stream when hatching adults are on the surface, but underwater nymphs are always present. Spend some time studying the underside of stones and driftwood. You'll find some naturals that look just like these representative artificials.

A typical mayfly nymph. This style represents a swimming insect and suggests many species. It can be weighted with lead wire, depending on how deep the angler wants it to ride.

The Zug Bug is an excellent all-purpose fly that suggests a number of nymphal forms. Its peacock herl body looks buggy when wet because of its natural iridescence.

else. They undoubtedly do in waters that are rich in insect variety. As fish grow to more heroic size, 20 inches or longer, they tend to seek larger food such as minnows and crayfish, but even the big ones will feed on nymphs if there are plenty of them. This is especially true where the larger ones are available, such as green drakes, various dark stoneflies, and hellgrammites.

That trout do eat a lot of nymphs was not widely known until a half century ago. Maybe a few anglers knew it and kept it to themselves, but it's been just within the past thirty years that any great attention has been paid to nymphs as being something other than wet flies. Nymph fishing is currently an American specialty. A handful of British anglers have been advocating nymphs for some years, but in the United States nymph fishing has gone far beyond the fad state. As with dry-fly purists who fish only with floating flies, we also have confirmed nymph purists. I don't advocate one-system fishing of any kind (it's too much fun to try them all) but the truth is, when conditions are right, nymph fishing is the best way to go.

DEEP NYMPHING

The ideal situation for deep nymph fishing occurs when the water is slightly off-color. By that, I don't mean mud-colored or simply dirty, but about the shade of weak tea with a spot of cream in it. Trout can be taken on nymphs in extremely dirty water but drifting a nymph close to or on the bottom is best done during the early and late stages of a cloudy water period.

There's plenty of proof that trout have amazing ability to spot natural food and artificial flies in cloudy water. However, they won't move far from their feeding station to search for food when the water is heavily loaded with silt and debris. Their feeding area expands as the water becomes clearer and contracts as it becomes more turbid. When using nymphs, a good rule of thumb is to fish slower, deeper, and more

methodically as water color darkens. Cloudy water prevents the trout from seeing your silhouette clearly, a built-in advantage for the short casts and close approach necessary to deliver sunken nymphs in the most deceptive manner.

Unlike most other forms of sunken fly fishing, weighted nymphs are best fished *upstream*. In order to give the nymph a lifelike appearance, short casts are necessary. Because the nymph itself will be weighted, or the leader weighted in some way, classic casting techniques don't apply here. To flip, lob, or swing a weighted nymph twelve to fourteen feet (and sometimes much less) is not a graceful act. But when conditions are right, it's a highly effective way to fish for trout. In many situations, the skillful angler fishing nymphs near the bottom will outfish those using live bait. I've seen it happen so many times it can't be merely chalked up to luck.

The first move in basic sunken nymph fishing is to wade to a position that's close—I mean really close—to the moving stretch of water you intend to fish. Wade carefully, even if the water is cloudy. The crunching and grinding sounds of rocks against each other and your boot soles are magnified in the water. The trout may not see you but too much in-water noise may alert them. For such short-range fishing you won't need a long leader (6 feet or the length of the rod is plenty) nor such a fine tippet as you would for most dry-fly fishing. Tippet diameters of .007 or .008 are good choices to start with (4- or 5-pound test). Begin with a single nymph. It can be controlled easier and it's more economical; you will lose some flies fishing this way so it's better to lose only one instead of two as you might with a dropper. When the water is less cloudy, the addition of a dropper may prove very effective, however, and we'll get into that shortly.

Armed with a suitable leader, a nymph that looks much like the ones you found on the underside of a couple of streambed stones, the next thing to consider is how to make the nymph

Drifting a nymph along the bottom is best done with a short line and rod tip held close to the surface in order to feel the difference between snags and strikes. Keep a close watch on line or strike indicator for the slightest movement.

sink quickly and then ride along with the current at the most effective depth. The idea is to cause the artificial to drift along in an unfettered manner to resemble a swimming or accidently dislodged nymph. Remember, the trout is not going to move a great distance to grab it, so you've got to drift it to him. Some weight in the nymph or some added to the leader is usually necessary, and the various ways of doing this form the essence of deep nymphing.

Expert nymph anglers are divided on how best to apply weight, which adds still another big question mark for the novice. (Gee, should I have taken up tennis after all?) Practically any method of sinking the nymph will work reasonably well and the fish won't mind much. It's just that some ways are easier than others. Small

split-shot, thin strips of lead (known as wraparound), "soft lead" (a kind of putty-like material), and sections of lead-core line are the four most popular kinds of nymph sinkers. In addition, lead or copper wire can be wound around the hook shank before tying the nymph, thus keeping the weight in the nymph itself.

Weight within the fly eliminates the need for extra sinkers much of the time but increases the chances of getting hung up on rocks, limbs, and other bottom flotsam. Another drawback to having the weight in the nymph is that it just sort of hangs there in an inert manner and doesn't undulate with the natural flow of the water. Many anglers, this one included, seldom use weighted flies for that reason. If soft lead is used, and gets caught beneath a rock, it can be

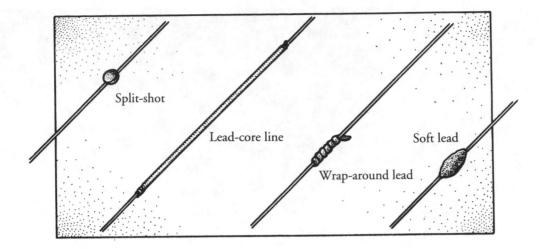

Here are some different ways to weight the leader in order to sink a nymph or streamer fly. The more weight used, the more difficult it is to cast in a conventional manner. At times, a sinking or sink-tip line will accomplish the job, but not when using less than twenty-five feet of line and leader. Split-shot can be applied quickly with pliers or hemostats but are not always easy to remove without damaging the leader. Wraparound and soft lead come off without any difficulty and can be attached with the fingers. A section of lead-core line is more bothersome to attach, but it casts better and seldom hangs up on the bottom.

pulled loose easily without losing the nymph. The same is true of the lead strips that are pinched on over a leader knot or with split-shot that are squeezed on *lightly*. If a sinker pops off it's not a great loss. Another one can be quickly attached.

A growing number of anglers who do a lot of nymphing tie sections of lead-core line into their leaders. Lead-core line, developed primarily for deep trolling, works perfectly as a fly fishing "sinker." Six- to twelve-inch lengths can be added by breaking the lead core inside the braided line in such a way that a loop can be tied into each end. These loops are then interlocked with corresponding loops within the body of the leader. Depending on where the loops are located, the weight can be placed at any distance from the nymph. This arrangement requires more fussing but casts better than most sinker options in situations calling for a

long-range presentation. The bottom line? Stick with the wrap-around strips or the soft lead at the outset.

When you're drifting a sunken nymph through a likely looking spot, the leader and no more than two or three feet of line may be all that's needed. If more line is required, a float of some kind or a strike indicator will be a great help. Plastic tab indicators are sold under a variety of names, and while they will do the job, the best ones I've found are the homemade kind. Half-inch squares of plastic-foam packing material, mentioned earlier, are perfect. Cut a slot halfway through the cube with a razor blade and pull the leader into it. The cube is positioned on the leader at the point that will allow the nymph to drift in such a way that it just "ticks" the bottom.

As you move from pool to pool or decide to alter the depth of the nymph, you simply

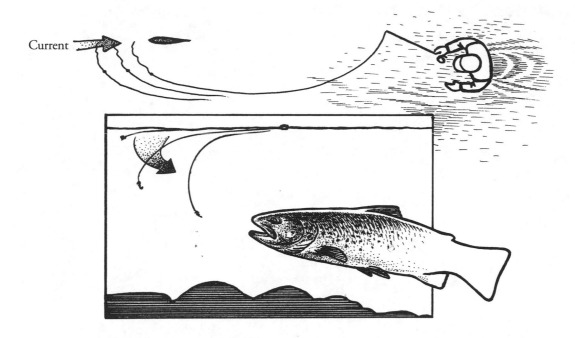

Current

There are many situations when casting a sunken nymph upstream and allowing it to drift back towards you is the best approach. Depending on the character of the stream bottom, you may or may not want the nymph directly on the bottom. If you choose to have the nymph drift at mid- depth or slightly deeper, attach some weight eight inches or so above the fly and use a floating strike indicator. Depending on water depth and current you may want to try casting at a right angle to the target and drift the sunken nymph on a very short line.

change the weight and its position. Most of the time the sunken nymph will produce best on or very close to the bottom, but there will also be situations when coasting it at mid-depth or quite near the surface will be required. Using a float allows for easy adjustments.

THE IDEAL SITUATION

It was raining hard when our Bill got out of bed. On arriving at streamside, he estimates that the water has risen a couple of inches above the previous evening's mark. It's a milky-gray shade. No surface insects are evident and low cloud cover indicates the probability of a sunless day. It's late May and under clear water conditions

some large flies would probably be hatching come evening. But if the water remains so cloudy, will the trout spot them if they do? Visibility could also be a problem with a string of wet flies, fished downstream. Bill's got a selection of nymphs he ordered from a mail-order house. They include a few generic mayflies, a couple of dark stoneflies, small scuds, and some peacock-bodied Zug Bugs. A pretty good group of nymphs for most trout streams. Hmmmm. Which one to try?

Remembering the advice he received earlier in the year from a local angler, he kneels down to peek under some rocks. There's some form of life under each one he studies. A few of the little creatures are of size 18 and smaller while others

Short-line nymphing in pocket water, as shown here, is not unlike fishing with a drifting worm or other natural bait. The nymph should bounce along the bottom in a lifelike manner without too much rod manipulation.

are nearly an inch long. The water is only about six inches deep where Bill is searching, and as he replaces one of the stones he spots a big nymph wiggling out of the silt. It's a brownish-gray, three-tailed, fat-legged thing that scoots away quickly. Bill has a good enough look at it to recognize it as being a mayfly and not a stonefly. Close enough. What he sees is a Green Drake nymph *(Ephemera guttulata).* To his delight one of the size 10 nymphs in his fly box appears to be the right size and color.

Bill's got the greenish-gray nymph tied on now and he pulls a small packet of plastic strike indicators from a vest pocket. He's added his own touch to these little floats by painting them bright yellow. He guesses that placing the float about three feet above the nymph should be about right in the tail end of the pool he's decided to try first. He'd fished here last evening

so he's got some idea of how deep the pool is. About ten inches above the nymph, he squeezes on a small dab of soft lead which he'd rolled between his fingers to form a ball.

Wading quietly into the tail end of the pool, he's surprised by how quickly he's up to his knees. Well now, the water did rise quite a bit, didn't it? He strips about four feet of line from the reel and tosses the nymph up and slightly across. The lead drags the nymph under; its drop is checked at the three-foot mark by the plastic float. Bill follows the float's progress with the tip of his rod. The slightest jerk or wiggle of the float and he wants to be ready to strike. The current is a bit stronger than Bill guessed and the nymph is not ticking the bottom. After four drifts of ten feet or so, he decides to slide the float another foot up the leader.

Three more drifts with the float repositioned

doesn't seem to be getting the nymph down deep enough either. Bill is still not feeling that "bump-bump-bump" through the rod that will tell him the nymph is on the bottom. He rolls another chunk of soft lead onto the first one. The next sidearm lob brings a pronounced "plunk" as the nymph and sinker meet the water. Good guessing this time. He can feel the bump-bump as the nymph touches bottom and the float vibrates each time it does. Whoa now! The float ducks under and there's a hard pull. Bill pulls back too—but it's not a fish. The hook had obviously caught the edge of a rock or something and hung up for a second. Watch it Bill, don't strike too hard on these false alarms. Deep nymph fishing is a game of touch and a lot of those rock strikes do feel like the real thing. Bill should be consoled by the fact that the best nymphers in the world do a lot of extra striking!

Ten more drifts bring a couple more rock strikes, but Bill is getting the feel of his weight bouncing along the bottom and has confidence that he's doing it right. He takes two steps upstream. That's it. Don't move too far in cloudy water. The trout aren't dashing about either. They're waiting patiently for food to come to them. A foot upstream, or left or right of the last cast, may be the magic spot.

In two-step increments, Bill is moving up through the pool. Twice more, he adjusts the float an inch or so in order to keep the nymph at the right depth. It's a busy way to fish and Bill is enjoying the strategy. As he reaches the center of the pool it occurs to him that he's been drifting the nymph at about the same distance from his rod tip for every try. Maybe the fish are closer. He reels up a couple feet of line and flips the nymph again. This time the float is directly beneath the rod tip as it passes in front of him. This is really *close* fishing but it's not uncommon when fishing sunken nymphs. Tick-tick-tick, the nymph is working just right. The plastic float suddenly jerks towards the opposite bank and Bill reacts with a twist of the rod

hand. The tip bends instantly, throbbing from the head-shaking action of a hooked trout.

Bill's excited about his fish, his first on a sunken nymph, but the excitement is heightened by not being able to see it in the cloudy water. It's not making a run like some of fish he's hooked on wet or dry flies. Instead, the fish is choosing to slug it out almost in place, allowing the current to help it. Steady pressure will tire it soon.

It's up on top now and Bill sees that it's a rainbow of about 14 inches. A nice fish in most streams. He's going to net this one instead of hand-landing because he doesn't want to make a mistake in the discolored water. He unclips the net from the D-ring on the side of the vest and swishes it through the water a couple of times to soak the mesh. Bill lifts the fish's head slightly and leads it, head-first, into the net. He raises the net smoothly, not with a wild sweep. No need to lift the fish completely out of the water to thrash about frantically. He keeps the trout in the water so it will calm down for unhooking. If the hook barb has been pinched down flat, removal will be easy.

Bill backs out of the strong current and allows the fish to swim out of the net. Good show. And now, Bill's ready to do it again. He's got the technique down pat!

Of course, our hero, and the rest of us, don't always do so well. Real fishing situations can include long periods of fruitless casting, and days when it seems everything we try catches fish. The wonderful thing about all fly fishing is the diversity of the fish's behavior. Fishing sunken nymphs is no different in this respect than fishing dry flies, wet flies, or streamers. The right presentation, pattern, and size will vary from day to day. In nymph fishing, however, the correct presentation will often vary from *hour to hour*. As the water changes in color, height, and velocity the fish and food they're feeding on act differently. Approaching to a rod's length of a trout (as Bill did when he caught that rainbow) when the water begins to run clear, will surely spook the fish. That's when longer casts and downstream techniques are called for.

FISHING THE NYMPH DOWNSTREAM

A sunken nymph can be fished across and downstream much like standard wet flies are handled with a float or strike indicator. The indicator hampers smooth casting to a considerable degree but sometimes we must sacrifice form for function. When the nymph must be drifted at a depth greater than four feet, or stronger current simply won't allow the fly to sink fast enough, sinking or sink-tip lines are a great help. Additional sinkers aren't the answer because any more than two BBs of weight prohibits manageable casting.

On the largest and swiftest of rivers, a full sinking line is often the only way to send a nymph close to the bottom. On most trout streams, however, a sink-tip line will do the job. Such a line is much easier to lift out of the water for the next cast. The same leader used for standard nymphing will work well but the nymph itself must be weighted to achieve a deep drift.

Cover the water as you would with standard wet flies. Begin with short casts and gradually extend them until you've swept the area. Move a few feet downstream and begin again. At first, don't add any action to the nymph. Allow it to coast along naturally, as close to the bottom as possible. If you don't feel the nymph touching the bottom occasionally, try casting upstream a bit in order to allow the nymph more time to sink. As the nymph travels downstream, strip in just enough line to maintain contact (less slack line) with the nymph itself. If you allow too much slack to form, you may not feel the strikes or react to them in time.

Facts must be faced when trying to fish flies of any kind in very strong current. There are some pools and stretches of steep gradient runs where productive fishing can't be done during periods of high water. Some anglers move to other pools or to another stream when deep water appears to be a problem. Six feet or more is the working definition of "deep" to most anglers. In such pools a sinking line will take a nymph to the bottom without added weight if the current is not too strong. A cast or two will quickly determine if it's possible. If the pool is not too wide, some soft lead may be added—but keep the weight close to the nymph. Fish in deep water are seldom spooked by seeing a sinker placed ten inches or less behind the nymph. The extra thrill involved in fishing nymphs in deep water is that that's where the largest trout usually are.

In deep pools that are quite calm, the dead-drift method is not very effective. Some movement must be added to the nymph in order to attract the trout's attention. A slow strip, hand-twist retrieve, or combination of the two is the best way to start. A slight jerk or two on the rod can also be added from time to time. Just as with fishing wet flies downstream, what we're searching for is the blend of action that appeals to the fish on a particular day. If anything, lean towards the *slow* rather than the *fast* or erratic retrieve combinations. Trout in cold, deep water usually move slower than they do in shallow water. The quick, skittering action that works so well with traditional wet flies is not good nymph technique. Natural nymphs in deep water move much like the trout do—slowly and deliberately. Move that nymph accordingly.

SHALLOW NYMPHING

Two of the most frustrating situations that confront the fly angler are the "bulging rise" and the "tailing rise." The former happens when a fish takes a drifting or swimming nymph that's attempting to reach the surface. The surface is not penetrated by the fish's jaws; instead, the top of the head or the back pushes the water into a momentary hump or bulge. A tailing rise occurs when a trout is searching for and eating nymphs or crustaceans on the bottom in shallow water. As it does so, the entire tail fin, or part of it, thrusts through the surface film. Both types of rises can form rings on the surface that appear to the angler like typical rises for surface food. You've got to be watching carefully in order to tell the difference.

Casting a dry fly into the vicinity of these two rise forms usually results in nothing. In the case of a tailing rise, the solution is to fish a nymph just under the surface film or about a foot deep. The slight subsurface drift is quite easy. All that's required, on reasonably calm water, is to coat the entire leader, except for the front twelve inches next to the nymph, with fly floatant. Soak the nymph with saliva and try a short test cast before you aim for the last bulge. The leader should float and the nymph should sink quickly. If all isn't working well, you may want to add a small chip of plastic foam to keep the nymph at the correct depth. This will serve as a combination float and strike indicator.

Bulging fish that are feeding on mayfly nymphs that are about to emerge as adult flies may switch to the floating insects. In this case it's a simple matter to tie on a dry fly. Curiously, though, some individual fish remain partial to the nymphs long after many of their companions have zeroed-in on floating food; and these are usually the larger fish. Moral: Stick with the nymph for a while.

The subsurface food that brings on bulging activity might be mayfly nymphs, caddis pupa, mosquito larva, or one of several dozen other insect forms. It may also be drifting scuds, a type of freshwater crustacean that looks like a miniature shrimp. Trout eat a lot of scuds, and here again there are some excellent scud patterns available from mail-order houses. If you tie your own, they're little more than a pinch of natural fur or synthetic yarn wound around the hook and wrapped with spiral ribbing of fine

tinsel. Pale olive, pink, and yellow are the best colors, with sizes 16, 18, and 20 most useful. When using such small hooks, remember to pull when a fish takes instead of striking with a pronounced jerk.

Fishing downstream with nymphs, when a deep drift is not desired, is similar to wet-fly fishing. Droppers may be used with nymphs in the same way and can be very effective. If the water is four feet or less in depth a floating line works best. It will act as a kind of strike indicator. When the nymphs are drifting, you may not feel a strike, but by watching the line you will usually *see* it.

In deeper water a sink-tip line will work better. As the nymphs move downstream with the current or sink at the end of a long cast into still water, some movement must be added. Allowing the nymphs to drift about at random will eventually cause strange curves and curls to form in the line, thus preventing you from feeling a strike. Stripping line or hand-twist retrieving are the best ways to do it. While a fast retrieve will often work with winged wet flies, more fish are attracted to a slower moving nymph. An excellent technique is to allow the nymph to sink close to the bottom and then raise it by stripping for about three one-foot pulls and allowing it to sink again. Repeat this routine, until the leader/line connection is almost touching the rod tip. Trout will often follow the undulating nymph for several rise-and-fall sequences before grabbing it.

As with all fly fishing, varied presentations are the mark of the experienced angler. The one-system fly fisherman will eventually catch some trout when conditions suit his style—but only then. Mix up the presentations, change flies when you must, and be observant about what's on or in the water and how the trout are reacting. Trout fishing is a continuing game of puzzles, but like all puzzles there's always a solution. The solution may not be revealed every time, but by keeping past experiences in mind the next puzzle may be solved more easily.

I can't resist two final personal observations about nymphs and nymph fishing. The first is about color. Since various forms of algae seem to be in water everywhere, and cling to caddis cases and nymphs, it's my belief that the color green is important. Therefore, I'm very partial to artificial nymphs that wear some green. Not a bright green mind you, but a sort of dull-olive or greenish brown. The vast majority of natural nymphs are this color, and my fishing diaries indicate more success on olive-colored nymphs than all other colors combined. Therefore my first choice of nymph patterns always has some olive in its makeup.

The second observation is about barbless hooks. I do nearly all of my fly fishing with barbless hooks or with pinched-down barbs. There are two reasons: Barbless hooks are easier to remove from the fish *and from me* (yes, it happens to every fly fisherman sooner or later). It's easier to catch fish on a barbless hook. Far less striking force is needed to set the point. Trout often take a nymph positively and deeply. Prodding and pecking about in a trout's throat while trying to dislodge a barbed hook can easily cause fatal damage. The byword of today's anglers is indeed "catch and release" most of the time, but that means releasing them *alive*. Even if you choose to use barbed hooks for other kinds of fishing, go barbless with nymphs. Everyone's future fishing will be better if you do.

8

Fishing Streamer Flies

All gamefish are predators and their largest prey are other fish. The freshwater predator's only requirement is that the prey can be swallowed whole. (Sharks, barracuda, and other toothy saltwater species don't make this distinction and frequently gobble up fish much larger than themselves.) Where trout are the target species, streamers have long been considered to be the "big-fish" fly. Conventional angling wisdom holds that trophy size trout are always on the lookout for a substantial meal and seldom turn down the chance to gulp a catchable minnow.

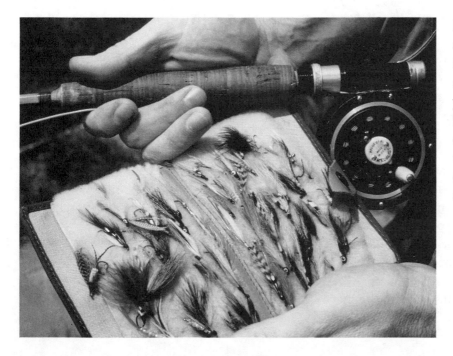

Many anglers consider streamer flies to be big-fish flies because large trout eat a lot of minnows and young of their own kind. But don't overlook streamers on small streams. Few trout will turn down an easy-to-catch baitfish that's smaller than they are.

Unlike some old angling "truths," this one is mostly true. Not only are big trout fond of minnows, they are not adverse to eating the young of their own kind. Since streamer flies are tied to look more or less like small fish, their importance in fly fishing is obvious.

If it's generally agreed among experienced trout anglers that streamers are highly effective on big trout, why do so many fishermen carry streamers in their fly boxes yet use them infrequently if at all? With a half century of fly fishing to draw from—which has included a lot of time watching and talking with other anglers—I'm convinced there are two major reasons. First, fishing streamers correctly is a "busy" way to fish and many anglers just don't want to be that busy. Second, and this may be more important than the first reason, most anglers simply don't know how to fish with streamer flies. I'm continually amazed to see otherwise competent fly fishermen tie on a streamer, make a few half-hearted casts, and then quickly change to something else. The good, downstream wet-fly angler is more likely to do a passably good job with a streamer, but many of them also fail to grasp the essence of "long fly" technique. Proper streamer fly fishing requires that *the fly be kept moving 99 percent of the time and that it move like a minnow in distress.* Following these requirements come size and pattern— but how the fly is fished is vital.

STANDARD STREAMER TECHNIQUE

The basic cast with a streamer is precisely like the cast with wet flies. Aim across and downstream at such an angle and range that your fly will pass in front of the area you think may hold a trout. Allow all of the line to snap up tight against the rod as the fly meets the water; no slack line is wanted at the outset. As soon as the fly is in the water hook the line beneath the first finger of the rod hand and begin to strip the streamer in snappy, four- to six-inch pulls without long pauses between pulls. *Do not allow the rod to rise much above horizontal.* In fact, if the rod tip occasionally touches the water so much the better.

The reason the rod tip should be kept low is to prevent a sag in the line between rod tip and the surface of the water. Line that is in the air is not working for you. Each time a pull is applied to move the streamer, the sagging slack line must be straightened in order to impart any movement to the fly; otherwise, it's wasted effort. Secondly, if a fish strikes when there's a lot of sag, chances are you won't feel it. Even if you see a flash or a swirl in the vicinity of the fly, you'll still miss the strike. The extra slack just can't be picked up in time. Keep the tip low, the line under control beneath the index finger, and strip often and fast enough to maintain taut contact with line, leader, and fly.

The character of the water often determines how fast the fly is stripped and how it's otherwise manipulated. If the current is strong, it will help keep the line tight, thus allowing for a shorter and slower-paced retrieve. In still or shallow water, with no current to help, a more pronounced and perhaps faster retrieve may prove more effective. At times, the hand-twist retrieve, so useful with wet flies and nymphs, will be just right. However you move the flies, don't fall into the habit of jerk-jerk-jerking the rod tip ever higher in trying to make that streamer look like a little swimming fish. Sooner or later, you'll have a solid strike when the rod is pointed straight up and possibly break off the top six inches of rod tip. Following car and screen door accidents, this mistake breaks more rod tips than fish.

If you must jerk the rod tip (and sometimes you must if a fish is still following the streamer at close range), sweep it to one side or the other instead of in an upwards direction. Twist the body as the rod is moved in such a way that you've still got enough arc to strike through. Put another way, the body should be facing slightly away from the fish.

While the advice to keep the streamer moving always applies, don't interpret this to mean that it must move at breakneck speed following every cast. Depending on the depth, the velocity of the current, and the "attitude" of the fish on a particular day, keep on experimenting with various retrieving speeds. When the water temperature is in the 40s or low 50s, trout move correspondingly slower. They also tend to be less frisky when it's heavily colored or silt-laden. At these times, a streamer close to the bottom, moved at a slow, *steady* cadence, can be deadly. A favorite pattern for this kind of work is the Muddler Minnow. This pattern is my choice as the best all-around sunken fly yet created. Not only is it an excellent suggestion of the family of sculpin minnows, it looks a lot like many large nymphs and does a better than passably good impression of a grasshopper.

When the water temperature rises into the mid-50s and slightly higher, almost any retrieving speed may attract trout on a given day. Practically any trout of 12 inches or longer can be coaxed into taking a look at a streamer if the right action is applied. The chance of grabbing a substantial and easy-to-catch meal is all the reason a trout needs. This attraction is often so great that fish will come back for several more looks. This built-in curiosity works to the angler's advantage more so when fishing streamers than with *any other type of fly*. For this reason, don't give up on a fish that splashes at the fly or follows it without taking. Keep working on any fish that shows interest. The chance of catching it is always there until it grows tired of the game or becomes frightened. This is what sets streamer fishing apart from other forms of fly fishing.

TRICKS WITH STREAMERS

If an angler fishes more than a half-dozen times a season and there are some big trout in the streams he visits, he will probably see the telltale signs of minnow chasing. A V-shaped wake may suddenly appear in shallow water to be punctuated by some wild thrashing with water flying in all directions. Or a huge, looping swirl will form near the tail end of a still pool. At other times a flash of white belly will be spotted beneath the surface followed by a minnow leaping clear of the water. Any and all of these antics may take place during a single chase. When a trout decides to take off after a particular minnow, it seldom gives up until it's successful or the prey finds safe cover. If the minnow has been injured as a result of being tail-nipped by a trout, or was previously injured in some other way, the trout usually wins. If the minnow is showing a spot of blood or is "sick" in any way, the trout always wins. (Mother Nature is an unforgiving parent. The sick and injured don't last long in the water.) Suggesting a minnow that's in trouble is the key to good streamer fishing. Imperfect or dead minnows are seldom seen in a trout stream. They've been eaten.

If a particular retrieve routine results in seeing a fish follow your streamer but not grab it for a try or two, it's time to switch tactics. Slowing the retrieve is a good next choice, particularly in swift water. While minnows seldom fight the current to stay in one place for long, having your fly do that will sometimes work. As the streamer is retrieved through a good looking spot, say behind a large rock or sunken log, pause for a few seconds and shake the rod tip. The streamer should present a trembling minnow that's trying to decide what to do next upon finding itself in a vulnerable location. No, I don't believe that minnows do any "deciding" at all, but we've got to interpret their actions in human terms.

A favorite stunt of practiced streamer anglers is to actually try to *take the fly away from the fish*. As crazy as this sounds it works about one out of ten times when a fish shows interest; those are good odds for any kind of fishing. The predatory instincts are at work here again. If a fish has made a start for your streamer and you see it or the resulting flash or swirl, cast back immediately and increase the retrieving speed. Strip the fly through the water at breakneck speed and if you see the fish coming, try to strip it even faster. I guarantee you can't move that fly fast enough if a frantic trout makes up its mind to grab it. It may strike a bit short but that may be exactly what the trout is trying to do. When chasing a single minnow or charging into a school of them, trout are not fussy about how they grab one. Actually, they merely nip the tails much of the time, and if a minnow's tail is pinched or cut it will be slowed a bit and therefore become an easier mark. The tail is the "engine" of every fish.

If you experience a couple of short strikes and the super fast retrieve is no longer creating inter-est, the "crippled" routine should be tried. During the next retrieve, try switching the rod from side to side, all the while stripping at varied speeds. This causes the streamer to swim in a zig-zag manner as it moves toward the angler and often brings the trout back for another look.

STREAMER FLY COLORS

As with all forms of fly fishing, certain techniques and certain flies work better than others on certain days. The flies vary tremendously in size, color, style, and weight. Even if you were to fish but one stream during your entire life, you'd experience days when one pattern worked much better than another. The trout decide which one appeals more and no angler in the world can explain why. Experience helps in making educated guesses, so let's make a few.

This foot-long brown trout had no trouble grabbing a size 6 Black Ghost. This pattern has caught trout the world over. Using hemostats to remove hooks greatly reduces damage if the fish is to be released.

An 18-inch brown that went for the No. 1 streamer fly in the world, the Muddler Minnow. There are many variations of this fly, but the common ingredient is the spongy, deer-hair head. Carry it in sizes 10, 8, 6, and 4.

I will never forsake the three favorite patterns which have served American anglers so well over the past half century. They are, once more: the Muddler Minnow, the Black Ghost, and the Mickey Finn. The Muddler is basically a somber, brownish fly that suggests the bottom-dwelling sculpin minnow. It also looks somewhat like a small crayfish, and I'm certain that that's what it's often taken for when fished slow and near the bottom. The Black Ghost has a black, silver-ribbed body and white wings. This combination offers the same general appearance of many minnows that are basically white on the belly and dark on the back. The Mickey Finn wears yellow and red bucktail wings and a silver body. It is my firm belief that these three flies in sizes 10 through 6, tied on 4X long hooks, will cover most streamer fly needs on any trout water 80 percent of the time. But what about the other 20 percent?

For those situations when the proven patterns don't work, fly tiers have spent long hours at their vises working on different combinations. Dave Whitlock's Sculpin Minnow patterns, Keith Fulsher's Thunder Creek streamers, Carrie Stevens' Maine patterns, and the unknown tiers who first made Zonkers, Woolly Buggers,

Matukas, and Marabou Leeches have added greatly to streamer fly effectiveness. The flowing, undulating action provided by maribou (stork) feathers adds amazing life to the now generic Woolly Bugger flies. It's the same with the Zonker flies that feature a strip of rabbit hide, with the fur attached. The shaking, wiggling action of this material is irresistible.

The Mickey Finn is one of the three most famous and popular streamer patterns in North America. Nothing more than a silver body with red and yellow wings, this fly has a lot of trout on its conscience. A painted eye improves it.

Two Woolly Buggers and a Woolly Worm. Such soft, wiggling flies suggest many underwater creatures and have proven their effectiveness everywhere. Green, black, and brown are favorite colors.

It's impossible to know what trout take some of the fancy attractor streamer flies to be. We think they resemble some sort of small fish, but I'm not so certain this is always the case. The fur and maribou flies probably suggest freshwater leeches, and some of the brown, black, and green ones do resemble crayfish. Smallish streamers could be taken for nymphs and the big ones may be taken for salamanders, leopard frogs, tadpoles, and heaven knows what else. This is why changes of pace when retrieving streamers is so important. All of these creatures move differently in the water and it's smart for the angler to switch patterns, sizes, and styles as often as the mood strikes him.

Some broad statements do apply when selecting streamer fly patterns. Brown, black, white, and various tones of gray are the foundation colors of most successful streamers. Those are the colors of most natural trout foods. A bit of flash in the form of silver or gold tinsel ribbing adds a touch of sparkle or iridescence—also present on many minnows and immature trout.

The primary colors of red, yellow, and blue, from which every other color is derived, are chosen mostly by whim but there can be some logic involved. Red is the color of blood and indicates an injured prey. Too much red on a trout streamer, however, can have a negative effect. Even on the Mickey Finn, a hint of red over a yellow wing is better than vice versa. Yellow is an attractor in streams where fingerling brown trout are plentiful. These little fish have bright yellow bellies and flanks dotted with tiny red spots. The larger trout know what they look like. Blue is mysterious. There aren't many live

The Hornberg is a great trout fly that can be fished as a streamer *and* a dry fly. When fished beneath the surface it looks like a minnow. When dressed with fly floatant and fished on top, it resembles a grasshopper.

Flashy, attractor-type streamer flies come in many sizes and colors. The bizarre and downright weird sometimes works better than more natural-looking patterns, especially for brook and rainbow trout.

creatures in this world that are blue except among the bird families. Underwater experiments have proven that blue is more easily seen in deep water than most other colors. That accounts for the success of blue lures when trolled deep in both fresh and salt water, but the jury is still out on blue for stream trout. Purple, on the other hand, a blend of blue and red, has proven to be an excellent color for rainbow trout. Small rainbow trout are sort of purplish in many waters and that may explain it.

The best advice on fly patterns always comes from the anglers who fish any stream regularly. A morning of fishing a famous Catskill stream proved this in spades when a young man, twenty years my junior, suggested not only where to fish but exactly what to try. I had caught a couple of smallish trout at the head end of a long, calm pool. I had decided to fish the top of the pool, where there was more current, to give my streamer maximum action. I was both right and wrong. After watching me fish through the pool, my informant walked up and announced I hadn't done it right. What was he talking about? I'd caught a couple fish and thought I was performing quite well, thank you. The young man told me there was a deep slot at the head of the

pool and that I was merely scratching the surface. "The bigger fish are deeper, beneath the fish you caught. Tie on a mostly black streamer and fish it real deep in front of a split-shot and I'll bet you catch a good one."

I did exactly what he suggested and the result was exactly as he predicted. After replacing my Mickey Finn with a Black Ghost, I hooked two dandy browns by casting across the deep run, allowing the streamer to sink, and bringing it back with a slow, hand-twist retrieve.

As much as I hate to add weight to my leader, there's simply no question about the need to do it at times. Some streamer specialists swear by weighted flies—that is, weight within the fly. As with nymphs weighted similarly, I think they tend to be sluggish in the water and not as effective as a fly and sinker arrangement. As a streamer is retrieved, the added piece of weight bobs up and down, forcing the streamer to do the same. This introduces a sort of yo-yo effect that works very well in deep water.

As with nymphs, split-shot, wrap-around strips, soft lead, or sections of lead-core line may be used to sink a streamer. In heavy current, sinking and sink-tip lines may be needed. Such lines must be retrieved almost to the boot tops before being cast again. They're simply too heavy to be plucked out of the water with one stroke. The use of a full-sinking line forces the streamer fisherman to continue retrieving until the fly is very close. Fishing each cast to its fullest in this way will lead to a lot more strikes.

EYES ON STREAMER FLIES

Some anglers are convinced that the addition of a painted eye on the head of a streamer fly adds to its effectiveness. Various kinds of glass and plastic eyes are also touted by many experienced anglers. Certain natural feathers, notably the neck hackles of the jungle cock, have been used

The idea behind most streamer designs is to suggest a small fish or minnow. Soft materials that flow together and form blended colors are often the best choices. While many famous streamer patterns don't wear them, painted eyes or some other way of suggesting them, seem to increase the number of strikes. Regardless of the style of streamer, the angler must move the fly in order to suggest the erratic movements of a live minnow. Fishing a streamer fly is busy work, but it will frequently pay off with larger fish.

for centuries to suggest fish eyes. (Among fly tiers, the jungle cock neck feathers are referred to as "eyes.") An equal number of fly fishing veterans pooh-pooh the value of eyes on flies and insist that the fish don't care one way or the other. This group declares that it's the movement of the fly itself that attracts the fish.

I believe that the addition of eyes is very important in deep, slow-moving water and more so in discolored water. In shallow water and in fast, rippling stretches it probably doesn't matter much. Put another way, where fish have less time to study the fly or may have some difficulty in seeing it, an eye acts like a beacon. It indicates the presence of something alive and edible. In fast, clear water the fish have to make up their minds quicker; food has to be grabbed now or never. The answer? Like "mother's chicken soup," eyes may not solve every streamer puzzle but they certainly don't hurt anything. If the water is even slightly discolored or over four feet deep, I'll choose an eyed fly over a plain one every time.

HOOKS FOR STREAMERS

The overall shape of a minnow is an extended, slim oval. Therefore, conventional wisdom tells us that the hook for streamers ought to be a long-shanked model in order to carry a sleek, minnow-like body. This is correct, but if the feathers, hair, or whatever forming the wing or upper half of the fake minnow extend too far behind the bend of the hook, a lot of strikes will be missed. While it's true that gamefish are inclined to aim for the head (or eye) when they attempt to seize a minnow, they don't always connect. Actually, they'll grab one any way they can and in a fast chase will often "tail-nip" a live minnow. They do the same with flies and if there's too much material behind the hook they won't touch the point. This is why some streamer-fly tiers like 5X and 6X hooks. (The number in front of the "X" means the hook shank is that many times longer than a normal hook.) They want the wing to end very close to the bend of the hook. More wing movement can be achieved with longer wings, but they'll lead to more short strikes and tangled flies. Long wings have a tendency to wrap around the bend of the hook when cast. The trade-off is, flies that undulate and pulsate do attract more strikes.

Another group of tiers approach the streamer hook problem from another direction. They choose shorter hooks, of standard shank length or perhaps 3X longer, and begin the wing at about the midpoint of the hook or even closer to the bend. This allows the wing to flow well behind the hook bend, thus preventing tangles. If the fly has an eye, they reason the fish will zero-in on it and probably be hooked.

The best of both theories can be put into service by tying a "trailer-hook" to the shank of the fly hook before making the fly. This is done by tying another hook to a short piece of monofilament and securing the mono with thread before finishing the fly. This method offers a two-hook advantage for eye-directed strikes and for the tail-nippers as well. The trailer-hook should hang directly under the tip of the streamer wing. Note: In some states and on some special waters, the use of more than one hook is illegal. Check the regulations. In any case, a two-hook fly should be fished barbless. If both hooks hold the fish they can be difficult to remove.

We'll be discussing long flies in other chapters and how they're used for species other than trout. But before we leave streamers a couple more thoughts are in order. It's worth repeating that streamer fly fishing is indeed a busy way to fish. The angler is doing something all the time. Some anglers are geared for this and some aren't. If streamers are fished diligently and some experimentation is tried the rewards can be great. Large fish tend to eat larger meals. Sizes 8 and 6 are large flies on most trout

streams but, just for the heck of it, every angler should tie on a much larger one every so often just to see if a trophy-size fish is looking. I mean something *big*, about size 2 or larger.

As outrageous as it may sound, streamer flies as large as 1/0 and even 2/0 have been responsible for catching some huge trout in supposedly fished-out streams. It's a case of tossing something in the trout's direction that just can't be ignored. Sure, such a huge fly may scare the spots off an ordinary sized fish, but more often than not that huge hermit trout that's seen its share of small flies, live bait, and spinning lures during its life may pay attention. A pal of mine once caught a 30-inch brown trout on a tarpon fly that was a full *6 inches long*. I was there on the evening when he tied on the giant fly in a fit of desperation. Another (quite large) trout had chased his streamer several times without touching it. He announced that he was going to go for broke with the biggest fly he owned. Besides, it was time to go home. Two casts and bang! He hooked and landed the largest trout of his life. It was also the only trout he'd caught the entire day. Streamer fishing is like that sometimes.

As a parting thought on streamers, it's good insurance to stick with leaders that don't taper down to much less than 5-pound test, 2X or 3X. Trout tend to become excited when chasing larger food and aren't nearly so leader shy as they can be when feeding on insects and other small food. Even in very clear water, a leader about the length of the rod will be long enough and will also allow better control of the fly. Strikes on streamer flies are generally more aggressive and can take place very close to the angler—another good reason for using a somewhat hefty leader. The streamer angler should always assume that he's trying for bigger fish. Fish those long flies with a positive attitude and my bet is you won't be disappointed!

9

Fly Fishing for Bass

It is generally accepted that among fly fisherman the salmonids (trout, char, and salmon) are the most popular group of species. It may surprise some to learn that the most fished for species (by all methods) are the basses, primarily the largemouth and smallmouth bass. These fish are widely distributed, with one or both of them present in fishable numbers in forty-nine states (Alaska is the lone exception). Bass are plentiful in the eastern provinces of Canada and have thrived in recent years in many Mexican impoundments. They have also been transplanted in other countries.

The American angler was conditioned for many years by the outdoor journals and more recently by the advent of bass fishing tournaments to think of these fish in terms of spinning and baitcasting tackle. It's reasonable to assume, however, that early sport fishing for bass was done mostly with long rods, including fly rods. This was certainly the case in the New England states and much of the Northeast where fly rods were in use long before "plug-casting" rods appeared. Because bass are an aggressive fish and tend to attack large prey whenever possible, the creation of a workable revolving-spool reel changed the picture radically in the early years of the 20th century. These reels were an aid in casting large lures long distances, eliminating the need to get close to the fish for vertical bait-fishing. Following World War II, spinning reels extended the casting range of the average bass angler still more. A few diehards stuck with the fly rod for bass, but it appeared that the old way was on the way out.

During the early 1980s a new wave of interest in fly-rodding for bass swept the country as a new generation discovered that this was an exciting and productive way to fish. My guess is that fly fishing for bass will continue to grow in popularity, because these fish are made-to-order for the angler who likes action-packed fishing.

There are several species and subspecies of black bass, but the most important are *Micropterus salmoides,* the largemouth bass, and *Micropterus dolomieui,* the smallmouth. To scientists, black bass are not really bass at all since they belong to the family Serranidae. This family includes the freshwater perches and sunfishes, and the saltwater sea bass, grouper, black-

Largemouth bass are America's most fished for species. While not considered a fly-rod fish in some locales, bass are readily taken on floating and sunken flies and bugs. Not quite as fussy about color as other fish, they can be very specific about where and when they feed.

fish, and several others. Most of them have sharp spines on the dorsal, pectoral, and anal fins. Local names such as redeye, bronzeback, bigmouth, green trout, and dozens more are common throughout the range but all of them are closely related.

There are two identifying features that will help the angler to distinguish the largemouth from the smallmouth bass. The maxillary bone, that tablike extension of the upper jaw, *extends to or beyond the margin of the eye* on most largemouths. The same bone is shorter in the smallmouth, usually reaching the midpoint of the eye. The dorsal fin is separated at the midpoint on the largemouth but is *connected* on smallmouths. In addition, the flanks and back of the largemouth are generally dark green with a broken band of black extending

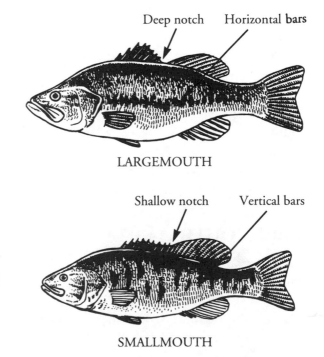

Two river smallmouth bass, caught from the same pool, showing the distinctly different marking patterns so often seen among bass. The bars on the cheeks of both fish identify them positively. The smallmouth is an American "exclusive."

from gill cover to tail. The smallmouth tends to be more brownish, and instead of a band wears a series of irregular bars or stripes on its sides. During spawning season, the smallmouth often displays a dark spot on the trailing edge of the gill cover (the opercular spot). All of these identifying characteristics are about 85 percent positive.

LARGEMOUTH HABITAT

The largemouth bass prefers waters with abundant weeds, grass, stumps, and submerged trash of all kinds. In short, this bass likes overhead cover and hiding places. It's happy in murky water, clear water, or in anything in between. It

tolerates a wide range of water temperatures and thus does well in near tropical latitudes and in lakes that form a foot or more of ice each winter.

The largemouth never stops feeding, north or south, but because of more available food during the entire year, grows to a much larger average size in southern climes. While the largemouth is primarily a lake fish it is found in many slow-moving rivers if there's suitable cover.

The largemouth is more resistant than the smallmouth to silt and manmade pollution. It can survive, even thrive, in water that would mean sure death to a smallmouth. Its ability to spawn in less than ideal locations is another strong survival factor. Of the two fish, it is slightly less cautious about food preferences—until it reaches trophy size. What is that? Most anglers who fish north of the Mason-Dixon line consider a 5-pound largemouth a dandy with an 8-pounder about as big as they could hope for. Southern bass are much larger. An 8-pounder is considered a good fish and one of 10 or 12 a trophy.

SMALLMOUTH HABITAT

Usually thought of as a northern bass because of its preference for cooler temperatures, the smallmouth is indeed fond of clear, moving water and rocky bottoms. It also does well in lakes that are not subject to extremely high temperatures in the summer or that become cloudy on a regular basis. In some southern states smallmouth bass thrive in dam tailraces where cooler, oxygen-saturated water is present. All of these habitat preferences combine with a reproduction requirement that makes the smallmouth a much fussier fish. Water temperature must reach the low 60s for successful spawning to occur. Prolonged water temperatures in the high 70s is not to their liking. For these reasons, the range of the smallmouth is much more restricted than that of the largemouth. They can and do occur in the same waters but will nearly

When a bass decides to strike a surface bug it's usually an exciting affair. When retrieving a bug, mix up styles and speeds. What works one day may not work the next.

always be in different areas of a lake or river.

North or south, a 4-pound smallmouth is an attention-getting trophy. A 5-pounder is an angling achievement, and one larger than that is legendary. Here again, the largest smallmouths tend to be caught on the downstream side of large southern impoundments. At these locations the cool water being drained from the deep stratum provides an ideal home for smallmouths. Because the water in these locations never freezes and is rich with small fish and crustaceans, the bronzebacks have a year-long smorgasbord.

Habitat preferences aside for a moment, both largemouth and smallmouth bass are mostly spring spawners (in Florida and occasionally Texas and southern California largemouth bass may spawn during any month). They are both aggressive battlers and often jump when hooked. The smallmouth is more likely to jump, but largemouth bass in the 2- to 3-pound range are almost as good at it. These antics make for lively fishing and wonderful sport on the fly rod.

Both bass are attracted to less than "natural-looking" lures of all kinds. These include flies, poppers, bugs, and other lures that can be easily cast with a fly rod. Bass, especially the largemouth, are very aggressive fish and appear to hit our offerings as much out of anger as hunger. If this isn't the case, most experienced bass anglers agree, how in the world can you explain why they hit some of the outlandish plugs, spinnerbaits, and plastic creatures that are cast their way? Yes, a streamer fly, deer-hair bug, cork popper, or huge dry fly may resemble some kind of *real* bass food; but how about the colors and sizes? No bass waters I know of contain 7-inch minnows that are solid chartreuse or dayglo orange. It must be sheer aggression or curiosity. Either explanation is good enough reason for the angler to have a wide range of bass lures in his fly box: some natural, somber-shaded creations and some of the really far-out attractors.

That said, it must be noted that smallmouths are somewhat less likely to go for the strange bugs and flies that are deadly on largemouths. For that reason, it's best to make the first casts into known smallmouth water with something less flashy. Conversely, on the opening try for largemouths it's better to use a more flamboyant bug or fly.

Like all gamefish, bass often cross up the best

theories and undergo a total change of personalities under changing weather and water conditions. In spite of what the trout purist may think, bass exhibit a wider variety of moods than most trout. Discover what the trout are eating on a particular day and the chances are good that you'll catch more than one. From one part of a lake or river to another, bass may act like they're on another planet. Even fish located within a few yards of each other may show an astounding difference in fly preference. But before we get into the flies and bugs we'll be aiming their way, we need to address what I consider the most important factor in knowing where to cast in the first place—it's water temperature. That's what determines where the "comfort zone" for bass will be. It's critical.

TEMPERATURE

It's probably safe to say that more fishing is done for bass in lakes and impoundments than in moving water. Because water in most lakes becomes stratified or layered in temperature belts, it's important to know which belt the bass prefer. Temperature is important in rivers and streams too, but there's not much the bass can do about it. In still bodies of water the bass can move to wherever they want to—and so can the angler. That's why boats were invented.

The sonar devices used by many anglers today are certainly a great help in locating bass in lakes. Reading one of them isn't difficult. Some of the screens and 'scopes actually pinpoint individual fish. Nearly always they are in the most comfortable temperature zone. A thermometer provides the same detective service. There are high-tech thermometers that coast along under the boat and can be dropped on a line to record temperatures on a digital dial; no need to raise and lower the thermometer a zillion times. Usually the bass will be at a depth where the temperature is between 60 and 75 degrees. During extremely hot or cold weather this range may not be available, but if it is, that's where you'll find the bass. Smallmouths are most active from the low 60s to just under 70. Largemouths, preferring slightly warmer water, really go on the prowl at about 67 to 73 degrees. Those are pretty narrow ranges to be sure, but most lakes with bottom topography that offers water deeper than thirty feet will allow for these ideal temperatures.

There is an overlapping of the ideal smallmouth and largemouth temperatures, and the alert reader will quickly notice that 65 or 66 degrees is just about right for both species. But there is no rule that states that bass won't feed above or below the ideal range. After all, largemouth bass are caught through holes in the ice every winter and smallmouths are just as regularly taken on super-hot summer days. (In both situations, however, the water is always closer to the ideal in deep water.)

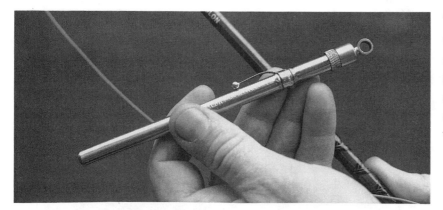

Thermometer is a good tool to carry, especially when fishing for bass. These fish are very temperature conscious and will always seek out the most comfortable water available.

In rivers, anglers don't have to be too concerned about temperature. The fish are going to be feeding or they aren't, and there isn't much to do about it—you simply aim your cast at likely -looking spots and hope for the best.

Largemouth bass are "lurkers." That is, they love to lie in wait near stumps, brush piles, overhanging banks, rocks, weedbeds, and lily pads—poised to dash out and grab a meal that appears inviting. Largemouths are good at lurking and this habit is the angler's best clue to finding them. This is particularly true during the spring when the water temperature is warming up and again in the fall when the reverse is occurring. In the middle of the summer, the bays, shoals, and river mouths where ample cover is abundant will also be productive before the sun rises and after it sets.

Many years ago, the legendary Ted Trueblood wrote, "When fishing a strange lake for bass, head for the lily pads." That became a joke among anglers whose lakes didn't have any lily pads. What Trueblood meant was to look for overhead cover. Not only do largemouths like the protection from predators offered by it, they also find more food there in the form of minnows, crayfish, frogs, salamanders, leeches, etc.

There is always more bass food in shallow water than in deep.

THE IDEAL BASS OUTFIT

There will be no beating about the bush on this. The perfect fly rod for all bass fishing is a two-piece 9-foot graphite stick designed to throw an 8-weight line. A case can be made for other configurations for specific purposes, but that's splitting hairs. An 8-foot rod is a little bit easier to manage in a boat, but for some weird reason, not many makers list an 8-footer for 8-weight lines. If you find one you like, buy it.

With a weight-forward, 8-weight line, the longest cast you'll ever need on a bass lake or river can be easily managed. The same line with the 9-foot rod will also plop a bass bug or fly twelve feet or so into a snag-infested spot with pin-point accuracy. You will, however, need two lines. The first is a floating one and the second a sink-tip or full sinking model for those days when surface fishing is out of the question.

A sturdy, single-action reel is the right choice, with the emphasis on *sturdy*. Fishing from a boat, which is how most largemouth fishing is done, involves a lot of banging about with rod-

Surface flies and bugs cast close to overhanging brush coaxed this smallmouth into striking. All bass are fond of shade during mid-day. Best colors for bass? All can be good but red-and-white is No. 1.

Single-action reel that will hold a weight-forward 8 or 9 floating line is the right choice for bass fly rodding.

dropping being a common part of it. Fragile fly reels don't last long in this environment. The very expensive fly reels that are so popular with salmon, steelhead, and saltwater anglers are not needed for bass fishing. These reels feature dependable, adjustable drag systems in anticipation of a long first run and prolonged battle. No bass in the world every pulled out the full 90-foot length of a fly line. This doesn't mean the bass fly rodder should settle for a cheap pot-metal or plastic reel. Excellent reels for 8-weight lines are offered by most fly reel manufacturers for less than $75.

LEADERS FOR BASS

Most of the time, the bass fly rodder will be casting flies and bugs that are heavier than those used for trout. These are generally bulkier and more air resistant than small wet and dry flies and require a thicker leader to make them turn over. If the diameter of the leader is not thick enough, the heavier fly has a tendency to double-back on it and cause a tangle.

Some anglers simplify leader selection by attaching a 6-foot section of 20-pound-test monofilament to the fly line, tie on the fly and

go to it. When casting no more than 25 feet this works better than many trout purists would guess. Actually, there is an advantage in using such a level leader when fishing in weedy water. There are no extra knots, which have a tendency to pick up grass, floating algae, and other flotsam. When fishing from a boat, after easing into a weedy or stump-filled bay, short-range casting is often the rule of the day. In addition, the short, level leader is easier to manage when a fish must be brought in close for unhooking. There are no leader knots to go bump-bump over the guides.

When casts of more than twenty-five feet must be made, a tapered leader of three or four sections will deliver the fly more accurately. But even with a tapered leader, the tippet section should still be reasonably stout. When hooked close to dense cover, bass generally try to dive into the thickest weeds or debris in the vicinity and can do so in a flash. You'll need a stout leader to turn their heads. Six-pound-test mono (.008 or .009 in.) is about as light as I'd recommend. In extremely heavy cover, or where you might expect to find bass of 4 pounds or more, 10-pound test would be a better choice.

A good basic bass leader begins with a 3-foot

section of 30-pound mono, a foot each of 20, 15, and 12, and a 2-foot tippet of 10-pound test. If you want to go lighter reduce all sections by 6 inches to allow for a 2-foot 8-pound tippet. If you want to go heavier, extend the 20-, 15-, and 12-pound sections to 2 feet each and eliminate the 10-pound portion. In all cases you'll end up with a leader about the length of the rod.

TACTICS FOR LARGEMOUTHS

There's little argument among fly-rod advocates about which is more exciting, seeing a surface strike or feeling an underwater tug. When a lurking largemouth zeros in on a surface bug and sends water flying in all directions as it engulfs the supposed prey, any angler who doesn't blink has taken up the wrong sport. It's the reason the ubiquitous popping bug is so popular. Nothing else seems to inspire such savage strikes or is so effective when bass are in the mood to hit top water offerings. The best part of it is, they're in that mood much of the time.

Popping bugs have long been fashioned from cork, balsa, and other buoyant woods. More recently, plastic bug bodies have become common. The synthetics are easy to mold, easy to paint, and nearly indestructible. The front end of some poppers are dished, or of concave configuration. Others are slanted, or angled in an upward or downward direction. If slanted up, they tend to skip when retrieved. If angled down, they duck under when jerked or twitched. Popping bugs are usually equipped with feather, hair, or synthetic legs and tails which add color and extra movement or action when retrieved.

The number one feature of popping bugs is their built-in ability to make a noise or "pop" when they are spasmodically retrieved. Well, it isn't actually a "pop" in all cases. Some poppers gurgle or chug whereas others don't do much more than set up a wake or ripple. As with streamer flies, the angler is in control of what the popper does or doesn't do. Good popper fishing requires manipulation but the extra effort is usually well rewarded.

Traditionally the most popular colors for bass lures of all kinds have been red and white, black, green and yellow (frog-spotted), metallic silver, and florescent chartreuse. Black, frog-spotted, and silver make good sense because they suggest colors found in nature. A large number of creatures are black or nearly so, frogs are spotted (bass love frogs) and silver flashes like a minnow's sides. Blood, of course, is red and the bellies of small fish are white. Chartreuse is open to discussion, as are other florescent colors that seduce more than a few bass. Whatever the reasons, the above mentioned colors and combinations should be in every bass-bugger's box.

Hook sizes from 6 to 2/0 will be useful with a No. 2 probably being the best all-around size. Most legal bass can wrap their jaws around a 2, but this size will not hook too many tiny bass—which you don't want to hook anyway.

Bill Goes Bass Bugging

During late spring or early summer, depending on the latitude, a couple weeks of ideal bug fishing conditions usually occur on every bass lake or pond. The water has warmed to a near perfect level and the bass are anxious to move from the protection of deep water to the "fringe" areas of the lake. Of course, there's protection in these places too but it's of a different form. Cattails, lily pads, weeds, and grasses attract most of the live food that hungry bass are seeking. The added cover of stumps, sunken logs, rocks, brush, and trash of all sorts provide perfect lie-in-wait spots.

It's on one of these beautiful June mornings that we next catch up with Bill. He's here with a pal in a flat-bottomed boat. The pal knows the lake pretty well. Bill's got a 9-foot rod, the right leader, and a selection of bugs. Let's tag along.

 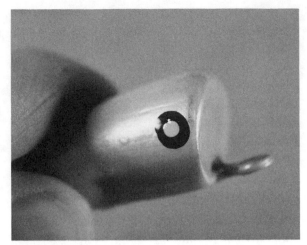

Hollow head of this bug will cause it to pop or gurgle when retrieved in short jerks. The sound and the disturbance pattern on the surface both contribute to the effectiveness of this design. The rubber legs help too.

Slant-head bug will dip and dive in an erratic fashion as it's retrieved. If the slant is formed in the opposite direction, it will duck under the surface with each jerk on the line or rod tip. Here again, the painted eye is an asset.

Bill's pal, Ted, has some fishing behind him. The experience shows; he stopped the motor at least fifty yards from the cove they intend to fish. From here on Ted will move the boat with an electric motor. Quiet paddling would work just as well, but the electric motor is quicker and can cover more water in less time.

What a great-looking spot this is. The cove is dotted with grass hummocks, a stump sticking up here and there and a scattering of emerging lily pads. The water is about two feet deep across the cove with an occasional hole a foot or so deeper. Ideal bass cover.

Ted eases the boat to the grassy border that marks the edge of the cove. By cruising along this border Bill can hit most of the good-looking spots with no more than a twenty-five-foot cast. He selects a red-and-white, hollow-headed popper in size 2, and attaches it to his line. He peels a few strips of line from the reel, false casts a couple of times, and aims for the left side of a grass hummock. The bug plops to within inches of it.

Bill is happy with his cast, but as he lowers

the rod tip to begin retrieving, he doesn't have time to congratulate himself. Pow! From beneath the hummock a 9-inch bass grabs the bug almost before it strikes the water. The little fish must have seen it coming. A frantic jump, a quick scoot here and there and the bass is out of gas. Bill swings the rod toward Ted, who grabs the little bass by the lower lip. He removes the hook easily.

It only requires a couple more casts aimed among the hummocks and Bill is fast to another small bass, a near duplicate of the first one. He hooks two more bass of similar size without much rod work. The little guys are smacking the bug the second it strikes the water. Ted, as we noted, is an experienced angler and has fished this lake before. He decides to change position. Instead of casting into the hummocks, Ted suspects that the larger bass might not be so deep into the cover. Maybe they're lying along the edge of the cove.

Ted paddles the boat deeper into the hummocks and stumps. Bill will have to cast over them to reach the edge of the open water. He'll then retrieve the bug back through the hummocks and stumps; it's just the reverse of what they were doing.

Bill's doing it right. The bug is landing about four feet beyond the edge of the cove. By switching the rod back and forth, he guides the bug between the hummocks and stumps. That's it, Bill, just as you did with the streamer flies, keep the rod down low and strip in short, choppy jerks. Allow the line to pass under the forefinger of the rod hand. Each strip makes the bug sound off: bloop, bloop, blurb, bloop. Oh, oh! Bill strikes hard as a huge wake appears behind the bug and ends in a loud splash. Nope. The bass made a pass but didn't get hooked.

Bill flicks the rod back for a false cast, but as he tries to shoot the stripped-in line from the deck the bug stops in midair and smacks him in the back of the head. The surplus line in the boat had somehow wound around a protruding bolt and also around the tab of a soft drink can. This is the most important lesson to learn and never forget when fly rodding from a boat: when stripped into a boat, a fly line will magically seek and attach itself to any protruding object. The easiest way to prevent such foul-ups is to cover the area where the line will fall with a piece of smooth canvas. Some anglers use a basket or cardboard box with all flaps smoothly cut off.

Bill solves the stripping problem by positioning his rain jacket so that it will catch the retrieved line. (I'm sure he'll bring a piece of canvas the next time.) Bill aims another cast not far from the last one and returns to the blooping retrieve. No long wait is necessary. Splash! Bill sets the hook with a sharp jab to the right and a 3-pound largemouth cartwheels into the air!

After the first jump, the bass makes a run for deeper water and Bill allows it to take line from the reel. Had the bass elected to run into the hummocky area, it would have been necessary to apply some pressure to prevent the fish from wrapping the leader around a snag. This is not the place for leaders that test a couple pounds!

A minute or so of spirited pulling, a final half-jump, and the bass is under Bill's control. Largemouths hit hard and put on a good opening act, but they don't last long. Bill leads the bass toward Ted's waiting hand, lifts its head slightly, and Ted grabs it by pinching the lower lip between thumb and forefinger. The hook backs out easily and the bass is back in the water. Ted doesn't worry about the bass biting his fingers. The lips feel more like coarse sandpaper and provide a good grip. Grabbing bass around the body may cause injury to the fish, if a release is intended, but can also harm the angler. Bass, like all members of the sunfish family, have sharp spines on all fins except the two pectorals and the tail fin.

Bass might remain in the kind of cove where Bill was fishing from April until October if the water doesn't become too warm or too cold. In either case they would seek deeper water. They would also look for new feeding areas if the food supply is insufficient. As a hypothetical case, let's assume that hot weather made the cove water too warm for comfort and the bass moved on searching for a cooler environment. Cruising the perimeter of the lake, they may come across a rock-bottomed area that is eight feet deep or more. It's not only cooler there, but there's also a plentiful supply of crayfish. Food, comfortable temperature, and all those rocks to supply cover—the best of all worlds as far as a bass is concerned. If the fly rodder finds these bass, a surface popper won't catch them. He'll have to switch to an underwater fly and get it down to where they are.

Fishing Sunken Flies

Bass spend more time dining *under* the surface than they do on top. While surface fishing for bass is very exciting, bass are more likely to fall for a sunken fly. Fishing for bass with the fly rod was originally a sunken lure operation. A hundred years ago, a fly and spinner combination was the standard lure. Floating flies and bugs for bass were scarce if not nonexistent. The fly and spinner was usually trolled from an oar-driven boat. Not much casting was involved. But the old-timers were aware that bass tended to go deep in hot weather. By moving the boat slower or by adding weight to the leader (or fly), they could increase the trolling depth. A lot of bass were caught on these fly/spinner rigs and so were trout, pickerel, landlocked salmon, and several other species. The fact is, the fly/spinners will still work as trolling lures, but casting them any distance is difficult, as the spinner blade will tangle and twist the leader into unbelievable knots. Besides, we now have sunken-fly designs and patterns that are much more effective—and they cast like a rocket.

Reviewing the streamer fly chapter in the section on fly fishing for trout is a good idea, since the basics of retrieving and adding life to the fly are much the same. There is, however, one important difference: when fishing a streamer for bass, continual action or motion is not critical. In fact, it's advisable to add a few pauses or dead stops now and then. Because bass tend to lurk in cover for their prey, a change of pace,

including pauses, will often elicit a strike.

All methods of sinking a fly will be useful at times. When you're using a sunken fly in lakes, however, the less weight, the better. Most of the time, a sink-tip fly line will take the fly deep enough to cover most situations. If the fly must be delivered deeper than five feet, a section of lead-core line tied into the leader itself is the best choice. When retrieved, the lead-core line imparts a seductive up-and-down jigging action and is much less likely to snag on bottom rocks or drifting weeds. When fished near underwater cover, a snakey-looking streamer can be just as effective as the highly popular plastic worm.

The flies that have more of this built-in action include the Marabou, Leech, Woolly Bugger, Zonker, and aft-tied saltwater groups. These fly types are represented by a long list of special names, and about the only way to determine which is which is by studying the catalogs and examining the flies at tackle shops. This is fun and educational too, since most tackle store personnel are anglers and may offer some worthwhile advice.

Unlike surface bugs and poppers of all kinds, the bass flies that work best underwater are sub-

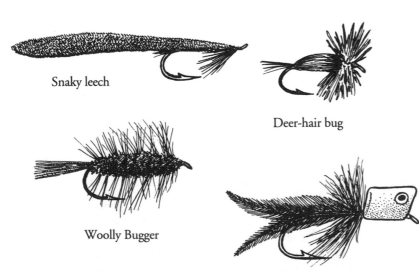

Snaky leech

Deer-hair bug

Woolly Bugger

Wooden popper

Flies for bass are generally larger than those used for trout. These are among the best.

dued in color. The most productive seem to be black, brown, deep purple, or a shade of green. White with a touch of red or silver may do very well on sunny days, but for some reason white seldom attracts many bass when fished much deeper than three feet. This seems to be true with other bright colors such as orange, yellow, and the various florescent tones.

Many bass anglers are keen on having eyes of some sort on all bass flies. It can be argued that freshwater leeches don't have eyes, but plenty of flies tied to suggest black leeches do include some sort of painted, plastic, or chain-bead eye. And they catch a lot of fish.

A good first choice among underwater flies would be a size 1 or 2 flowing-tail pattern such as a Woolly Bugger, Maribou, or rabbit-fur strip fly. I'd go with black or dark brown. Cast into the open pockets of the thickest cover you can find with no more than the length of the leader and about eight feet of line. Soak the fly in the water or with saliva to be sure it sinks the instant it lands. As it strikes the water, begin to strip immediately in short, choppy jerks. Do it for a count of three and then allow the fly to sink for the same count. Continue doing this, guiding the fly through the weeds and flotsam until the line to leader connection is at the rod

tip. False cast once or twice if necessary and aim for a new spot. Work the entire area around the boat, or what you can reach if wading or fishing from shore. Two or three casts are enough to direct at any single spot. If a lurking bass doesn't respond to three tries he's probably not going to. Move on ten feet or so and try again.

If you get few or no strikes in the thick cover, try working the open areas and then the deeper water adjacent to it. Position yourself so that a longer cast can be made along the edge of the cover. If the bass are doing their lurking here, retrieve that streamer parallel to the cover. Large minnows frequently do this, instinctively knowing that to swim into the cover invites disaster.

Deep spots along rocky cliffs or over submerged river beds and other naturally deep holes may be the only places bass can be found during extremely hot or cold weather. A full sinking line or longer section of lead-core line built into the leader is the only way to reach them with fly tackle. Eighteen or twenty feet is about as deep as flies can be fished effectively. It's possible to sink them deeper but feeling a strike is difficult and so is setting the hook. Fortunately, bass aren't usually found much deeper than twenty feet, except in ice-covered lakes or during extremely hot weather. (It's wise to

Molded streamer body with maribou tail is a good minnow imitation in most bass lakes and rivers. This one is painted black and white with red and yellow eyes. The hard body will sink quickly in deep water.

Sculpin design, with deer-hair head, works as well on bass as it does on trout. Fish these flies slowly and very close to the bottom. If you don't get hung on snags occasionally, you're not fishing it deep enough.

spend those days indoors tying flies, making leaders, or reading about fishing.)

Where bass are on the bottom, say fifteen feet or so, or suspended at about that depth in even deeper water, they can be vulnerable to a fly that has a touch of silver or a hint of white belly. There are some wonderful minnow imitations being made today with molded epoxy bodies that have a touch of metallic flash built into the material. Streamers with silver Mylar strips in the wings or as body material are also good choices. There are several other good streamer ideas that I haven't experimented with but may be just as good. The idea is to present a fly that looks like a nervous baitfish. When bass are in deep water, and particularly when they are suspended, they can be extremely fussy about eating. Your fake minnow may glide past them a dozen times without a glance, but the thirteenth time they'll strike. This is contrary to the behavior bass usually display in shallow water where they usually hit a lure the first time or not at all.

Ahead of a full-sinking line and a 6-foot leader, the fly should be cast at least forty feet away from the boat. A longer cast would be even better because additional line in the water will make it sink faster. For the first try, count to ten, slowly, as the fly sinks. Observe the angle between rod tip and water and begin to strip with six-inch strokes. If you have a strike, go right back to the same routine, remembering the line angle. Stick with the same counting rhythm and you may hook another one. Then again, you may not, in which case the count, the angle, and the cadence of the retrieve should be altered.

Fly rodding for largemouths is a game of trial and error in most lakes. Mix up the retrieves. Try different water types as well as depths. Experiment with flies of different colors and sizes. The goal is to find the combination that turns them on at that particular hour. Find it and chances are you'll catch a lot more than one.

TACTICS FOR SMALLMOUTHS

Of the two major bass species the smallmouth is more like the freshwater trout in its liking for moving water. Smallmouths are found in lakes as well, plenty of them, but they grow larger in rivers and are physically stronger in such environments as a result of having to swim against a current most of the time. They are also frequent feeders on mayflies, stoneflies, and other insect forms that are enjoyed by trout. Of course, in rivers they have a greater opportunity to feed on such creatures.

In rivers or lakes, don't look for the larger smallmouths in the weedy or stump-filled coves and bays nor over grassy shoals or any place that has too much mud or silt on the bottom. Smallmouth bass prefer the clearest water they can find, preferably with a lot of rocks. Find a rocky cliff on a smallmouth lake, places where fractured stones of all sizes have fallen into the water, and the odds are excellent that you'll catch some bass.

In rivers be alert for the hollowed-out places where flood waters have churned out the soil leaving the bottom laced with rocks the size of washing machines. Smallmouths also love to frequent the looping bends in rivers where high spring flows have gouged out grooves and notches in shale. Below manmade, hydroelectric projects, the blasting that was done during construction and the ensuing force of the rushing water from the turbines create perfect smallmouth feeding areas. The fact that the water being discharged from many of these projects in southern states is very cool is part of the reason smallmouths in Dixie grow so big. While the smallmouth is generally considered to be a northern fish (and there are a lot more of them in the northern states and Canada than in the South) the largest of the species are Southerners.

Large rocks, of three feet square or so, and flat stones the size of dinner plates are ideal smallmouth hangouts because *that's where the crayfish are.* There is little doubt among most long-time bass specialists who fish rivers that crayfish are favorite smallmouth food. Crayfish love to putter around the rocks and flat stones because they offer so many escape hatches and hiding places. So do minnows, which are probably number two on the menu.

Crayfish and minnows aren't the only creatures that smallmouth bass eat. Like most gamefish, they are opportunists; when a food supply is plentiful and easy to capture, they'll go for it. Where hellgrammites, the nymphal form of the dragonfly, are there for the taking the smallmouth will oblige. Also surface insects, small frogs, leeches, salamanders, moths, and butterflies. But unlike the largemouth bass, the smallmouth does indeed show preference for slightly smaller prey. These fish really do have a slightly smaller mouth than the largemouth and this is reflected by lure sizes preferred by plug fishermen. The fly rodder must also pay attention to this difference and choose bugs and flies accordingly.

Sunken Flies

Streamer flies are very effective for smallmouths. Brown, black, and olive-green are my top three choices. This is chiefly because these three colors suggest the shades of most crayfish. Following these, white, orange, yellow, red, and silver are most productive.

A strong case can be made for that same Muddler Minnow that is so famous as a trout producer. The traditional Muddler and the entire family of Muddler-types, such as the Whitlock Sculpin, Chaucy Lively Sculpin, and several others, have the dual advantage of resembling small, brownish minnows and crayfish. If smallmouth bass are the target fish of the day, and they're feeding beneath the surface, a muddler type of fly in size 2 or 4 is as close to a "guarantee" as you can find. Come to think of

it, when a muddler is retrieved slowly along or near the bottom, it also looks something like a hellgrammite.

A close second choice would have to be the Woolly Bugger and Zonker families of streamers. Small eels, leeches, minnows, pollywogs, and heaven knows what else are suggested by these flies. Here again, brown, black, and olive-green are top choices with the addition of a ribbing of silver tinsel or a touch of Mylar flash in the wing or tail.

Fly creations aimed directly at imitating crayfish are a bit of a puzzle. For some reason, the very best looking crayfish look-alikes seldom live up to their billing. Conversely, highly suggestive

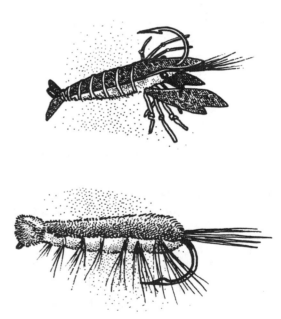

Crayfish imitations are highly effective on all bass wherever these crustaceans exist. Good flies have been fashioned from fur, yarn, feathers, and more recently leather. Because crayfish crawl and swim backwards, propelling themselves with the tail, imitations should be made accordingly. Fish these on or near the bottom with some weight attached to the leader about a foot above the fly.

crayfish patterns do catch smallmouths. Perhaps the reason is texture more than a realistic appearance. I think that a soft feeling in the mouth has more to do with a fly's success than any other factor where smallmouth bass are involved. This fish is famous for picking up live baits of all kinds and tasting or fiddling with them before closing its jaws. A smallmouth may also smack a real crayfish with gusto if it's in the mood, but just as often it will pick it up gently and swim away with it, holding it only between its lips. When it does that with an artificial, setting the hook can be extremely difficult.

There are several very good crayfish patterns on the market but not all tackle shops carry them. In parts of the U.S. where trout and smallmouth bass coexist crayfish copies are more common because trout eat crayfish too. (In fact, in some eastern trout streams crayfish are the preferred food of any trout over 15 inches long.) The important feature to look for is a soft overall feel. While real crayfish are hard and unyielding to the touch, fish prefer the individuals that have recently shed their outer shell. These are very soft and must taste better. Pennsylvania angler Chuck Furimsky has recently added a new twist to an old idea. He has created a highly effective crayfish imitation from very thin glove leather by trimming small bits into tail and claw shapes and attaching them with thread to various size hooks. The beauty of these leather crayfish is that the texture of the leather, once it becomes water soaked, is amazingly soft and spongy. When retrieved slowly, close to the bottom, these leather lures are fantastic producers. The leather material is marketed by Phil Camera Inc., P.O. Box 4031, Woodland Park, CO 80866. I haven't seen such a commercial leather crayfish (as this is being written), but I'll bet they'll be around soon. This material has great potential for all sorts of fly applications.

When fishing with a crayfish imitation or drab-colored streamer in rivers, the best plan is to follow the same procedure used with trout. Keep the fly close to or on the bottom and scoot and scurry it along in a crablike manner, now fast, now slow, now in between. It doesn't matter a great deal how you mix up the action because crayfish can and do make a lot of moves. The style I've found best is the hand-twist retrieve (as discussed in the wet-fly chapter) in still pools. Strip faster in faster water. But that's not an unbreakable rule: as with any kind of underwater fly fishing, some experimenting is usually necessary before the best pattern is found. Smallmouth bass are tremendously moody fish and may follow a fly for several feet before deciding to make their move. As with all kinds of underwater fly fishing, never become too addicted to one retrieve style.

Most standard trout streamer patterns will work with smallmouths. A somewhat larger size is suggested, however, with Nos. 2 and 4 being the best choices. The Black Ghost, Muddler, and Mickey Finn in certain waters may catch a trout on one cast and a smallmouth on the next. Streamers featuring grizzly or barred hackles as wings are especially attractive to smallmouths. Perhaps the barred effect resembles the markings of certain small fish. Whatever the reason, be sure to have a few barred wing flies in your box.

Floating Flies and Bugs

The same kinds of bugs suggested for largemouth bass will work equally well for smallmouths except those for smallmouths should be slightly smaller and more subdued in color. Size 1 is about as large as many fly anglers carry for smallmouths, with sizes 2 and 4 being most popular. All of the colors mentioned for largemouth bass apply for smallmouths at times, but it's best to stick with the blacks, browns, and olive-greens.

A type of bass bug we haven't mentioned is the hair bug. This is an American creation that was probably devised because we have so many deer. Deer tails and body hair are wonderful fly materials. Deer body hair can be tied onto a hook and trimmed with scissors to suggest all sorts of creatures that bass like to eat: frogs, mice, baby birds, large insects, and random shapes that resemble absolutely nothing. The longer tail hair serves as wings, tails, legs, and feelers. Deer-hair flies catch all kinds of fish but seem to work better on smallmouths than on other bass.

As with the leather crayfish, the effectiveness of hair bugs may be a matter of texture. A hair bug must feel like something natural when a fish seizes it. Most anglers agree that a smallmouth is not nearly as likely to reject (or eject) a hair bug as quickly as it sometimes does a hard bug of cork, wood, or plastic.

Deer hair bugs (hair from caribou, elk and antelope is just as good) float well and can be colored with felt-tip pens. While they don't make noises as hard poppers do, hair bugs wiggle and twitch when retrieved like nothing else. The simplest versions of these hair bugs usually feature a pair of legs that point rearward. Casting along a river or lake shoreline at dusk, at night or early in the morning with a hair bug can be a fly rodder's dream.

A hair bug is worked like a popping bug. Retrieve it in short, choppy jerks for a few tries and then with longer pulls, until you find the pattern. In lakes and still river pools, allow the bug to pause every so often. In faster water, keep it moving at all times. The best color? Natural deer-hair tan is No. 1, with black being a close second.

On many rivers and lakes, hatches of mayflies and stoneflies often trigger fantastic smallmouth action. If this happens, fish for them exactly as you would for trout. Dead-drift a dry fly over the last rise you saw in moving water or cast close to the rise form in a lake and twitch it a time or two at ten-second intervals. Select a dry fly that's close in color and silhouette but go up a size or two. Smallmouth bass will take small naturals to be sure, but they don't mind if your offering happens to be a size 10 when the real thing is a size 14.

Fishing After Dark

All bass are active nocturnal feeders where available food and water clarity permit. Smallmouth bass in rivers and clear lakes are particularly vulnerable at night and if you're accustomed to fishing after dark you'll catch some fish. When a hatch of insects continues into the night hours, surface fishing with a high-riding fly, hair bug, or popper is effective. During the heat of summer, when shallow bays and shorelines are too warm for fish comfort, the nights may not be. Here again, crayfish are usually the big attraction. These crustaceans aren't fond of warm water either, and will retreat to the depths or crawl under rocks when the sun is blazing. At night they'll move back to the lake or river edges and the bass are sure to follow.

Cruising the shoreline of a smallmouth lake after dark, under power from an electric motor or paddle, and just listening, will often tell you where the fish are. When bass move into shallow water to grub along the bottom seeking crayfish, nymphs, pollywogs, or what-have-you, they can't help but make some surface disturbances. You'll hear them and see them—once your eyes adjust to the dark. Move the boat to easy casting distance and try to put the lure practically on the shore. Retrieve it from shallow to deeper water with slow, jerky strokes. It's exciting fishing!

Night fishing can be done from the shore of many lakes. If you're not familiar with the lake, some scouting will be necessary. Look for those stone-laden beaches that will harbor crayfish and hellgrammites and do some listening and watching when the sun goes down. The detective work is half the fun!

10

Panfish

Anglers and the folks who ponder the meanings of words have yet to resolve the *panfish* issue. Are they called panfish because they fit in a frying pan or taste so good when they come out of one? Both statements are correct, but from a fly fisherman's standpoint, panfish, particularly the bluegill sunfish, are an important group owing to their wide distribution and willingness to strike most of the time.

The panfish group considered here includes the sunfish, perch, and crappies. Some anglers lump pickerel, catfish, suckers, and a few other plentiful species under this general heading, but catfish and suckers are not taken on flies with any degree of frequency and pickerel will be discussed under another heading.

TACKLE

The same rod, reel, and line combination recommended for trout is the perfect outfit for panfish: an 8- or 8½-foot rod rated for a 6-weight line. The only tackle alteration needed is a reduction in leader length. Shorten all sections of a tapered leader in order to end up with one

One of the reasons panfish are so named is because they are so good in the frying pan. More than a few are needed for a serious fish fry and this angler has a good start. Small popping bugs can fill the fish basket in short order.

6 feet long. When fishing for panfish, one should expect to catch a lot of them and the shorter leader is easier to manage; it won't have to be reeled through the tip guide so often. In addition, you'll be casting a lot of small bugs and the short leader will deliver them more accurately. Panfish are not leader shy.

BLUEGILLS

Bluegills are found in nearly every lake and pond that also contain black bass, and in many more that don't. In short, bluegills are plentiful in every state except Alaska, and there may be some there. Bluegills have been transplanted to other countries with some success, but the U.S. seems to be home base for this feisty little fighter.

The bluegill, *Lepomis macrochirus,* is a pretty

The well-distributed bluegill is a plentiful, willing striker. Surprisingly strong for such a little fish, it puts a deep bend into a light fly rod. It's also one of the best training fish for beginning fly fishermen.

little fish at all times but especially so when dressed in spawning colors. The gill plate, for which the fish is named, becomes a rich cobalt blue and its flanks are brilliant rosy-gold. The males are brighter than the females, but even the girls shine brightly.

Bluegills spawn in the spring, generally, but the month varies from latitude to latitude. It appears that spawning takes place when water temperature reaches the mid-60s. In most ponds and lakes, the females make their spawning beds along the shoreline in shallow water. They aren't all that fussy, however, and will nest much deeper if they can't find a shallow spot that suits them.

Coaxing the male fish to strike is easy when they are guarding a nest of eggs or watching over a female that is in the act of spawning. Bluegills are outrageously brave for such a small fish and will actually attack a much larger bass or other fish that attempts to interfere with the spawning act. Because of this pugnacious behavior, retrieving a small popping bug across a spawning area—where dozens of bluegills are congregated—can't fail to bring a strike. However, fly fishing for 'gills or bream, as they are known in the South, is not confined to the spawning period.

The wonderful thing about bluegills is they always seem to be ready to do battle at some time every day. And they do perform very well when hooked, putting much more of a bend into a fly rod than such a small fish seems capable of. Bluegills from any lake will seldom average much larger than an adult's hand. A 10-inch 'gill would be a dandy and anything longer than that is a trophy. The world's-record bluegill appears to be one caught in Alabama back in 1950 by "Coke" McKenzie. It weighed 4 pounds and 12 ounces but was only 15 inches long. Its girth, however, was 18 inches. Once an angler discovers how hard these little fish can pull, a bluegill the size of McKenzie's fish can be appreciated!

Bugs and Flies

Selecting the best fly-rod lures for bluegills is not on the same level as rocket science or brain surgery. Practically any bass bug, trout fly, or attractor-type streamer will get a bluegill's attention and bring a strike. Size is the most important factor. In the case of bass bugs, it's necessary to downsize, and with some trout flies upsizing may be necessary. The trick is to choose a bug that is just about the same diameter as a bluegill's mouth opening. If the bug or fly is too small it will be swallowed, making hook removal difficult. If it's too large, the fish won't be able to engulf it. The best way to gauge this, of course, is to catch a typical bluegill from the water at hand and see how large the mouth opening is. I've found that a cork, balsa, or plastic body should be at least a quarter inch in diameter but not more than a half inch. The tails, wings, or

The bluegill's small mouth requires a tiny popping bug. The fish sucks it in instead of gulping it. Small trout flies, nymphs, and streamers will work equally well on panfish if they are fished slowly.

Bluegills are not highly selective, but rubber legs on small bugs seem to bring more strikes. These are made by Gaines Poppers, the nation's best-known maker of cork-bodied fishing lures.

legs of any bug should add up to no more than an inch or slightly less. Many so-called panfish bugs and flies are longer than this—so trim the feathers, hair, or rubber bands a bit if necessary. Bluegills will attempt to swallow larger bugs but they just can't manage it, and you won't hook them with any degree of regularity. Hook sizes 8 and 10 are the only two necessary.

As for color, bluegills are quite undiscriminating, but I've had best luck with solid yellow, black, and white—or combinations of these three. The Gaines Company, which makes the widest assortment of bluegill bugs in the United States, reports that their most popular colors are chartreuse and black. This company, incidentally, markets a bluegill bug named Sneaky Pete which must be the most well-known commercial 'gill-getter in the world. More orders come in for the Sneaky Pete in chartreuse than for any other color. Take heed.

A standard wet fly or streamer pattern of almost any color combination will catch bluegills, but when the fly is underwater, a touch of white seems to draw more attention. The traditional Royal Coachman and the tinsel-ribbed patterns such as the Professor and Grizzly King are terrific bluegill patterns and so is the famous Mickey Finn streamer—as long as they aren't much over an inch long. As with the bugs, a size 8 or 10 hook is the best choice.

Technique for Bluegills

If you see bluegills hovering over cleaned-out depressions along shorelines your approach won't matter much. Simply cast the bug or fly to a point just beyond the spawning bed and retrieve it over or through the bed with short, jerky strips. You'll have a strike within two seconds or quicker. Don't jerk when you see the splash—wait until you feel some resistance and just pull back smoothly. After a short initial run, the bluegill will turn its body sideways and go into its typical chug-chug-chug routine.

If you've never caught one before you'll be surprised at how strong these little fish are. Ease it in, grasp the hook, and shake it off into an ice-laden cooler if you intend to eat it. If not, shake it back into the water. It's best to pinch down the barbs on all bluegill bugs. These fish often take the bug deeply and it's much easier to remove a debarbed hook. When handling bluegills be careful of the pointed spines on the dorsal, anal, and pectoral fins. These become sharp and erect when a bluegill is stressed or excited. By folding them down with the thumb, you can hold the fish easily with the thumb on top and the other fingers beneath the belly. Some anglers find it convenient to use a cotton glove for bluegill unhooking operations, and one is recommended for youngsters.

When bluegills aren't engaged in spawning, finding them can be more of a problem. This is seldom difficult in a farm pond or small lake, but it can be in larger bodies of water. Electronic fish finders can save time here, but bluegills, like bass, are keen on finding a comfortable temperature zone. They seem to like that same mid-60s range that bass are fond of, except they are seldom found in water deeper than 12 feet. Being an active surface feeder and not keen on eating minnows or large underwater prey, the bluegill likes to keep its eyes on the surface. In lakes that have small streams flowing into them be sure to check these areas, especially if there are some shallow coves close by. A few casts with a surface bug will soon let you know if bluegills are around.

If the 'gills are in deeper water, a period of trolling with wet flies may be called for. Tie on a size 10 ten wet fly—a brightly colored one—or a pair of them attached as described in the wet-fly chapter, and do some near-shore trolling. A sink-tip or full sinking line will help a great deal. Pay out forty feet of line and cruise along, say, forty feet from the bank. Try different depths until you get a strike. If it's a bluegill, mark the spot. Anchor and begin casting. When you find the right depth, the chances are good that you'll catch several, enough for a fish fry, anyway. Of course, the fish you catch trolling may not be a bluegill. It could be a crappie, yellow perch, or some other member of the sunfish family. No matter, they're all fun to catch and good to eat.

Most of the other members of the small sunfish group, such as the pumpkinseed, longeared sunfish, yellowbreast sunfish, and redear sunfish all react much the same as bluegills do. The same methods will catch them, and when you locate one you'll usually find more since they travel in schools when they're not spawning.

CRAPPIES

Crappies are the second most popular panfish following the bluegill. Millions are caught on tiny live minnows each summer and almost as many through holes in the ice in the winter. The two subspecies, the black and the white, are distributed across the contiguous forty-eight states in almost the same numbers as the bluegill. However, the crappie is not a fly fishing pushover like the bluegill. I suspect the reason for this is the crappies' preference for minnows

Surface bugs fashioned from deer hair and plastic foam are alternatives that often work as well as cork bugs. The foam bug, when fished deep with the aid of a small sinker and a sink-tip fly line, does equally well on crappies.

and deep water. So they present a much more difficult challenge for the fly fisherman. But they can be caught on flies if the angler persists.

Because minnows like to hang around thick cover for protection, sunken logs, tree tops, submerged brush piles, and overhanging rock

Crappies are the favorite panfish in many southern lakes. Ordinarily found in slightly deeper water than bluegills, crappies respond well to sunken nymphs, cricket imitations, and small streamers.

ledges are good places to try. My best catches of crappies on flies have been made near sunken brush piles in about twelve feet of water. Use a fast-sinking line (or sinker on the leader), make a cast that will eventually hang straight down from the rod tip about two or three feet from the brush. Once the line is straight, begin to jig it up and down, as if it were a frightened minnow. Mix up the jigging with a bit of side to side movement (this is easy to do with a fly rod), and finally strip the fly rapidly towards the surface for six feet or more. Then allow it to fall back again for another sequence.

For this kind of crappie fishing, trout streamers work best, and a size 8 or 10 Black Ghost is a good choice. Painted eyes or eyes fashioned from chain beads or plastic are a great help. Crappies really do zero in on the eyes. Trolling a streamer fly is also effective for crappies if you're having trouble coaxing them to hit the jigged fly.

YELLOW PERCH

Yellow perch present the same set of problems that crappies do, only more so. You've got to fish deeper for them. I can never recall catching a yellow perch on a surface fly or bug of any kind. They will take a trolled streamer, probably more often than crappies will, and they are vulnerable to small Zonker-style flies when cast and retrieved. Being avid minnow chasers, yellow perch usually hit a rabbit-fur Zonker undulating in front of their nose. Marabou streamers in sizes 6, 8, and 10 are almost as good. The best colors for yellow perch are yellow-red and white-red combinations. Painted eyes on the head of the fly for this minnow-chaser are a great advantage.

ROCK BASS

The other panfish mentioned thus far are primarily found in lakes and ponds. The rock bass does inhabit ponds and lakes that have sizable

inlet or outlet rivers, but it really prefers moving water. The rock bass is considered to be a northeastern species, but it's now found in most states east of the Rocky Mountains. As a rule of thumb, where smallmouth bass are found, rock bass probably will be too.

As with bluegills, find some beds of spawning rock bass and you'll enjoy some fantastic surface fishing. They hit like a small ton of bricks and are very likely to strike a large fly or popper intended for smallmouth bass. When fishing for smallmouths, some anglers consider "rockies" to

Yellow perch, like crappies, are fond of minnows and crustaceans. Grublike nymphs and small, silver-bodied streamers will catch them if a sink-tip line is used. Perch are temperature sensitive; if you catch one, try to return the fly to the same depth.

be a trash fish, but I've never felt that way. A small fish that hits so hard and fights so valiantly is always a worthwhile catch.

Rock bass hang around the same kinds of cover that smallmouths do and sometimes in even faster water. In slower-moving pools, surface poppers and hair bugs in sizes 8 and 6, and sometimes as large as 4, yield the most fun. In stronger currents, a sunken fly stripped very fast is a better attractor, but the surface bug will also catch rock bass if moved fast. These small fish—they're seldom longer than 10 inches—have no trouble catching up to a rapidly retrieved streamer.

The selection of colors is seldom important with rock bass, but I have found them to be particularly fond of yellow. A favorite is the Yellow Muddler with a yellow-winged Edson Tiger being a close second. Yellow popping or hair bugs are also excellent producers, and unlike bugs for bluegills, don't trim the wings or legs. The rock bass has an oversize jaw for such a short, chunky fish and will surprise you with how large a fly it will go after.

Just like its stream mate, the smallmouth bass, rockies will also feed greedily on hatching mayflies and stoneflies when they get the chance. Fish for them just as you would for trout—except jiggle the fly more often; rock bass are aggressive lightweights.

11

Pike, Muskie, and Pickerel

NORTHERN PIKE

The long-nosed members of the *Esox* genus share a long and mixed history of being admired and loathed, even feared, by some anglers. In the British Isles and across much of western Europe, the northern pike, *Esox lucius*, is mostly hated as a vicious predator of their beloved trout. Many are the legends of huge pike that were large enough to eat swimming pigs and occasionally small children. North American tales abound of monstrous pike attacking boats and people. Northern pike of nearly 50 pounds have been caught in U.S. and Canadian waters, and a few are caught every year that tip the scales around 30 pounds. The average is much smaller than that, however, with a 10-pounder being considered a "nice" fish and one over 15 approaching trophy size. The North American average is much closer to 4 or 5 pounds.

Recognition of the northern pike as a fly-rod fish has not come about easily. The salvation of many Canadian fishing excursions, the plentiful pike has been (and is) the number one target for anglers who cast red and white spoons rigged with a single treble hook. The aggressive pike has willingly obliged. Without the pike, several hundred Canadian fishing lodges would be out of business.

A few dozen serious fly rodders were tossing flies at pike fifty or more years ago and loving it. The violent strike, a sudden first run, and an occasional leap make the pike an exciting fish to catch. But fly fishing for pike didn't catch on in a big way until recently. Perhaps it was a lack of proper tackle. Maybe the lodge owners didn't promote the sport well enough. Or perhaps many guides were not keen about handling the sharp-toothed pike. The picture is rapidly changing, with anglers now heading for Canadian and U.S. pike waters armed exclusively with fly fishing gear. The appeal is the thrill of catching the largest freshwater fish many of them will ever see.

Tackle

The basic fly tackle for northern pike and muskellunge consists of a 9-foot rod rated for a

An average-size northern pike about to be released. The bean-shaped markings on this fish are perfectly formed as are the stripes on the tail. The often maligned pike is a wonderful fly-rod fish that is gaining admirers.

9 WFF line. Practically all manufacturers of quality fly rods offer more than one 9-foot rod, which makes the selection process a bit tricky. Some makers, helpfully, describe certain rods as being designed for pike and muskies. Others leave it up to the buyer to decide. Go for the rod that's a bit on the stiff side when "test wiggled" at the tackle shop. As with all rods, try to arrange a few practice casts to see how it performs. Extra-long casts of more than sixty feet are seldom required when pike fishing but extra "lifting" power will be needed.

Pike are often hooked in or adjacent to weeds, brush, and rocky-bottomed bays and will need to be pressured by the rod to prevent an escape. At netting or release time, the rod must be strong enough to lift the pike's head close enough to the surface for capture. "Lifting power" is an elusive trait. Some rods that are excellent casting tools simply don't have the

With a face that only a mother could love, the northern pike strikes savagely and loves long, wiggling streamer flies. Large, debarbed hooks are easier to remove from the pike's tooth-filled jaws.

necessary backbone to control a big fish when landing time arrives. I use a simple test to determine if a 9-weight rod has enough power: run the line through the guides and attach the leader to a 1-pound weight (a plastic bottle with a handle is ideal). Hold the rod by the grip with one hand and grasp the butt section of the rod about 10 inches ahead of the grip with the other hand. Slowly lift the weight from the floor high enough to place it on a chair. If the rod will do this without much effort it will handle pike nicely. You'll be surprised how heavy the 1-

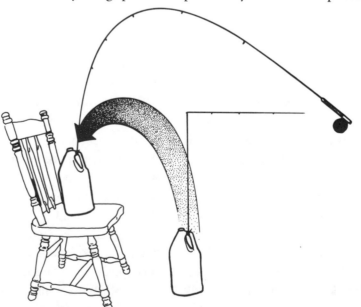

Tackle shop owners may not enjoy seeing this test done on their premises, but it's good to know if the rod you choose for northern pike (and other fish that could weigh 30 pounds or more) has the necessary lifting power.

pound weight feels. *Don't* try this test with any more weight attached—you might break the rod. The reason a big pike of 15 pounds or more can be lifted with such a rod is because the water is supporting more than 90 percent of the fish's weight.

Most pike fly fishing can be handled well with a weight-forward, 9-weight floating line (WF9F). Occasionally, where pike are not anxious to come to the surface or are too close to it, a sink-tip line will be useful. This is an excellent reason to choose a reel that allows for a quick exchange of spools. Keep a floating line on one spool, a sink-tip on the other, and you're prepared for any situation.

The same single-action reel previously recommended for bass will be suitable for pike and muskies if it holds 50 yards of backing and a 9-weight line. Neither fish makes long runs, so the backing will seldom be needed, but fast reeling is often necessary. A spool diameter of at least 3 inches takes up line quickly, which will help keep excess line from causing problems in the boat.

Leaders

It only takes one glance at a pike to see that the fish is well endowed with mean-looking teeth. Stories abound about their ability to bite through almost anything short of a half-inch steel cable. As a result, anglers who throw spoons, plugs, and live bait at the toothy ones have traditionally opted for wire leaders. Short leaders, or "traces," are the usual choice, those sections of braided wire with a snap-swivel on one end and a barrel swivel on the other. Early fly anglers used them too and some still do. Not only do wire leaders have a tendency to kink into annoying shapes when fly casting, they frequently spook the fish.

The best leader for pike and muskies is one borrowed from saltwater fishing. Instead of wire next to the fly, a better idea is to use a 12-inch section of heavy monofilament, of 40-pound test. All of the advantages of wire are enjoyed and none of the disadvantages. Such thick monofilament is not unwieldy or wiry if you buy the type used for trolling leaders for sailfish, tarpon, or white marlin. It is extremely flexible and takes a knot beautifully.

If you're not concerned about fishing for the record book, start your leader with a 3-foot section of 30-pound-test material at the line. Attach that with a nail knot. Next, add a foot of 25-pound test, followed by another foot of 20-pound. Use an Albright knot to connect the 20-pound material to the 40-pound mono. In saltwater parlance this last section is known as a shock leader. If fishing *for* the record book is the plan, shorten the 25-pound and 20-pound sections by about half and add a foot of whatever pound test material you choose. Connect this to the 20-pound section with interlocking loops. The fly is then tied to the shock leader with a loop knot. Something other than a turle or clinch knot must be used in order to keep the fly from locking in position when casting. The loop knot also makes it much easier to hook fish because the free-swinging connection can turn in a big pike's mouth as a strike is made.

Pike cannot actually *bite* through leader material no matter how thin it is. The leader breaks from being pulled or see-sawed across the jaws as the fish is shaking its head during the battle. A pike or muskie's pointed teeth are sharp only on the tips and the tips don't touch, they interlock. Of course, thin mono wears through quicker than thick material will. I've been using 40-pound-test mono on northern pike for 25 years and have yet to lose a fish from a bite-off. If even more insurance is preferred go up to 50- or even 60-pound mono. Pike are not terribly leader-shy but will often spook at the sight of wire.

When fish are hooked in such a way that the entire shock leader is outside the mouth there

ALBRIGHT SPECIAL

This knot is used for tying a light line to a heavy monofilament leader or a wire leader.

1. **Double back a couple inches of heavy line and insert about 10 inches of the light line through the loop in the heavy line.**

2. **Wrap the light line back over itself and over both strands of the heavy line. While doing this you are gripping the light line and both leader strands with the thumb and finger of your left hand, and winding with your right.**

3. **Make ten turns, then insert the end of line back through the loop once more at the point of original entry.**

4. **Pull gently on both ends of heavy line, sliding knot toward loop. Remove slack by pulling on standing and tag ends of light line. Pull both standing lines as tight as possible and clip off excess from both ends.**

will be no fraying. When hooked inside the mouth, eventually some visible abrasion will occur. If the shock tippet is cut into by more than a third of its diameter, cut the fly off and retie it. If you think that all this sounds like too much knot-tying, attach a barrel swivel to the 20-pound test, tie the shock leader to the other end of the swivel, and go to it!

Flies and Bugs

Northern pike have attacked almost anything that moves on or beneath the surface at some time or other. If any fish is a born attack specialist it's this long-nosed predator. Birds, ducklings, muskrats, mice, lemmings, frogs, and, of course, fish of all kinds are all fair game. I've seen pike seize a variety of items that have fallen overboard, including flashlights, cigarette lighters, teaspoons, and pocketknives. When pike are hungry, which they seem to be most of the time, fly and lure color is not usually much of a consideration. But a disclaimer of some sort must be inserted here, because there are times on certain waters when they can be quite fussy.

All fish that eat other fish are attracted by a touch of red. Many fish, however, such as trout, salmon, and several saltwater species want their red in measured doses. But the northern pike is absolutely crazy about crimson. The famous Dardevle wobbling spoon in traditional red and white is the number one pike catcher of all time. It's followed closely by the same spoon in "5 of diamonds" pattern, which is bright yellow decorated with a quintet of red, diamond-shaped spots. The most successful flies and bugs are therefore red and white, yellow and red, red and silver, and red and black. The "hot" florescent colors such as chartreuse, blaze orange, and neon red have also proven their worth in cloudy or discolored water, as have dark purple and black.

Floating bugs should be the same colors except for the addition of solid white. While there is considerable doubt in some anglers' minds about fish being able to distinguish color on a floating lure, pike seem to prefer reflective colors on the surface. Since white reflects more light than the other colors, I wouldn't be without a white floater on bright days.

Pike will hit a wide variety of flies and surface bugs. Retrieve them at a rapid pace and make the bugs "pop" noisily. When caught on single-hook flies, most pike are stuck in the corner of the jaw instead of throat hooked, as is often the case with treble hooks on lures.

Pike have huge mouths. Even a small one of a couple pounds or so (called "hammer handles" on Canadian lakes) can easily swallow a large ear of corn. A 15-pounder is capable of eating a bushel of it—basket and all. For that reason, the best hook sizes for bugs and flies begin at 2/0 and end at 5/0. Yes, these are big hooks, but even small pike have no trouble grabbing such a large fly: and when the barbs are pinched down, a large hook is much easier to remove from a dangerous part of a pike's mouth. With pike, pinching down the barbs is not merely good sportsmanship, it's a form of protection for the

angler or the person who does the unhooking.

Both jaws, the inside edges of the gills and the top of the throat are dangerous for the unsuspecting. Grab a pike by the lower jaw and you'll think your fingers just went through a meat-grinder. Never fish for pike without having large hemostats or a hook-out device close at hand. We'll end this chapter with a discussion of landing and unhooking the toothy ones, but for the moment, let someone else handle the hook removal chores.

Most flies and bugs for pike should be in sizes 3/0 and 4/0. These two hook sizes will hold

Large popping bugs with suitable hooks are great pike catchers. All pike strikes are violent, but those to surface bugs are even more so. Red, orange, yellow, black, and combinations of these colors, are favorites.

securely in a big pike's jaw. Hooks much larger than this are more difficult to cast. Gravity being what it is, the bigger piece of steel wants to come down faster.

The most productive styles of flies for pike are the long snaky ones that quiver and undulate when retrieved. This group includes the Zonkers, Buggers, Marabous, saltwater splittails, Dahlberg divers, eel configurations, and just about any fly that is long and slinky. A bit of flash in the form of Mylar, tinsel, Flashabou, Estaz, or other sparkling-metallic material is also helpful. Regardless of the materials used in pike flies, they'll take a terrible beating from the sharp teeth and the slime that pike exude. Be sure to have plenty of spares.

Poppers that give off with a resounding "bloop" when retrieved in fits and starts are excellent pike catchers. So are the slant-headed models that tend to duck under the surface when moved sharply. In addition to being pugnacious, pike are also extremely curious and will often swim for ten yards or more to investigate a strange sound. Tails, wings, and legs on cork, wooden, or plastic bugs should be long and

floppy just like the appendages on flies. The more action and color the better.

Tip: Wood and hard plastic lures are better for pike than cork or balsa wood. Pike will chew up the latter two materials in short order.

Locating Pike

Northerns are not unlike largemouth black bass in that they are fond of lying in wait in hope of ambushing an unsuspecting prey. Their favorite hides are the edges of weedbeds, near sunken logs, brush, and rock piles, grassy coves, and connecting waterways between lakes and ponds. They are fast swimmers for short sprints but not long on endurance. For that reason, they don't do a great deal of foraging in deep water. Unless the surface temperature exceeds 70 degrees, they'll usually be found in water less than six feet deep and frequently much less than that. Some of the best pike fly rodding I've enjoyed has taken place in shallow bays that weren't much over three feet deep.

During the first thirty days following the last ice cover, pike are going to be in the shallow bays and coves because that's were the food is and the water temperature more to their liking. The same situation exists in the fall immediately following the first frosty night. But even in midsummer don't expect to find pike too far from shallow water and cover. The first drop-off adjacent to a shallow bay, or where the water temperature falls to the mid-60s, is where they'll be watching and waiting.

Technique

The most exciting form of fly casting occurs when you spot a pike cruising in a shallow cove or resting motionless at the edge of a clump of lily pads or grass. The cruising fish is on the prowl and the resting fish is on alert waiting for a morsel to pass by. Either fish is vulnerable and almost sure to take a crack at your offering if it isn't spooked. If you're in a boat, and 99 percent of the time you will be when pike fishing, the first thing to do is stop the motor if it's running. Paddle slowly and as quietly as possible to within casting distance and place the fly about ten feet in front of the pike's nose. Allow the fly to sink for a couple of feet—not to the bottom—and begin a quick, staccato retrieve. Within two or three strokes, the fish may rush the fly and have it. If not, keep up the retrieve until the fish turns towards the fly. At the first sign of interest, increase the retrieve speed. If the fish increases its speed, do the same. Don't worry, you can't move the fly too fast. Keep on bringing the fly toward the boat and chances are better than even that the pike will nail it. If it

doesn't strike, don't immediately cast again *at* the fish, which is probably suspended at mid-depth staring balefully at the boat. Cast at least six feet *beyond and to one side* of the pike and strip the fly *towards* it. Most of the time this routine drives *Esox* absolutely nuts, and he'll inhale that fly. If he doesn't, locate another pike or let your partner try his fly or bug.

Pike may follow a noise-making surface bug, or one that merely makes a wake, for a half-dozen looks before slamming it. The combination of movement and noise may be too much to ignore. But if a pike shows interest in the bug, keep on trying for a few more casts.

There is one trick that works for pike but seldom fools a muskie. That's the sudden stop. If a

Holding a pike just behind the gills, as this angler is doing, is the correct grip. Sticking fingers in the eyes is not only poor form but will blind the pike, dooming it to die of starvation if released.

pike is following your streamer or bug at a pretty fast clip, but remains a uniform distance behind it, stop the retrieve instantly. Allow the fly to sink for a count of three and then crank it up again. Do the same with a floating bug by just letting it float motionless for the same count. At the next pull on the line, the pike is likely to have it in a heartbeat.

At the strike, almost all pike snap their heads to one side and often set the hook themselves. If there isn't any slack line between rod tip and fly, the angler won't have any doubt of when it happens. A sudden jolt, a quick run, and perhaps a jump let you know in a hurry. As with all big fish, try to get slack line on the reel as quickly as possible to avoid loose coils getting tangled with other items in the boat. Northern pike fight furiously for the first twenty seconds or so after being hooked and then settle down to a steady pulling contest. As a rule they can then be led towards the boat without too much force being applied. About the time they see the boat or a net coming toward them they go into another frenzy. This is when most pike break free. Don't try to hold them with a death grip on your rod and reel handle. Allow the fish to make another short run or two and it will quickly give up the battle.

MUSKELLUNGE

This fish, *Esox masquinongy*, is a cousin of the pike. In lakes and rivers with good muskie populations, the small ones of under a couple feet long are sometimes easy to catch. Not so with muskies over 30 inches in length. As muskies grow bigger they seem to become more cautious or, as some anglers believe, more intelligent. They certainly don't come to lures, flies, or even live bait with the reckless abandon for which northern pike are famous.

There isn't a wealth of information about fly fishing for muskellunge because not many anglers have caught them on a fly. In fact, few anglers spend much time even trying to coax

The muskellunge is much more cautious about hitting flies than is the northern pike. Catching a muskie on *anything* is a major angling accomplishment; catching one on a fly is beyond that. Locating a muskie lurking place is half the battle.

these mysterious fish with flies; most try it a time or two and decide it's more fun to cast for species that are more cooperative. I must confess to feeling this way myself, at least some of the time, but when muskies happen to be in the water I'm fishing, I've got to give them a decent try. Such is the attraction of big fish. And muskies are among the largest of freshwater gamefish. The world's record is just under 70 pounds, and larger ones have been netted and speared through the ice.

Muskellunge share the pike's ferocity and its appetite for a wide variety of food items. A muskie of 25 pounds or more can eat about anything it wants to in freshwater. It is also the champion at lurking for something tasty to come close to its lair. The muskie's hiding place is also its lair. Once a muskie decides that a particular spot is where it wants to spend the feeding year, it will remain there until driven out by excessively warm water, a reduced water level, or human annoyance. Even at less than trophy

All muskies are trophies, but coaxing one like this to take a fly will be long remembered. The bigger, the better is the rule for flies. Some jumbo-size saltwater models are used with good results.

size, the muskie is not bothered much by other aquatic predators.

Veteran muskie anglers, wooden lure specialists for the most part, know where the muskie lairs are on waters they fish. They also know that if they do things right and are persistent, they'll eventually hook a particular fish. The fly rodder who hopes to hook a muskie must think the same way.

Locating Muskies

Muskies are generally found in waters that eventually flow into or out of the Great Lakes. They have been introduced into other waters where food and water temperatures are suitable. Muskies spawn at water temperatures between 48 and 60 degrees and, as a rule, seek out water that seldom rises above the mid-60s. Muskies

won't remain in water that's too shallow—three feet or less—during the summer months. They may be in such locations in early spring and late fall, but expect to find them mostly in water between five and fifteen feet deep where they can prey on large fish such as suckers and chubs.

Muskellunge are considered to be more of a lake fish than a river dweller. They are, however, found in moving water and especially in very large rivers such as the St. Lawrence, Allegheny, and Ohio in the U.S. and in dozens of Canadian rivers that flow into Lakes Huron and Superior. They are not fond of swift current, so look for them in the calmer sections of rivers, especially back eddies and along snag-infested shorelines. All muskies, even very small ones, love overhead cover, and the largest of them will always dominate the choice spots. Sunken weedbeds (where nothing shows on top), logs, rocky ledges and, not infrequently, little-used boat docks are ideal muskie hangouts. The common requirements seem to be water deeper than four feet, shade, and enough overhead protection to hide their silhouette.

In lakes or rivers that lack abundant shoreline cover, muskies will be found in somewhat deeper water. Even at such depths they'll still hunt for cover of some sort. If they can't find it they'll go even deeper. Anglers who troll large lures in the St. Lawrence, for example, hook a lot of muskies at well below the twenty-foot mark. The same is true in some deep lakes in Pennsylvania, New York, and West Virginia.

When muskellunge are spending most of the their time in water deeper than fifteen feet, the fly rodder must troll his flies on a deep sinking line or try for another species. Fortunately, many productive muskie waters are far enough north to preclude this. The best way to seek them is to team up with another angler (or guide) and cruise the edge of a lake, river, or connecting flow between lakes and cast your fly or bug to every possible hiding place. If there are other species in the same water, you'll occasionally hook something and every once in a while there will be a hydraulic explosion. That will be a muskellunge!

Technique

There's no reason to repeat tackle recommendations for muskellunge—all gear, including leaders, is the same as that needed for northern pike. The only exception might be the flies; bigger is better for all muskie fishing.

Casting a fly or popper for muskies is just like casting for pike, bass, or any other stillwater fish—with one major exception: never, repeat never, allow the fly to remain motionless. Once the retrieve is started, keep on moving at a *steady* pace. Fast, slow, or anywhere in between, keep the fly or bug moving at the same speed. Muskies want their food alive, and

for some reason known only to them are not keen on chasing anything that changes course or speed too often. It doesn't matter if you see a fish behind your fly or not, don't alter speed during any single retrieving sequence. Alter it after the next cast if you want to move the fly faster or slower.

When I first began my personal quest to catch a muskie on a fly rod I was sure a stop-start fly action was the right thing to do. It worked for nearly everything else. After watching a half-dozen different muskies follow my fly without striking, it dawned on me why they were turning away after a ten-foot chase. Each time I'd see the dark torpedo behind the fly I'd change the retrieve speed—force of habit. Invariably, the muskie would stop in its wake and turn away. They do this a lot, even when you keep the fly moving, but constant motion is the only way to hook one.

After a heap of casting and retrieving, and a muskie finally does strike, there's one more basic difference between northern pike and muskellunge. Pike inhale a fly and almost always snap their head sideways in such way that they usually hook themselves. Muskies prefer to grab their prey and shake their heads from side to side while holding their jaws *clamped shut* for several seconds. This action drives their backward-curving teeth deeper and deeper into the captured fish, rendering it incapable of escape once they loosen the grip for swallowing. This is important to remember because you must strike hard enough to *move the hook*. Otherwise, when the fish relaxes its grip, the fly will simply drop away. Hit it hard—once, twice, and a third time for good measure.

Muskies grab a fly or their prey with a great rush, and if the strike takes place on or near the surface you'll certainly know it. They fight very much like a northern pike after that: a strong initial run, an occasional jump, and then a lot of twisting and chugging. They'll almost always go through a last-gasp bit of serious thrashing at boatside, so be alert and drop the rod tip in order to accommodate this.

Flies and Bugs

The same types of flies that will coax pike will work for muskellunge. Forget any hooks smaller than 4/0 or 5/0 and try to find patterns with feathers or trailing wings that are at least 5 inches long. If you don't tie your own, such long flies are not easily found near freshwater lakes. Flies tied for sailfish, those 6- and 7-inch giants, work great on muskies. It must be remembered that fly rodding for muskies is not a common pastime. Many excellent muskie guides have little or no faith in flies and fly rods. This is changing slowly, as more fly anglers are extending their horizons, but in the meantime, the best bet is to tie your own muskie flies or have someone make them for you. Use the Zonkers, leeches, strip flies, and split-tail saltwater styles as models and tie them on 5/0 hooks in 6- and 7-inch lengths.

Any color could coax a muskie on any given day but red-white and yellow-black combinations have proven to be better than most. As with pike, a touch of metallic flash is helpful.

To be honest, the largest muskie I've hooked fell for an all-white, split-tail pattern that sported chain-bead eyes. I've tried an all-white fly many times since without having history repeat itself. Red-white combinations, however, have been responsible for three muskies. The most "follows" have been behind black-yellow patterns. Muskie fishing with flies is not yet high science!

The fact is, catching muskies is not an easy matter with any sort of artificial lure. Even the best muskie plug casters see many days pass without a strike or even a hint of one. These strange fish seem to feed on exactly what they want to and precisely when they choose. Perhaps their metabolic rate is different from that of their cousin the northern pike. There is some evidence that pike do seem to digest food faster than muskies. There is also the matter of feeding times. Pike are not nocturnal creatures, whereas muskies do eat at night. It could be that when most of us are out there fishing for them, the muskellunge are resting, fat and content, in their secret hiding spots. Then again, it may be character-building for fly enthusiasts to be blessed with such elusive adversaries. When you catch one, or even coax a strike from one of

Flies for pike and muskies should have soft, undulating feathers and other materials that wiggle when retrieved. Some metallic flash helps.

these awesome fish, it's fair to consider either an angling milestone!

PICKEREL

There are either two or three important angling species in the pickerel family depending on which scientist is doing the explaining. The largest of the group is the chain pickerel, *Esox niger,* and the smallest is the grass pickerel, *Esox americanus vermiculatis.* The third pickerel, the redfin is the *Esox americanus americanus.* The chain pickerel reaches a maximum size of about 7 pounds while the grass and redfins seldom exceed a single pound. All pickerel have scales on the *entire* cheek and gill cover. (Pike have scales on the entire cheek and *upper half* of the gill cover only and muskellunge are scaled on the *upper half* of *both* cheek and gill cover.) The chain pickerel, as the name implies, wears chain-like markings on its flanks whereas the grass and redfin carry indistinct bars or stripes. A less scientific means of identification is: if you're south of the Canadian border and the fish looks pike-like but not as large, it's a chain pickerel. If it's less than a foot long and has reddish-tinged fins, it's probably a grass (or redfin) pickerel. In the case of the two small ones, you won't be punished for not knowing the difference.

Pickerel are much like their larger pike and muskellunge relatives in that they prefer to lie in wait for food to swim by. When the unsuspecting minnow, frog, tadpole, or salamander is close enough, the quick pickerel makes a dashing sprint for it and it's gone in one gulp. The teeth, while smaller than those in a pike's jaw, are sharp as needles and prey has little chance of escape. Look for pickerel in thick grass and weeds and under logs and bushes where they have a vantage point to watch over a patch of open water. They are not fish of the depths and are most often found in water less than three feet deep.

Tackle

Rods, lines, and reels for pickerel are easy calls. Go with the basic trout outfit discussed earlier in this book: an 8- or 8½-foot rod for a 6-weight floating line and a single-action reel. Pickerel have sharp teeth, but a short leader of 10-pound-test monofilament will handle them nicely.

Pickerel flies are not highly specialized. Nearly any streamer pattern used for trout, bass, or pike will fill the bill. Try sizes 4 and 6 for chain pickerel and size 8 for grass pickerel. Surface bugs and poppers in red and yellow are also effective. Any fly smaller than that will be difficult to remove from the toothy jaws. Hemostats, pliers, or needle holders are a must for pickerel fishing—they help prevent a lot of cut fingers.

Technique

Like all members of the pike family, pickerel smack a fly with gusto. Because of the exciting strike, these fish are fun to catch and in spite of their small size in some waters are amazingly good in the pan. But there may be some surprises in the size department. In some ponds in southern New Jersey and West Virginia, for example, chain pickerel may average 2 pounds or more. Fish of this size put up a fine battle on a 6-weight fly rod. The best approach is to locate a shoreline featuring heavy vegetation—grass, weeds, cattails, water lilies, or windfall brush. Cruise the edge of this cover in a boat or wade carefully in such a way that the fly or bug can be presented to fall about two feet clear of the protective greenery. Even if the fish doesn't see your offering touch the water, it will hear the "plop" (if it's within five feet or so) and quickly swim closer for inspection.

I've found that a combination *pause and hurry* routine is an almost sure-fire pickerel technique if they're in a feeding mood. Allow the fly or surface bug to stay put for a fast count of one-two-three. Then, strip it fast in very short strokes of six inches or so. If a pickerel is in the vicinity you'll get a look, at least. If a strike comes, you can't miss hooking it.

In very thick cover, the surface bug will work better than a sunken fly—it won't hang up so much. It's also a good idea to use a leader no longer than 6 feet. Pickerel are not leader-shy and don't seem to be terribly spooked by the sight of a boat.

Pickerel are somewhere in between northern pike and muskellunge in feeding characteristics. Pike seem to be hungry most of the time and muskellunge on rare occasions. Pickerel fishing can be fantastic one day and dismal the next. All of those other things that influence fishing apply here, but with pickerel it seems that they just go nuts at times and strike anything that moves. Then there are days when a *live* minnow, swimming two inches from their noses, will be ignored.

IN CONCLUSION

At the risk of sounding like a broken record, I'd like to advocate the use of pinched-down barbs for all of these duck-nosed, toothy fish. They all have the habit of clamping their jaws together when a hook is inside, and if there is a barb on it the removal job can be very difficult. A pair of soft, cloth gloves help a lot and so do hemostats or needle holders. Wire "jaw-spreaders" are useful on larger fish, but be careful not to tear the fish's mouth with them. If the tension is too great, bend the wire a bit to ease up on the pressure. With a fish you intend to eat there's no worry. Knock it on the head with a wooden billy and jerk out the hook. In cold northern waters, big pike and muskies, the producers of more big fish, grow very slowly. Unless you're fishing for the pan or think you've caught a potential record, try to release them carefully. All of those sharp teeth do make it difficult at times, so if there is any question that you won't be able to do it without an excessive amount of probing and jerking, simply cut the leader and say goodbye. Flies aren't that expensive.

12

Atlantic Salmon

Without any preliminary rambling, I must declare that the Atlantic salmon is my favorite fish. While I'm happy to cast a fly at any species that's inclined to grab it, my favorite is *Salmo salar*. Atlantic salmon are found in beautiful rivers and are fished for with the most beautiful flies ever created. If that isn't enough, the salmon's life cycle remains a partial mystery and its willingness to take flies a fascinating conundrum. These and other enigmas have intrigued anglers on both sides of the Atlantic Ocean for centuries.

In North America most of our Atlantic salmon are found in the provinces of eastern Canada—Quebec, New Brunswick, Nova Scotia, Newfoundland/Labrador. In the United States, Maine is the only state that offers authentic angling for the species, with that being limited to about a dozen rivers on the extreme northeastern coast. Atlantic salmon have been transplanted to other locations in the United States with some success, but unless the fish has access to the sea it seems to lose some of its gameness. Progress has been made towards restoring salmon runs to the Connecticut River

(which was once, arguably, North America's most productive Atlantic salmon river). Let's hope the good work there succeeds!

Atlantic salmon are available in fishable numbers in England, Scotland, Ireland, Norway, Iceland, and in several Russian rivers that empty into the White Sea. Limited numbers of salmon are caught each year in Spain, Sweden, and Finland. The rivers of Russia's Kola Peninsula deserve special mention. These waters have only recently become available to western anglers (to any anglers for that matter), and early indications are that the fishing there is superb.

Before we get into the matter of angling for this wonderful fish, it's important to point out that the Atlantic salmon, is the only salmon indigenous to rivers that flow into the Atlantic Ocean. Unlike the Pacific salmon, of which there are several subspecies, there is only one Atlantic salmon and it is totally unlike its Pacific cousins. Pacific salmon are genetically programmed to die upon completing the spawning act; Atlantic salmon are not. The rigors of spawning and the associated piscatorial pitfalls of entering a freshwater river after months of

Fishing for Atlantic salmon is a sport loaded with tradition. Native to rivers that flow into the cold waters of the Atlantic Ocean, it is the king of anadromous fishes for all fly fishermen who seek it.

growing in the ocean does take a toll—but many Atlantic salmon do survive to have another go at it. Atlantic and Pacific salmon are *anadromous*, meaning they are born in freshwater, travel to saltwater for feeding and maturing, and then return to freshwater for reproduction chores. Large numbers of Pacific salmon are caught by sport fishermen in saltwater and freshwater. Atlantic salmon are caught by angling methods only in freshwater.

It is particularly appropriate to deal with Atlantic salmon in a book devoted to fly fishing, because in North America fly fishing is the only legal method. Lures and natural baits are used in several other countries (an old habit that

ought to be banned), but on most rivers fly fishing is the accepted method.

Unless an angler lives near a salmon river, a fishing guide who knows the water is usually required. While they look a lot like trout, salmon don't act like trout, nor are they found in the same locations. From here on, we will assume that while fishing for Atlantic salmon the reader will be accompanied by a guide.

TACKLE

Experienced anglers are divided into several camps in the matter of the ideal Atlantic salmon rod-and-line combination. The differences stem from the size of the fish that enter the river they usually fish and the size of the river itself. If most of the pools can be covered with a cast of 60 feet or so, and the fish caught are mostly *grilse*, (juvenile salmon of between 3 and 5 pounds), an 8½-foot rod rated for a 7-weight line will do the job. If 90-foot casts are the norm and 12-pound fish are commonly hooked, a 9-foot rod throwing an 8- or 9-weight line is a better choice. If the river is really wide and fish of 25 pounds or more are taken, many anglers choose an extra-long, two-handed, 10-weight rod. Into this assortment of possible combinations, the sporting factor must be added.

A 4-pound grilse can be whipped in three minutes when overpowered by a 15-foot, two-handed shaft. Conversely, in a huge river where size 5/0 flies are cast to salmon that may weigh 35 pounds and more, a 7- or 8-weight rod will be hard pressed to handle the work.

As most fly fishermen come to understand, the ideal solution is to own several rods in order to have all situations well covered. Realistically, a 9-foot rod rated for a 9-weight line can be depended on to handle 99.9 percent of all Atlantic salmon fishing. The most useful line for such a rod should be a weight-forward floater (9WFF). Occasionally, a sink-tip will be needed in heavy currents or deep pools.

When Atlantic salmon fishing, you should always assume that you might hook a large fish, of 20 pounds or more. For this reason, the reel chosen should have enough capacity to hold at least 150 yards of 30-pound backing, and 200 yards would be better. Even 4-pound grilse are capable of making a run that will pull out all of the fly line (about 30 yards) and 50 yards or more of backing. Generally, this means a single-action or multiplying reel with a spool diameter of 3 inches or more. The rated pound-test of the backing material should be 30. Some anglers opt for 20-pound-test backing in order to have more yardage, but 20-pound backing is much more susceptible to being abraded on rocks during a long-distance battle. I came to be a 30-pound backing fan after several salmon broke off on 20-pound line. Use the 20-pound on trout reels.

Following capacity, the next most important feature a salmon reel should offer is a reliable drag. The fact that a drag can be adjusted so tightly that the reel will barely turn is not a good test. Such a tight drag is not needed for salmon because the fish must run in order to expend energy; it's got to tire before it can be captured. Even if you hooked a fish on a 50-

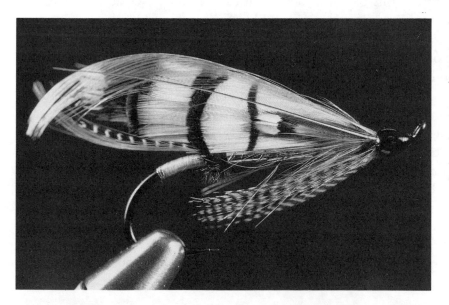

The Lady Amherst, a classic salmon pattern, is typical of the colorful flies that were developed in Victorian times. While still used by some anglers, most of these complicated flies are now being framed as wall decorations.

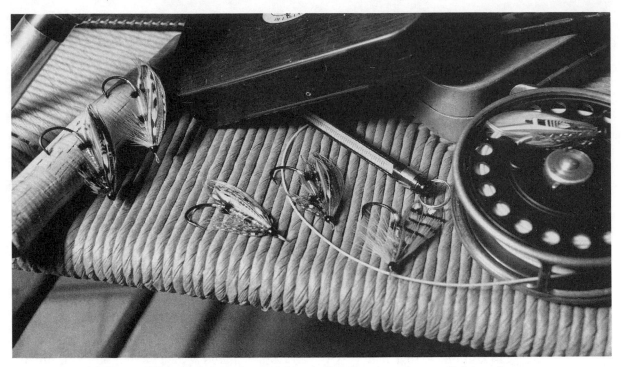

The tackle, tools, and trappings of Atlantic salmon fishing have remained much the same for a hundred years. It's not uncommon to see flies, fly boxes, cane rods, and battered reels on many salmon rivers. They've been passed on through the generations.

pound-test leader, and held on tight, it's initial run would probably tear the hook from its jaw. These fish simply cannot "horsed." What's desired is a drag mechanism that functions smoothly. When a fish goes through its bag of fighting tricks it stops and starts, jumps and thrashes in long runs and short spurts. There's a lot of jerk-jerk-jerking going on, and if the drag system doesn't operate smoothly you may lose the fish.

To adjust the drag on their reel, some experienced anglers pull a few feet of line from the spool, see how it feels for the tippet they're using, and make a correction. Others recommend a drag setting of one half the breaking point of the leader. That system works with spinning or casting line but makes matters a bit scary when a fish is close and does some last second thrashing. If you don't trust your intuition,

attach a half-pound weight (8 ounces) to the end of the leader after passing it through the rod guides. Lift the weight off the floor or ground with the drag set very tight. Reduce the drag until the weight moves down slowly and smoothly. With most reels, this setting will work perfectly for Atlantic salmon on leader tippets between 6 and 12 pounds. Set the drag a tad less for lighter tippets but don't tighten it too much more for heavier material. Remember, the fish has to run or you'll lose it.

LEADERS

Leaders for Atlantic salmon handle best when they are about the length of the rod or slightly longer. I like a 2X leader about 12 or 13 feet long because I change flies a lot, so I want to begin with an extra-long tippet. The formula for easy-casting salmon leaders is not complicated. Next to the line begin with about 30 inches of 30-pound monofilament. Attach this with a nail or needle knot. Next, tie in 25 inches of 25-pound mono, 20 inches of 20, 15 inches of 15, 12 inches of 12, and 30 inches of 10-pound. This will result in about 11 feet of leader. That's fine for starters. If you want to use an 8-pound tippet, reduce the 12- and 10-pound sections to 6 inches and add 30 inches of 8. If you want to drop to 6-pound, shorten the 20-, 15-, 12-, 10- and 8-pound sections in equal amounts, and add a 30-inch piece of 6-pound. For connecting sections, use the blood or surgeon's knot. A tippet lighter than 6-pound for Atlantic salmon is your call. Don't worry if the leader sections are a few inches longer or shorter than what the formula calls for. It won't make any difference to the fish or affect casting.

THE SALMON'S LIFE

Adult salmon enter freshwater rivers from the sea for one purpose only—to reproduce. Prior to the spawning act, they do not eat. This means that some salmon which come into a river during the months of May and June will be fasting until November. They survive until then by living off stored body fat. To appreciate the phenomenon of catching Atlantic salmon on flies, one must have a basic understanding of the fish's life cycle.

While the precise timing of the various stages of development vary from river to river, the sequence remains the same: Stirrings in the eggs, which were dropped in the fall, begin to occur during early spring. An eye takes shape, now a tail, and then fins. The yolk sac will nourish the tiny embryo until the mouth and digestive tract have formed. At this point the tiny *alevin* will swim out of its protective gravel nest and begin to hunt for food. Microscopic insect larvae, some vegetable matter and, later, adult insects nourish it to minnow size within a few months. As it grows, it begins to feed on even larger insects snatched from the surface. These little fish, known as *parr*, will remain in the river for two or three years, occasionally four, until another spring day arrives and a magical happening occurs. The larger parr, between 8 and 14 inches, take on a silvery sheen which replaces the red spots and bars on their flanks. As quickly as this transformation occurs, the fish, now known as *smolts,* rapidly leave the river and enter the ocean.

In yet another example of nature's way of guaranteeing survival of a species, some of the fish stay in saltwater for less than two years while others remain there from two to occasionally six. The number of "sea years" a fish spends feeding and growing in saltwater can be determined by scale examination. Each additional year of ocean feeding adds weight and length. Sooner or later, all salmon heed the call of their natal rivers and return. The first-time returnees are the 3- to 5-pound grilse, which make up the bulk of the catch on many rivers. The salmon that fed for two full years may weigh in excess of 10 pounds and those that remained for longer periods correspondingly more. In addition to varying size, individual fish and groups of fish enter the rivers at different times; another safeguard in perpetuating the species in case of flooding or drought conditions.

When the adult fish are in the rivers, they pause to rest in certain pools. While in these resting places they frequently rise to the surface to examine drifting bits of flotsam, insects, or anything else that strikes their fancy. And here lies the major mystery of Atlantic salmon fishing. Since they are not actually feeding (their stomachs are usually empty), why in the world do they grab our flies? Many theories have been advanced over the centuries, but the most accepted answer is that the fish somehow recall their insect feeding days as parr and smolt and simply can't resist the impulse to try it again. Curiosity and anger, many anglers maintain, are

An average grilse, or one sea-year salmon. Somewhat over 20 inches, these fish have spent at least 12 months feeding in the ocean. By law, they are the only salmon that may be kept in several Canadian provinces.

also at work here. On a few salmon rivers, insects are taken and swallowed by pre-spawning fish. Another mystery, since they appear to ingest but do not digest.

As autumn's approach is signaled by falling water temperatures, the salmon change colors again and become coppery-brown on the flanks and the red spots they wore as parr reappear. The fish move still farther upstream until they reach a place in the river that suits them for mating and egg-laying. The females create a depression in the gravel, deposit their eggs, and the males quickly eject sperm, or milt, over them.

If the surface of the river hasn't yet turned to ice, the spent salmon will quickly head downstream in an attempt to get back to the ocean. Many don't survive due to spawning stress,

predators, low water, and other factors. In some rivers, the post-partum salmon are forced to remain under the ice until the spring thaw. When these fish descend the river they are mere shadows of their sleek summer forms. Slim and hungry, they lunge at and eat anything that looks like food. In this stage they are known as black salmon or in Europe, *kelts*.

Regardless of when a spawned-out salmon gets back to the ocean, it will quickly regain its metallic silver color and handsome form as a result of the rich food there. It is not out of the ordinary for some of them to make still another upstream trip.

Curiously, Atlantic salmon are rarely caught in saltwater or as smolts in freshwater. The little parr, however, strike at flies as large as they are and the fresh-run grilse may go for anything that drifts over them. Then again, they may not, which is why this game is called *sport* fishing!

SALMON FLIES

As with so many sporting activities that became popular in North America, fly fishing for salmon was born on the British Isles. England, Scotland, Wales, and Ireland had substantial salmon fishing traditions long before they began to take shape in Canada, the United States, and several other nations. Flies for salmon had become a highly stylized art form in Great Britain by the early 1800s; before the century was over it had been written about at great length. Pattern names such as Jock Scott, Silver Doctor, Durham Ranger, Black Dose, and hundreds more were well known and revered as fish-getters by the time serious sport fishing for

Atlantic salmon began in the New World. 12-5

For the most part, these traditional British flies were ornate creations that required a dozen or more different bird feathers to make correctly. Toucan, jungle cock, Indian crow, macaw, florican bustard, chatterer, and almost every exotic creature you can think of was a source of feathers. The old-time tiers had a field day competing to see who could design the most spectacular salmon fly. Since Great Britain ruled the sea lanes and had colonies around the world, they certainly had access to the raw material for such flies.

Today, because of environmental and legal constraints, fancy traditional flies are impossible to make according to the original formulas. Some exceedingly handsome duplicates can be fashioned out of substitute materials, but now these copies are tied more for show purposes than for fishing. The old styles still catch fish to be sure, but it's safe to say that well over 75 per-

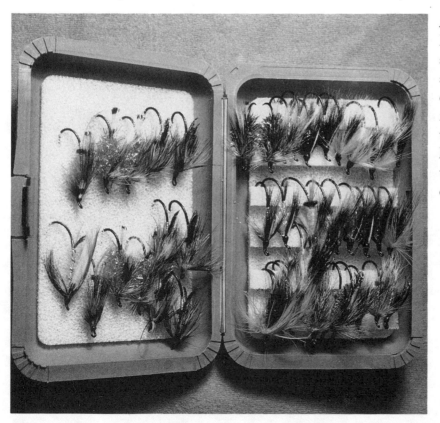

A box of salmon flies is a lovely sight. Plenty of color and variety. Since salmon are not much interested in eating when they enter rivers, the reason they strike these pretty creations is largely mystery. Selecting the one they'll take is part of the fun!

cent of the flies cast in the direction of salmon today are hairwings. The salmon don't seem to care. If the colors suit them, the size is right and it's presented correctly, one of today's flies will work just as well as one from the Victorian Age. Why one pattern works today and not tomorrow, however, baffles us all.

Color

A glance at any display or illustration of salmon flies will quickly reveal that they contain almost every color imaginable. Salmon can be caught on flies of any color, but fish of certain rivers are more likely to rise for a fly of a particular color, or a combination of colors—that's the mystery.

The basic colors an angler needs on his salmon wet flies are black, silver, and gold. Slight touches of the primary colors— red, yellow, and blue—add some dash and originality, but for the most part please the angler more than the fish. There are, however, some combinations of colors, along with the metallic tones of silver and gold, that perform amazingly well on specific waters. As when trout fishing, pay attention to the local favorites.

Personal experiences, and those of many salmon anglers, have proven the worth of blue and silver patterns on many rivers. Few Atlantic salmon anglers with a half-dozen seasons behind them would think of setting out without some black flies in their box. Green-bodied patterns, or yellowish-green ones, are also popular, as are flies that feature an ample splash of orange in their make-up. We can never be totally objective about colors and patterns because no one knows why these fish take flies in the first place. We just have to depend on what they've taken in the past and build on it.

If I had to limit myself to ten patterns for Atlantic salmon, here's what they'd be:

Silver Rat. Covers the silver-gray combinations; tie it or buy it with a red head.

Black Bear/Green Butt. The best all-around black pattern I've ever used. This fly has thousands of salmon on its conscience.

Blue Charm. In either traditional style with featherwings or hairwings, this old standard black-and-blue combination is a must-have pattern.

Cosseboome. A green-and-yellow combination that continues to catch fish everywhere.

Rusty Rat. The orange-bodied version is more popular than the yellow-bodied model on Canadian waters with good reason.

Blue Rat. Identical to the Rusty Rat except the rear half of the body is blue instead of orange. It can make a difference.

Ingles Butterfly. This wet fly is nothing more than a Hairwing Coachman tied with long,

The "rat" series of hairwing salmon flies are standards on most Atlantic salmon rivers today. Plentiful fox and gray squirrel hairs are used for the wings.

Typical Bomber salmon fly. This buglike pattern has accounted for thousands of Atlantics. Fished on the surface as a dry fly, it will catch fish on a dead drift or when skittered across the surface.

white wings that are designed to flutter in the water.

Thunder and Lightning. A triple-threat fly combination of black, blue, and orange (usually the first fly I try on a strange river). The last two flies are dries, to be fished on the surface when the water is 60 degrees or higher or when water levels are somewhat lower than normal.

Bomber. This elongated "bug," resembling a pregnant caterpillar, will sometimes bring fish to the surface when nothing else will. It's made in a multitude of color combinations but my favorite has a natural deer-hair brown body and an orange hackle.

Royal Wulff. All of the Wulff series of dry flies have caught a pile of salmon, but the Royal is more commonly available and as good as any variation.

Hooks

Salmon flies are tied on hooks of stouter steel than trout flies because salmon put up a more violent battle. Wet flies are tied on standard-weight hooks and occasionally on "low-water hooks," which are about a third lighter and usually employed when salmon are in shallow water. Bombers are tied on long-shanked 3X and 4X hooks. Regular dry flies are tied on low-water or salmon dry-fly hooks that traditionally are painted with black enamel.

For many years, the English and Norwegians supplied practically all of the salmon fly hooks sold in the world. The swelling interest in tying these pretty flies has brought several other hook makers into the business. Excellent quality hooks are now being produced in Japan and Taiwan. The most famous American hook maker, Wright & McGill (Eagle Claw), is now offering black enameled hooks.

On most Canadian rivers, a size 6 fly will be most useful with sizes 8 and 4 tied for second place. On some larger rivers, bigger flies from 2 to 4/0 (a 4/0 is a very large fly) may be needed. Advance information from the lodge or camp will fill you in on this. Conversely, some rivers call for flies as small as 10s and 12s. For these reasons it's always a good idea to have a few extra-large and extra-small flies in your box.

WET-FLY TECHNIQUE

Assuming that you're properly rigged with rod, leader, and flies, let's approach a typical salmon pool with a guide at your side. He'll point out where you should make your first cast because that's what he's paid to do. The spot indicated may not look like a place fish might be but keep in mind that these are not trout. They are not waiting for food to drift by. They are resting, waiting for the time they will move again to find a spawning place. The guide may suggest a particular size or pattern or ask to see your fly box. For the initial try, take his advice.

The best way to start is to cast several feet in front of the supposed hotspot in such a way that the fly drifts down and over the lie. The idea is to have the fly sweep across the salmon in a more or less natural drift, curling as a wet fly does when it reaches the end of the drift. If the current is strong enough to maintain a slight pull on the line, no other action may be needed to bring a rise. If the flow is not fast enough to prevent slack line from forming, strip the fly, just as you would a trout streamer, except not quite so fast. Salmon will take a fly that's simply hanging in the current at the end of its drift, but more often they'll come when it's drifting at an even pace or just as it begins that little buttonhook maneuver at the end of its trip.

After making about a dozen casts, move slightly downstream and repeat the same drill. Keep the line fairly tight between you and the fly by retrieving it a stroke now and then or by continually retrieving it if the current requires. Don't worry about seeing or feeling a strike. If a salmon takes a drifting fly there will be a splash and a strong pull will bend the rod tip. Then raise the rod, not with a sudden jerk but with a pull about equal to that delivered by the fish.

About 50 percent of the time, the first rise to the fly will not lead to a hooked fish. The salmon is merely looking things over. When it decides to grab that fly it will do so with amazing accuracy and hook itself, if the angler doesn't make the most common beginner's mistake of striking too soon.

Hooking a salmon on the typical downstream drift requires that the fish be given enough time to make a half circle in the water. While the fish will occasionally engulf the fly in a headlong rush, usually it adjusts its pectoral fins so it coasts to the surface. It approaches the fly from one side and takes it at the same instant the circle is half completed. It then heads for its former position near the bottom. This is a full-circle movement if carried to completion. At the time the current begins to apply pressure to the fish's broad side, the fly is soundly inside the mouth and that's when the pull will be felt. Pull back, and 95 percent of the time the fish will be solidly hooked in the cor-

ner of the jaw, at what's known as the "hinge."

If the angler strikes at the first indication of a surface disturbance, the chance of a hook-up is slim. You may see the back, dorsal fins, or tail of the fish, but it hasn't yet made its full-circle arc and doesn't have the fly in its mouth. The rule is, *don't apply any pressure or move the rod until you feel some weight.*

The game of cat-and-mouse with Atlantic salmon begins when a fish boils or "shows" at a fly several times but doesn't make solid contact. At times, it almost seems like the fish is amusing itself by playing with the fly. To some anglers this can be downright annoying, but most find this the highlight of the sport. A fish that continues to show interest in a fly is a fish that can be hooked if the angler keeps his cool and tries the traditional (and sometimes untraditional) tricks.

The first thing to try with a reluctant taker is simply to stop casting after three or four rises and rest the fish. Admire the clouds, study the surrounding landscape, or talk to the guide or your fishing companion. After a pause of five minutes or so, put the same fly over the fish. Quite often the rest technique works and on the next cast you'll get a solid strike.

If the fish continues to rise without taking, a change of fly pattern is called for. Stick with the same size, however, since that's the size it came to in the first place. If a different pattern fails, try a size larger or a size smaller. Next, try a different stripping speed or move a couple of steps up or downstream. Keep in mind that the slightest change in presentation may trigger a strike. Exactly what salmon are looking for is *their* secret, but *how* the fly is presented influences the decision to seize it. Thousands of salmon have been given up by as many anglers, only to have them take on the first cast presented by someone else. It is well recorded in the logs of salmon fishing camps that while many fish are caught on the first cast, just as many are hooked on the hundredth cast.

There are times when salmon are not keen on rising to the surface. Then a larger fly or perhaps a double-hook fly is the answer. The additional weight of the double-hook will slow the speed of drift in swift water and sink it much faster in slower water. Double-hook flies do complicate casting in that the forward and rearward strokes must be adjusted to compensate for gravity; the heavy hook wants to drop faster. Double-hooks are also not the deadly hooking and holding tool some anglers think they are. In fact, double-hooks of size 2 and larger have a tendency to come unstuck after a prolonged battle because the twin puncture holes may create a much larger wound and the hooks simply pull out. Smaller doubles of 6 and under seldom do this.

DRY-FLY TECHNIQUE

When salmon rivers drop to normal flow or below, and the surface temperature climbs to 58 degrees or higher, dry flies may be the right choice. They are certainly the most exciting choice if the salmon are so inclined. Here again is another Atlantic salmon mystery. The fish in one river may be eager takers of dry flies whereas the fish in another just don't respond. If fish are seen in the river and they're not interested in wet flies, don't be put off by local talk of "their" fish not taking dry flies. I've enjoyed many great days of dry-fly fishing on rivers where dry flies were said to be ineffective. You never know until you try.

Dry-fly fishing for Atlantic salmon can be done just as it is for large trout. A dead drift over a good lie or a fish that's been spotted is often all that's needed. If the fish shows no interest or makes a half-hearted start for a dry fly, it's time to work the fly. Deliberately drag the floating fly over the salmon's nose or allow it to drift motionless for a few feet before twitching it in short, jerky dashes. The strike may come in an explosion of water. If it does, forget the advice about waiting to feel the pull. You can't react fast enough to a splashy dry-fly strike; by the time you see the eruption, the fish already has the fly in its mouth.

On the other hand, a salmon may rise to a drifting dry fly with merely a tip-up of its head, like a big brown trout taking a mayfly. In this case, strike at the instant the fly *vanishes*. It's important to wait until this happens because some fish will merely nudge or push the fly tentatively before making a second move to grab it. Sure, such a planned response requires patience and nerves of steel, but after you've snatched a few flies away from a big salmon—a wee bit early—you'll learn to wait.

FIGHTING A SALMON

Like all gamefish, Atlantic salmon don't always react in exactly the same way when hooked, but they do jump more than most freshwater species. This is particularly true of grilse. Grilse (3- to 5-pound salmon) can be counted on to make an initial run that will pull out the entire fly line plus a great deal of backing. They may make a jump or two before streaking off or they may not break water until after the first run. Any attempt to check the first run when the fish is at its strongest will seldom succeed. A salmon's jaw is not very tough or resilient, and the hook can easily tear out. Have your drag set as suggested earlier and don't change it during the fight. Let the fish run its heart out and the reel spool spin without applying any additional force.

The second the fish stops, reel up the slack line and try to keep the rod at about a 40-degree angle. As the fish gives up line, keep cranking. If it makes another run, allow it to move. If the fish jumps, drop the rod tip to the water in order to prevent the full weight of the salmon from falling on the leader or tearing the hook loose in midair. When the fish is in the air, its full weight may be directly applied to the tippet. Dropping the rod is known as "bowing" to the salmon and is the right way to handle any leaping fish.

Because of the curving way a salmon takes a fly, it may be hooked in either side of the mouth. When a fish is beginning to tire, keep an eye on where the fly is imbedded. Try to position yourself in such a way that the leader doesn't pull across the salmon's back or through its mouth. This is tough to do at times, but if it can be managed, it will save a lot of fish at the last minute.

If the fish is to be kept (on many Canadian rivers only the grilse may be killed), netting or skidding it onto the beach is acceptable. Netting a fish that's to be released should only be done if the net mesh is less than an inch across and of soft material. A coarse net mesh, made from hard nylon, cuts fins and gills and causes a great deal of damage. In calm water, slide the hand down the leader, wait until the fish stops struggling and back out

the hook. If it's deeply imbedded, cut the leader.

Hand-tailing a salmon of 8 pounds or more is not terribly difficult. Maneuver the fish into fairly shallow water. Put your hand underwater and guide the fish to a point just under it. With the thumb on top and the forefinger beneath the tail, clutch the "wrist" of the salmon's body between tail and adipose fin firmly. Hang on. The fish will struggle violently for a few seconds and then become amazingly docile. Tailing an adult salmon is possible due to the stout tail rays. They are so stiff the hand will not slip to the rear. This is not possible with grilse, as their tail rays have not yet developed.

Keep the fish in the water for photos and admiration no more than a couple minutes. After unhooking, hold the fish in mild current, with its head pointed upstream, and wait for it to regain its equilibrium before loosening your grip. Salmon handled in this way will recover quickly.

Some guides, and not a few anglers, still har-

Hand-tailing is the best way to handle a fish that's to be released. Lift it gently, with the other hand beneath its belly for picture taking. Don't raise it clear of the water by its tail unless the fish is to be eaten. Such treatment may damage internal organs.

bor the belief that released salmon are sure to die. I can assure you that this is not the case. Numerous experiments involving tagged fish have proven that the survival rate is high. Of course, some fish don't make it, but enough do to make catch-and-release salmon fishing beneficial to the overall good of the species. At this time in history, only the grilse should be kept for consumption.

Atlantic salmon have been relentlessly pursued as a commercial species for centuries. Great strides have been made over the past decade that may insure their survival. The ban on killing large salmon in several Canadian provinces, government buy-outs of commercial netting permits, reduced harvests on the high seas by international agreement, and self-imposed limits by anglers have all helped. In addition, it now appears that pen-reared salmon grown for the world's fish markets have the potential of supplying the commercial demand.

13

Pacific Salmon and Steelhead

Fly fishing for Pacific salmon and steelhead is largely a river-based activity. Fish can be caught in saltwater and at river estuaries, but the simple act of finding the migrating fish in such vast expanses of water is difficult. When they enter the rivers, however, we know where to fish for them. Like Atlantic salmon, Pacific salmon and steelhead trout tend to frequent age-old lies and specific pools.

The Pacific salmon belong to the genus

The chinook, largest of the Pacific salmon, is a strong, long-lasting fighter. This bright fish is not long out of the ocean and has not yet taken on the reddish flank color it will soon acquire in freshwater.

Pink salmon seldom reach the 10-pound mark but are great fly-rod fish in western Canada. Bright streamers with plenty of red and silver are very effective.

Oncorhynchus. Common names for the five major species abound, but for ease of understanding the following names will be used here: chinook *(O. tshawystscha),* coho *(O. kisutch),* pink *(O. gorbuscha),* sockeye *(O. nerka),* chum *(O. keta).* All of these fish spawn in freshwater after spending varying amounts of time feeding and growing in the ocean. Different races of fish from different rivers travel to the Pacific Ocean to begin feeding within a few months of becoming tiny alevins. Others remain in freshwater for a year or more. As with Atlantic salmon, in this parr stage, their trip to the ocean is timed to occur at intervals in a way that guarantees survival of the species. To the angler, this means that there are spring, summer, and fall runs of salmon into the freshwater rivers. The chinook salmon is the leading example of this staggered river-entry schedule. From February to November, *some* chinooks are in nearly every river that attracts them. Of course, one or another seasonal run is usually dominant. The same is true of steelhead, which may enter coastal rivers during any month, although far more steelhead ascend rivers between November and May than during other months. If you do not live close to a steelhead or Pacific salmon river, a trip to catch them must be coordinated with guides and fishing camps in order to be sure you're there at the correct time.

All of the Pacific salmon are programmed to die following their spawning chores. Their size at

A huge male steelhead that fell for a drifting wet fly. Now classified as a type of Pacific salmon instead of a true trout, this is one of the world's greatest gamefish. A great leaper and strong runner, the steelhead is a trophy at any size.

The break between dark back and silvery flanks is highly evident on sea-run fish. It's actually a camouflage system when the fish are in the ocean and are preyed upon by larger fish. Within a couple weeks this steelhead will become much darker and develop a bright red stripe.

this time is determined by how many years they spent feeding in the ocean, which is preordained by the species or race of salmon they belong to. Even though the steelhead, which is an ocean-going strain of rainbow trout, was recently renamed *Oncorhyncus mykiss,* it is quite capable of surviving the rigors of spawning. Formerly known as *Salmo gairdneri,* the anadromous steelhead is more like the Atlantic salmon in its habits and fly taking characteristics. Steelhead are included in this chapter because in most of the rivers where they are found they share their space with one or more Pacific salmons.

Chinook and coho salmon were introduced into the Great Lakes many years ago and are now well established there. Along with the lake steelheads, salmon in these large, inland "oceans" enter rivers in the spring and fall just like their Pacific cousins do. Fishing for them in the Great Lakes is not appreciably different.

TACKLE

Depending on one's casting and fish-handling skills, rods rated for several line weights have to be considered. In addition, the size of the river fished and the expected size of the fish hooked also have a bearing on rod choice. A 9-foot rod, regardless of the line weight chosen, is the most practical length. A longer rod is not out of place, but one any shorter than 8½ feet is a handicap on most S & S rivers where casts of 60 feet or more are often required. My personal choice for nearly all S & S fly fishing is a 9- or 9 ½-foot rod rated for a 9-weight line. If a fish of less than 10 pounds is the norm in the water at hand, then a rod of the same length geared for an 8-weight line would suffice. If Chinook salmon of 25 pounds or more are anticipated, or trophy size steelheads of the same weight may be in the river, a 10-weight two-handed rod, or one with a butt-extension, should be considered.

Fly rods for S & S fishing should be powerful from one end to the other. Soft, wimpy performers can't handle this job because you'll not only be hooking hard-fighting fish but often find it necessary to cast sinking or sink-tip lines and perhaps lead-core shooting heads in order to get the fly down to fish-eye level. Rods with butt-extensions are advisable and a rugged, locking-type reel seat is mandatory.

With the exceptions of summer-run steelhead, which may be encountered in lower and calmer pools, and the occasional situation where salmon are in shallow water, weight-forward sink-tip and full-sinking lines are the best choices. Anyone contemplating a trip for S & S should consider extra reel spools holding sinkers and floaters. A third option is the shooting head, which basically consists of a 30-foot section of heavy, level line and a long shooting section of monofilament, or running line, of smaller diameter. The major makers of fly lines offer these specialized lines and they are a great help for long-distance casting. Another choice is to use a section of lead-core

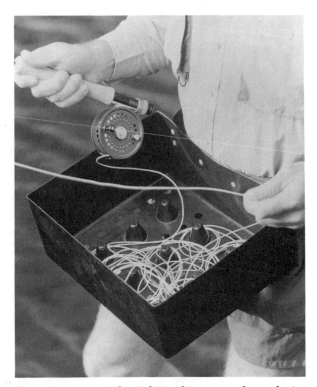

Longer casts with sinking lines are the rule in western steelhead and salmon fishing. A shooting basket for holding stripped-in line will make the next cast much easier. This device is particularly valuable when wading in deep water.

line at the front end. Choosing the proper amount of lead-core line for the river you happen to be fishing is a trial and error operation, but an 8-foot piece is a good length to begin with. Check the chapter on knots to see how the lead core is connected.

Reels for S & S must be rugged, reliable, and capable of holding an adequate amount of 30-pound backing. It's not wise to consider any reel that cannot accommodate at least 150 yards of backing. These fish may easily run that far and a bit more capacity is not a bad idea—just in case. An adjustable drag is mandatory and so is a handle that can be grasped easily without searching, and cranked with cold and wet fingers or when wearing gloves. Some the best fishing takes place in cold, wet places.

FLIES

The reasons leading to the design of flies for steelhead and Pacific salmon are almost as difficult to fathom as those used for Atlantic salmon—with one exception. The availability of salmon eggs in the rivers these fish inhabit is a strong factor. These eggs are mostly red, orange, and yellow. The S & S know what they look like and all of them will seize drifting fish eggs at one time or another. The curious part of this is that while the salmon do little or no actual feeding while in freshwater, they will grab eggs and hold them for a second or so before expelling them. A few observers insist that this is a protective act, and that the salmon's intention is to put the errant egg back in the nest. Maybe, but I can't believe a fish is that smart or so domestically inclined. Steelhead on the other hand do feed sporadically while in freshwater, and nourishment is the more logical reason. But even the steelhead isn't always in an egg-eating mood. In addition to red, orange, and yellow shades, some flies of other colors must also be in the fly box.

As a rule, flies for Pacific salmon are tied with materials that absorb water and sink fast. Most of the time, all of these fish will be on or close to the bottom so that's where the flies should be. However, steelhead will occasionally rise to or near the surface much like an Atlantic salmon does to snatch a drifting wet fly and sometimes a floating fly. Hook sizes 1 and 2 are the most popular, but a few as small as 6 are needed for low water conditions, and big chinooks and cohos are not reluctant to take flies as large as 2/0 and 3/0.

These fish pull hard and battle for a long time. A heavy hook that won't bend or break under terrific strain is needed. A Limerick hook with a round rather than flat cross section is the best choice. A flat, or forged, hook is much more likely to tear through a fish's jaw than a round one.

Heavy hooks sink faster, which is an advan-

Two-egg Sperm Fly is an all-fish favorite in western Canada, Alaska, and everywhere else there are steelhead and salmon in the same rivers. It suggests a pair of drifting salmon eggs. Fish it close to the bottom in a dead

tage most of the time on S & S rivers. At times, additional weight is added to the fly in order to get it down deep enough. Strips of lead foil, copper wire, or other soft metal can help. Tackle shops on the West Coast and a number of mail-order houses offer such flies. Traditional black hooks are used on many S & S flies, but just as popular are the nickel-plated models. Pacific salmon and steelhead do respond to metallic silver tones so the choice makes sense.

For steelhead, the Polar Shrimp, Silver Comet, Babine Special, and Skykomish Sunrise are four good flies to start with in the yellow/orange group. A black fly or two, with a dash of silver, is also needed. The famous Skunk pattern is a dandy in red and green-butted versions. The Jim Teeney nymph series have become accepted standards, as have the Purple Peril and Purple Flash. If the water drops and fish are seen rolling on or near the surface, the Royal Wulff and the Bomber designs will handle most dry-fly situations.

Flies tied as reasonably precise imitations of salmon eggs are absolutely deadly much of the time for steelhead and not infrequently for salmon. The Two-Egg-Sperm Fly is a dandy and so are the Glo-Bugs and Krystal Eggs. Most of these patterns are little more than round bumps of chenille or other soft material. A recent addition to the materials list is a fuzzy, metallic product named Estaz. Tied as an egg fly or used on fly bodies, this highly reflective material is quickly becoming known as an S & S killer.

Chinooks, cohos, sockeyes, and pink salmon may strike any of the steelhead flies but more often they want something even redder or flashier, and the big chinooks usually go for flies that are much larger. All salmon, however, are fond of flies that wiggle and pulsate in the water. This tendency makes the flies tied with flowing marabou or long hackle feathers good fish getters. The Zonker and Woolly Bugger types in red, orange, hot pink and chartreuse are very effective. Some flashy patterns featuring silver and gold metallic tones often work well on bright days, with the Karluk Flash Fly a good beginning choice. On dark, rainy days (and there are a lot on S & S rivers), black, purple, and dark-blue flies may bring more strikes than the brighter colors.

Many Atlantic salmon flies will do well on Pacific salmon and steelhead, especially patterns in red and orange. The Orange Parson, General Practitioner, Durham Ranger, and Rusty Rat patterns have proven themselves. In addition to these flies suggesting the color of salmon eggs, they also look somewhat like Pacific Ocean prawns which are eaten by all of the S & S.

Where salmon are sought in salt or brackish water, longer flies of the streamer sort are usually more productive, probably because the fish are still feeding on baitfish and have not yet become accustomed to seeing many salmon eggs. Whatever the reason, flies with more silver, white, and blue in their makeup seem to perform better. However, even in the salt, some red mixed into the wing is still a good idea, to appeal to the fish's predator instinct.

WHERE TO FISH

As with Atlantic salmon, first-timers will need the services of a guide who knows the pools, riffles, and runs in the river. Pay attention to where the guide tells you to cast, at least for the first day, until you learn to read the water. While the rivers S & S enter are often wild, rushing, and sometimes awesome flows, the fish seldom choose to rest in extra-fast water. They like *some* current but as a rule, if the water is too fast to wade in safely, the fish won't stay there for long. A slick glide just ahead of or below a stretch of rapids or a very deep pool is ideal for steelhead, sockeyes, and pinks. Chinooks will be found more often in somewhat deeper water with cohos apt to found almost anywhere.

A considerable amount of S & S angling is done from boats near river mouths and in wide rivers that are difficult to wade. At times trolling a fly will be the only way to cover the water. Some anglers don't consider trolling to be real fly fishing, but when a vast area must be searched, trolling is the only way to do it. In the ocean, in estuaries or in the Great Lakes, trolling is the most practical way to fish with flies. Fish are actively feeding and moving about in schools and hunting packs searching for pods of baitfish. On rare occasions, they might remain in one place for a short time, but mostly they're on the move.

TECHNIQUE

As with fishing streamers for trout or wet flies for Atlantic salmon, the standard across-and-slightly-downstream drift is the best way to present a fly to steelhead or Pacific salmon. If the current moves the fly at an effective speed, little else need be done other than a bit of stripping to keep the line and leader reasonably tight

Coho or silver salmon on the fly rod is a frequent jumper and will hit the same flies that catch steelhead. As with all Pacific salmon, flies must generally be fished close to the bottom for best results.

between fly and rod tip. If the water speed is slower, stripping the fly at a steady pace is the next move. Then switch to a faster or more varied retrieve.

The important difference with S & S is to keep the fly as close to the bottom as possible. These fish do not rise up in the "curving" Atlantic salmon manner. Their usual way of taking a drifting fly is merely to move their heads deliberately to one side or another, engulf the fly, and hold their position. The pull of the current on the line will feel like you've snagged bottom. You'll feel bottom many times if you're working the fly correctly, and you'll get some false strikes—that's part of the game. Strike at any indication that the fly has stopped its drift. When the "bottom" pulls back, you've got a fish on!

A passive strike is not the only way salmon and steelhead may take a fly. If they are excited or "hot," as fish fresh from the ocean frequently are, the strike may be a rod-banging, arm-jolting

punch. It can come so fast that the fish is hooked solidly and is off and running before you have time to hiccup. This is when you appreciate a large-capacity reel holding plenty of backing and a rod with some stiffness in the butt. The surge of adrenaline is a good feeling too—that's why you're fishing in the first place!

Play a steelhead or salmon on the reel and don't try to force the fish while it's running hard. If you're standing in hip-deep water, move cautiously to the shoreline or at least to knee depth to continue the battle.

In many rivers spawning sockeye salmon are abundant. Sockeyes are willing strikers and provide good training for novice fly fishermen. These bright-red fish with eagle beaks and garish green heads are strong, long-lasting fighters. They won't run or jump as spectacularly as steelhead or cohos but will give any rod a good workout and teach you plenty about fighting fish. Just remember to treat those sharp teeth with respect. Remove the hook with a hemostat to avoid serious puncture wounds.

Pink salmon are plentiful too in many salmon rivers and may often be found in extremely narrow and shallow pools prior to their spawning time. The "pinkie" loves red and silver flies of size 4 or smaller and puts up a great battle for its size. The average pink is 2 or 3 pounds lighter than most sockeyes, with most of them running about 4 pounds. If you travel with a trout-weight fly rod, the pink salmon will provide hours of fun. As the name implies, pinks are metallic-pink on their sides and are easily distinguished from other salmon by their irregular-shaped tail spots and white blotches near the belly.

Fly fishing for salmon in rivers that empty into the Great Lakes differs little in technique.

In spite of the freshwater environment, they are still the same species and react much the same. Salmon and steelhead have, however, a different choice of baitfish available to them and this is reflected in their fly preferences. Alewives, smelt, and shiners of various kinds are plentiful in the big lakes and all of them take on a bluish-green sheen in these waters. Oceanic baitfish are similarly colored, but the blue is not so prominent. For this reason, flies that favor blue with a touch of flash (tinsel or Mylar) and a spot of red are good choices.

At the mouths of rivers entering the Pacific Ocean and any of the Great Lakes that receive spawning runs of steelhead or salmon, flies made with "bead-chain" eyes can be very effective. These flies sink rapidly and the bug-eyed

Sockeye salmon in spawning condition, with the hump and grotesque "beak" they develop in freshwater, along with their bright red color, are unique, impossible to mistake. Not a jumper or long runner, the sockeye prefers to slug it out by turning its broad side toward the angler and using the current as its ally.

effect is fishy looking. Try using available current to carry the fly out much farther than you can cast until a hundred feet or more line is extended. Then, begin a steady stripping retrieve until the fly is nearly at the rod tip. This technique works best from a boat, but if the current is strong enough it will work from the shoreline as well.

Pacific salmon seldom display any leader shyness so tippet size is not a serious factor. If fish larger than 20 pounds are expected, a three-section leader consisting of 3 feet each of 30-, 20- and 15-pound-test material will be all the sophistication necessary. If steelhead are the primary target, the same leader specifications suggested in the chapter on Atlantic salmon will serve better.

Steelhead can be fussy at times in clear water and especially so when dry flies are being used. They seem to be wary of flies cast directly over them in shallow or very clear water. If you see a fish before casting to it, make the first cast upstream and slightly to one side of its position. If interested, a steelhead will move several feet to intercept it—if the leader doesn't coast over its head.

II

SALTWATER FLY FISHING

To some anglers who began their fishing careers with conventional trolling or "bottom" tackle, the use of a fly rod on anything weighing 50 pounds or more seems ridiculous. The fact is, really big fish, those of 100 pounds and more, were extremely difficult to subdue on a fly rod in the not too distant past. Coaxing them to strike was not a great problem but getting them to boatside or leading them into shallow water for landing purposes was. Rods broke, leaders and lines were flimsy, reels were not tough enough, and everything wore out faster from saltwater corrosion.

Fiberglass rods, high-quality monofilament, reels with smooth, dependable drag systems, plastic-coated fly lines, and dozens of other innovations came on us with a surge following World War II. Materials and techniques invented for military application were quickly

refined and adapted for angling use. All forms of fly fishing benefitted from this technology but the sport of saltwater fly fishing gained the most. As more anglers tried the long rod in saltwater, the innovative ones not only kept improving the techniques but searched for still more efficient tackle. Graphite rods, reels with superior drags, specialized lines, and more effective flies and saltwater bugs soon became standard gear.

The past four decades have seen a tremendous increase in the number of saltwater fly fishermen. Practically every sportfish that swims in any ocean has now been taken on the fly, including species once thought to be impossible to seduce, let alone capture. Marlin, tarpon, tuna, swordfish, sailfish, wahoo, and just about every kind of shark in the world have fallen to the fly. But it isn't just the "monsters" of the salt that lure fly rodders. Bonefish, redfish, bluefish, permit, seatrout, snappers of all kinds are now taken regularly on flies.

While some species are more difficult than others, it's fair to say that it's possible to hook any saltwater fish on a fly if that fish ever feeds within ten feet of the surface. Notice the word "hook," not catch. There has to be a limit on how large a fish can be handled on a rod that's cast with one hand. As this is being written, a 188-pound tarpon appears to be the largest gamefish yet taken on a fly. I have no doubt that some fish of 200 pounds or more will soon be caught on a fly.

14

The Big Ones

Tarpon, sailfish, tuna, wahoo, sharks, and marlin are the giants of the fly-rodding game. Tackle needed for these heavy, hard-fighting fish is highly specialized. With the exception of tarpon and some sharks, an offshore boat is needed to get to them. This requires that the angler either be a skilled boat handler or fishes with someone who is. For the entry level angler, fishing for these giants will be done by hiring the services of a skipper and crew for a larger boat or the combination captain/guide for species that are closer to shore such as tarpon and, at times, tuna. For the novice to hire a boat and then set out on his own is not merely unwise, it's foolish and dangerous.

FLY RODS

Rods for saltwater fish that weight over 50 pounds are chosen more for lifting power than finesse in casting. If a rod is capable of raising the head of a 150-pound tarpon or yellowfin tuna, it will not lay a fly down as gently as a light trout rod can. Nor is it designed to. Such a rod is made for sinking a big hook in a hard jaw, whipping the fish as quickly as possible and lifting its head at gaffing or release time. It is not made for continuous casting. Actually, a cast at all of these big fish is made only when one is seen. If an angler spent a full hour casting "blind," he'd be too tired to fight a fish even if he did hook one. Modern graphite rods are extremely lightweight, but the energy used in casting these stiff shafts can wear out the strongest arm in short order.

The vast majority of saltwater fly fishermen choose a 9-foot graphite rod rated for an 11- or 12-weight line. Although some special lines heavier than 12 are manufactured, most line companies don't regularly catalog them. Some big-fish anglers opt for 10-weight lines and rods, but the 9-foot/12-weight combination is considered the number one choice. Longer rods are awkward to handle in a boat and offer no leverage advantage. Shorter rods are too difficult to cast with large-diameter lines.

Sturdy, corrosion-proof guides and locking reel seats are mandatory. Beyond these requirements, only one other feature is really important: does the rod offer enough backbone to perform the hook-setting and lifting chores necessary? To their credit, rods offered by the quality manufacturers are up to the task. If you're not sure, ask for help. In most tackle shops catering to saltwater fly anglers, the personnel know what they're talking about. The last thing they want to do is misinform a potential repeat customer.

The test suggested for rods suitable for pike and muskellunge applies here, except the tarpon rod should be able to lift *three pounds* from the floor instead of one pound. Before you scoff at what may seem to be an easy challenge for rod and angler, remember that a 9-foot rod increases the distance of the power source from the weight. And the rod isn't as stiff as a broom-

stick—it's flexible. *Warning: Performing this test could break the rod or cause personal injury. Lift slowly!*

REELS

Practically any saltwater species hooked on the fly will out-pull a freshwater fish of the same size. In fact, most fish in the salt will outfight freshwater species by a two to one margin. For this reason, the reel used for saltwater fly rodding in the ocean must be rugged, able to hold plenty of backing, and highly resistant to salt corrosion. Reels receive rough treatment on boats even when they're not being fished with. Because these fish fight long and hard, the drag system must be reliable, adjust easily and pay out line without jerks and glitches. It's possible to pay well over $1000 for a saltwater fly reel. Excellent reels can be purchased for about half that amount and some good used reels are available. If you get involved in shopping for used

An old "wedding cake" Fin-Nor fly reel. Now collector items, these reels remain one of the best ever designed for the largest of fish sought with fly tackle.

Among modern reels the Abel is representative of the quality needed for rugged saltwater use—dependable drag, corrosion-proof construction, and a large handle.

saltwater reels enlist the services of a professional guide or experienced angler for advice.

Most quality saltwater reels utilize a *disc drag* system. This braking mechanism brings two round surfaces together when the drag-adjusting knob is tightened. The materials used in the opposing discs may be metal, cork, synthetic, leather, or some sort of treated fabric. Just about everything you can imagine has been tried at one time or another with varying results. Rapid dissipation of heat is one of the goals and the other is smooth braking. Some materials work well for a short time but may simply burn out with extended use. What's the best combination of drag materials? Frankly, I don't know. Teflon, Nylon, Rulon, and a number of other patented synthetics perform about as well as anything could. Leather and cork will do the job for a time if lubricated correctly. The latter two, however, are organic materials and subject to rot and deterioration. One of the synthetics is probably the best choice. A trout-reel drag system is not acceptable for saltwater use.

Many high-grade reel spools revolve on ball bearings, which provide smooth rotation when the line is coming in or going out. A few spins of the reel in the tackle shop will instantly reveal their presence. A counterweight on the reel spool is helpful.

Some reels have an antireverse mechanism that prevents the reel handle from turning when the spool is rotating as the fish runs. Line can be cranked in, unless the fish pulls with more force than the drag setting will allow. Such a system saves a lot of bruised and possibly broken knuckles. Some experienced saltwater anglers prefer direct-drive reels; they want to be in total control of the battle and gain a turn of line with each turn of the reel handle.

One other important detail to check before buying a saltwater fly reel is the size of the reel "scoop"—the base that fastens to the rod. For some reason, all reel scoops will not fit *all* reel seats. Be sure the two are compatible before finding yourself several miles offshore with rod and reel that can't be attached to each other.

LINES

The major makers of fly lines offer saltwater tapers. These lines feature a much thicker section near the front end of the line that enables the caster to shoot line without having to carry so much of it in the air. This is important, because standard procedure when casting from a boat is to make one or, at most, two false casts before the fly hits the water. The fly is held in the hand, loose coils are at your feet, the fish is spotted and zip-zip, the angler is expected to cast in a hurry. The heavy-ended, saltwater-tapered line will help you present the fly as quickly as possible.

Most of the time, a floating line will be the correct choice. On rare occasions, a sink-tip line will be advantageous, making an extra spool or reel a good insurance policy. Except for tarpon fishing in turbid water, there will be little need for a full-sinking fly line in saltwater.

LEADERS

The basic leader for big saltwater fish is a three-part setup consisting of butt, tippet, and shock tippet. If the angler decides to fish by the rules set forth by the International Game Fish Association, the butt section can be of any length but the tippet must be at least 15 inches long. The shock tippet can be no longer than 12 inches. The shock tippet is measured between the eye of the hook to the single strand of *class* tippet. Class refers to the pound-test category you decide to fish under. At present the fly rod categories are 2, 4, 8, 12, 16, and 20 pounds. (Of course, if you choose to hook and fight a big fish on a single strand of 100-pound-test monofilament there's no law that says you can't.)

A typical leader consists of 5 or 6 feet of 40-pound butt section, a couple feet of class tippet,

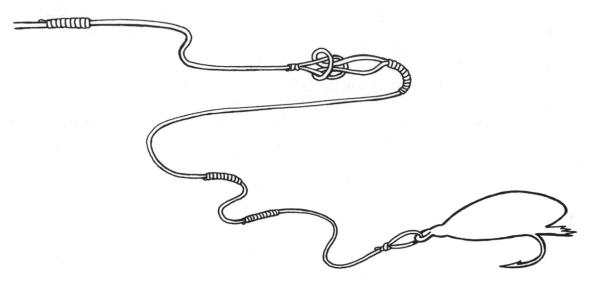

This is a typical saltwater fly leader. By varying the tippet section (which is in the middle of the leader instead of at the end, as with freshwater tapered leaders), any species can be considered.

and the compulsory 12 inches of shock tippet which is usually 80-, 90-, or 100-pound mono. If wahoo, sharks, or barracuda are expected, the shock leader is of braided or solid wire. These fish make short work of monofilament. The tippet section is best attached to the butt section by means of interlocking loops. The tippet to the shock tippet connection is usually an Albright knot. In order to accomplish these knots, it's first necessary to tie a Bimini twist in both ends of the shock tippet. I know this sounds like a knot-tying nightmare, but don't despair. The first mate on a boat specializing in saltwater fly fishing will tie these in a heartbeat.

FLIES

As more anglers head for the sea, there are a lot of innovative fly tiers among them and the flies this group have developed and continue to develop are fascinating. The inclusion of synthetic materials adds another dimension to the traditional feathers and tinsel. The modern "stuff" works to be sure, but one material continues to be the foundation of the most effective saltwater flies; long, rooster hackles from either the neck or the "saddle" of the bird. Few materials offer the same flowing, undulating action in the water or are so easy to obtain. Bucktail hair is almost as good and some of the synthetic "hair" is terrific—but plain old "chicken feathers" are still tops in my book.

In recent years, nomenclature for saltwater flies has begun to resemble that applied to many freshwater patterns. Surnames and first names have been attached to individual patterns and types of flies. All of them will catch fish and most of them have, but the more effective among them bear some resemblance to the bait fish that the offshore species like to eat. Mostly, this means they are long, contain some white, some bluish-green and a dash of flash in the form of Mylar, tinsel or some other synthetic metallic strands. The most consistently productive saltwater flies feature a white "belly," a dark "back," prominent "eyes," and a touch of red.

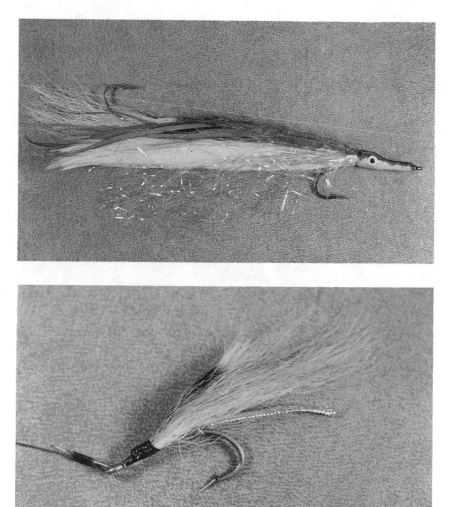

A tandem-hook sailfish fly. This one is blue and white with silver Mylar added for extra flash. The painted eye is a worthwhile addition for all offshore species.

A short saltwater fly that does a good job on tuna. When attracted to the boat by fresh chum, such abbreviated flies suggest chunks of cut-up fish. It's just like "matching the hatch" on a trout stream!

All saltwater gamefish are predators which feed on other fish. This fact is what makes the eyes and hint of red significant. Some of the florescent and "glowing" colors are proving their worth too and many anglers are convinced that these are better than the "normal" colors. Perhaps they are, but in the meantime, don't set out without basic white, silver, and red.

The mail order houses offer a good selection of "ocean" flies and so do the growing platoon of talented saltwater tiers. If you make your own, study the catalogs and work at duplicating the ones that suit you. Tie them on 4/0 and 5/0 hooks (nickel, cadmium-plated, or stainless) and tie them at least six inches long for offshore use. Flies for tarpon are generally shorter and somewhat smaller—which we'll get into shortly.

SALTWATER TECHNIQUES

By the time the shoreline vanishes, the novice saltwater fly fisherman begins to wonder how in the world *any fish* could be found in such a vast expanse of water. To stop the boat and begin to cast seems utterly silly—and it is. Freshwater techniques of any sort seem equally out of place.

There are two basic ways to fish offshore waters: search for the fish or try to get the fish to find you. With billfish (marlins and sailfish) and other cruisers that move about singly or in pairs, trolling a "teaser" is the most commonly employed technique.

A teaser is a lure that wears no hooks. It may be a baitfish or a belly strip from a larger fish. Teasers are also made from feathers, plastics, and even such strange items as glass bottles, sections of rag mops, or polished strips of metal. The idea is to entice the fish to chase the teaser, allow it *almost* to grab it once or twice and then snatch it out of the water. If the fish is in the right mood, the angler drops the fly in front of it and begins a fast retrieve.

In most cases, if the fish has shown interest in the teaser it will hang around the boat for a few seconds, wondering where the supposed easy meal went. Ideally, if the teaser was literally jerked from the fish's mouth, one extremely annoyed fish is ready to slam into the first thing it sees.

"Teasing a fish up" requires well-timed teamwork. The mate must pull in the teaser at the right moment, the skipper must slip the gears into neutral, and the angler must be poised to cast. The cast may not amount to much more than flipping fly, leader, and a few feet of line to one side or another. If the fish acts a bit "spooky," it may be necessary to cast fifty feet or more, or try to tease it up again.

Saltwater specialists are in general agreement that trolling a "spread" of different kinds of teasers works better than a single attractor. However, in order to pull this off, enough hands must be on board to handle the teasers when a fish shows up. Big fish may be gullible at times, but after taking a whack at a phony baitfish they soon get the idea that something's wrong. The people handling the fake teasers must not allow the fish to mouth one of them for more than a split second. A belly strip from a bonito, dolphin, or a whole ballyhoo is a different matter. It feels real because it is. If such a teaser is pulled from a sail's mouth, you'll have a really teed-off fish that will probably inhale your fly the second it touches the water.

Here is a string of artificial squids (rubber) about to be lowered into the water as teasers for sailfish. The fish will grab them and become so annoyed at not being able to eat them they'll nail the fly the moment it's spotted.

Every skipper and crew on boats that specialize in fly fishing for blue-water fish have their own methods of teasing. For your first encounter of this kind, let the crew manage the business at hand. They are geared to help you, the "sport" or client, hook a fish on a fly rod. They'll work hard to get the fish close to the boat and then it's your turn to go to work.

It's difficult to predict how much line should be stripped from the reel in preparation for making the first cast. The skill and luck of the people handling the teasers play a big part in

Teasing a sailfish before casting the fly is a team effort. The fish must be excited with a natural or artificial bait which does not contain a hook. The angler stands ready to cast as the mate works the teaser rod.

this, but as a rule, 35 or 40 feet of line should be adequate. Of the billfish I've caught and seen caught, I can't recall an instance when a cast of more than fifty feet was required. In nearly all cases the fish was easy to see and "hot."

When you see a hot billfish, you'll not forget the sight. The fish actually changes colors before your eyes, flashing green, blue, and yellow—in a kind of eerie, underwater light show. These iridescent colors are a trick of the chromatophores which lie just under the skin of many pelagic species and become much brighter when the fish is angry or excited, much like the hair on the back of human necks. When you see a billfish light up, your chances of hooking it are excellent.

CHUMMING

Big fish that usually move about the ocean hunting for food in pairs, or "wolf packs," can be coaxed to a drifting or anchored boat by chumming. Cut-up pieces of fish, crab, clam, squid, shrimp, or other oily, aromatic sea creatures are the usual chumming choices. Ideally, an oily sheen, or "chum slick," is created that floats on the surface. This slick, combined with floating particles of the chum material, moves with the current or wind. If there is little of either, the chum and slick may merely expand around the boat. The chum and slick itself may attract what you're looking for, but the big fish usually don't show up until some smaller ones begin to pick at the chum. When the small fish arrive in quantity, you can expect to see some larger ones quite soon.

As with teasing, boat skippers and mates have their own ways of doing things and their secret concoctions of chum mix. If you're new at the game, pay attention and watch what shows up at boatside. You may be amazed.

Chumming is standard procedure when the various tuna are sought. Yellowfin, or Allison's, tuna are highly vulnerable to chumming. So are blackfin tuna, albacore, bonito, mackerel and many fish not usually classed as heavyweights. But some of the more solitary big fish of the sea may arrive to inspect the chum picnic as well. Wahoo, sailfish, sharks, and not infrequently some bottom-feeding fish may come to the surface to see what all the excitement is about. Huge groupers, jacks, and snappers of various kinds have been caught in chum slicks.

Tip about flies when chumming: If the fish you seek are grabbing smaller fish in the chum, traditional saltwater streamer flies will probably work well. Some big fish, however, particularly tuna, will also eat very small pieces of the chum itself. In this case, a very sparsely dressed fly, consisting of little more than a short, white feather or two and a couple turns of silver Mylar, is all that's needed. If tuna are the target fish, it's wise to have some of these small flies ready for action. A 2/0 hook will be large enough. If the big fish are milling about in the chum, don't retrieve this small fly. Just allow it to float freely; you'll probably see the strike—and most certainly feel it!

THE STRIKE AND THE BATTLE

Casting to a big saltwater fish that's been coaxed close to the boat is fundamentally the same when teasing or chumming. The angler has to be a bit speedier about it when teasing (because the fish has lost sight of its "prey") than when chumming. It's "sight" fishing since the target fish is there to see. Try to drop the fly about four or five feet in front of its nose and begin to strip the instant the fly strikes the water. If it's going to take the fly, it will grab it before you can take another breath.

Any line you stripped through the guides should be lying on the deck in loose coils. Your rod hand should be poised for the sudden jolt, with index finger bent around the line against the grip. Bang! The rod tip bends down smartly and the left hand (if you're right-handed) grasps the slack line and pulls away from the rod as the rod hand moves in the opposite direction to drive the steel home. Do this twice or three times smartly—jab-jab-jab. Saltwater fish have tough flesh and very tough bones and cartilage. A limp-wristed strike won't set the hook.

Some fish don't react for a second or so when first hooked, but you can predict what most of the them will do when they suddenly discover that something unusual has happened. They will take off like a racehorse out of the starting gate. This is the time to form an extra guide with the thumb and index finger of the other hand and allow the slack line to coast through the fingers to the first guide on the rod. It will do so with blinding speed—if it doesn't get tangled around your feet or a boat cleat or form a mysterious knot. The mission is to get the fish on the reel in order to bring the wearing effect of the drag mechanism into play.

The sailfish, marlin, wahoo, and some sharks

Boating large fish on the blue water requires boat, crew, and stamina on the part of the angler. Specialized tackle makes the job easier, but it's still hard work with a measure of luck thrown in. This 7-foot sailfish was released.

may leap into the air before they run more than a few yards. Tuna will generally make a long run toward the bottom. If the fish jumps, treat it like a leaping salmon or trout and lower the rod tip to prevent the full weight of the fish from breaking the leader. When the fish is running fast don't fuss with the drag or apply any extra pressure. You can't stop the first run of these large fish, and the only thing to do is hang on, smile, and hope that you've got enough backing on the reel.

When the fish pauses, and it will, eventually, reel up until the line is taut and put some pressure on it by pulling slightly sideways on the rod. As the fish gives line, get it back by pulling upwards with the rod and reeling fast as the rod tip is lowered. Performing this lift-drop-reel sequence is called "pumping" and is the only way you'll ever boat a large fish without having to take a lunch break. If you give them a moment's rest, saltwater fish will regain strength and fight the angler all day long. You've got to keep the pressure on.

Florida angler Bob Stearns with a 117½-pound sailfish that was a world record on the fly for nearly ten years. Note the size of the fly hanging below Bob's hand. Fish was caught off the west coast of Costa Rica.

The hard-running, high-jumping wahoo is another saltwater trophy that comes readily to the fly—but few are landed. This fish requires a wire shock leader since its mouth is full of razor-sharp teeth.

If the fish takes off on a second run, which it probably will, wait out the spurt and go back to pumping. This run-and-stop routine may happen several times with individual fish, but each time it does the runs become shorter and weaker. As the fish shows signs of giving up, by rolling on its side or rising close to the surface, don't ease up on the pressure. Try to pull it closer to the boat with that sideways, pull-and-pump routine. Try to do this smoothly with no irregular motions. The leader, knots, and hook have been through a

lot of violent action at this point and all three may be near the point of collapse.

As a big fish is brought within gaffing or release distance, another moment of high drama may take place. It's best to decide long before the fish is at boatside if it's to be body-gaffed (killed) or released. With sailfish and marlin of 75 pounds or under, an experienced mate may choose to grab the fish by the bill to remove the hook or cut the leader. *Caution:* "Billing" a sail or marlin is not to be attempted by a novice. It

A white marlin off the coast of North Carolina that hit a 10-inch streamer fly. Two jumps later it was gone. Hooking big fish on flies is one thing and getting them to the boat is something else.

must be done with a heavy fabric glove to prevent skin loss or worse. The rapier-like bill is covered with rough bumps that feel like coarse sandpaper. If you do the grabbing you must be ready to hang on—no matter what happens. It's not a job for the faint of heart or weak of arms and hands.

If the fish is going to be kept, the best place to strike with the gaff point is six inches behind the gill covers at about the midpoint of the body. This entry spot will hit the heart. As with billing a fish, when a gaff is struck, the gaffer must be ready to hang on. There will be a serious amount of thrashing and lunging taking place and boat captains really hate to see gaffs (and customers) vanish into the depths. Until you're certain you can handle it, leave the gaffing to those who have done it before.

OFFSHORE TIPS

If you are prone to seasickness be sure to take your medicine *before* you step on board. I will not mention any specific medications because of possible legal complications. Your doctor will suggest one if you ask, and many good ones are available over the counter. Pay no attention to

The author with what he considers to be the strongest fish he's ever taken on a fly rod—the yellow-fin, or Allison's, tuna. Hooked on 10-pound tippet, this 42-pounder pulled hard for over an hour before being gaffed.

Veteran angler Boyd Pfeiffer has just sunk the gaff into an 8-foot shark and has both hands full. Going after sharks alone is not suggested, but Boyd wasn't alone. After this picture was snapped the photographer took over the gaffing chores.

the various "home remedies" for avoiding seasickness.

Another matter to attend to before the boat departs is to be sure you, the skipper, and his deck hands understand how the fishing is to be done. Saltwater fly fishing, while becoming more popular each year, is still not a common pastime out of some ports. Renting an offshore boat by the day is not an inexpensive undertaking. Depending on how far you travel, the size of the boat and number of crew members, the rate can run from $50 to over $200 an hour. At those figures the renter who wants to fly fish can call the shots. But be sure to do it *before* you're underway.

The other side of the coin is that the skipper is the captain of his boat and does not require any help in running it. If you're a beginner, ask the skipper and mate for advice and follow their suggestions.

15

Fly Fishing the Flats

In tropical and subtropical latitudes, the warm waters of the shallow bays and sandy shoals around islands, peninsulas, and reefs are usually referred to as the "flats." These areas can be but a dozen acres of sandy bottom or can stretch for hundreds of miles, as is the case around Florida, many Caribbean Islands, and along the coast of Mexico, Central, and South America. Africa and the South Pacific islands also have huge flats. As a means of reference, if the water is seldom more than ten feet deep at high tide and drops to three feet or less at low tide, the area could be described as a flat.

The species that roam the flats are mostly shallow-water feeders that are always on the lookout for crabs, shrimp, baitfish, water worms, sand eels, and the many other small saltwater creatures that thrive in near-shore environments. The most sought after of the flats fish are bonefish, tarpon, and permit. But the list doesn't end with this trio of gamefish. Barracuda, redfish, snappers of many kinds, boxfish, small drum, and a wide range of sharks are frequent visitors. Saltwater angling of all kinds is full of surprises simply because so many kinds of fish live in the ocean. Flats fishing differs from deep-water angling in a special way; the fish is *usually seen* before a cast is made. In this respect, flats angling is not unlike casting to a rising trout.

There are three basic methods of fishing the flats: *chumming* to bring fish to a stationary boat; *waiting* near a slightly deeper channel for tarpon and other cruising species to appear; and *stalking* a feeding fish by wading or slowly poling a skiff.

CHUMMING FOR BONEFISH

Chumming is a highly effective method of bringing bonefish to within casting distance when your boat is anchored or tied to a push-pole jammed into a sandy bottom. Experienced flats guides all have favorite places and methods for doing this. The beginner can try the technique on his own if he wishes, but until one has seen it done and knows how to calculate the options, it's wise to hire boat and guide for the first few attempts. What's required here is to locate a flat that maintains enough water to suspend a swim-

The guide is pointing at incoming bonefish that have been attracted
by pieces of shrimp tossed into the water. This chumming technique
is highly effective in the Florida Keys.

ming fish but is also situated at a high enough
elevation to allow some current as the tide drops.
A perfect setup is a hundred-acre flat adjacent to
a pocket of deeper water. By anchoring a hundred yards or so from the deep pocket or channel
and tossing some cut-up shrimp, crab, or baitfish
chunks into the tidal flow, the hope is that some
hungry bonefish will smell the food and
approach within casting range.   15-1

The usual practice is for the guide to toss a
handful of chum to a spot within easy casting
distance, say forty feet off the bow of the skiff.
The angler makes a cast or two to the chum in
order to estimate range. The surplus line is
stripped in and allowed to fall in loose coils on
the bow deck. The wait begins. If the guide
spots fish headed for the chum, he'll announce

that there's a fish at "11 o'clock" or wherever
and, if it's within range, tell the angler to cast ...
now! (The bow direction is considered 12
o'clock.)

If all planets are in the correct orbit, the wind
doesn't act up, or the angler doesn't blow the
cast, the chances for a hook-up are excellent.
The fish know that something good to eat is at
hand. If the first thing that moves happens to
be your bonefish fly it may grab it in a heart-
beat. All the angler needs to do is raise the rod
in a smooth, deliberate pull—not with an arm-
wrenching jab. The second the bonefish feels
the hook point it will go into overdrive, headed
for the horizon. The hook will be well set by the
time the bonefish hits the 100-yard mark.

Before we discuss fighting the bonefish (and

A bonefish is hooked and running and the angler shows proper form by holding the rod high to avoid snagging weeds. Bonefish are predictable in that they will make an initial run of 100 yards or more when hooked.

other flats species), it's necessary to point out that bonefish do not always grab a fly with total abandon. They will sometimes, but chumming can be as frustrating as any other kind of angling. A bonefish may come charging to the chum and decide not to eat your fly or even pick at the chum. It may eat a bit of chum *and* your fly. It may choose to come no closer than 200 feet from the boat. Then again, every fish

that approaches the chum may grab the fly with a savage lunge. Be prepared for anything and listen to the guide's advice. Until you acquire the knack for spotting fish in the glare of clear water over a reflective bottom, you'll quickly discover why guides earn their pay. The dark shape that you first think is a cloud shadow could be a fish and vice versa. Identifying the various species and look-alikes is frustrating at first but an enjoyable part of the game as you log more days on the flats.

Waiting on some flats, there are natural channels and feeding areas where chumming may not be necessary. When moving from place to place, flats species follow familiar avenues during incoming and outgoing tides. Guides earn their pay by finding these places as will anglers who come to know their home waters well. Seeing fish and hooking them may involve nothing more than tossing out the anchor or tying the skiff to a push-pole that's been rammed into a sandy bottom.

The boat should be positioned in such a way that the sun's rays do not bounce off the water directly into your eyes. If this is done correctly (and you'll know when it isn't), fish can be seen at an amazing distance. Many of them will pass the boat well out of casting range—the luck of the game—but happily some won't. Casting to these cruising fish is much like shooting clay pigeons: you've got to lead the fish by casting well in front of your target. Cast too close and the "plop" of the fly entering the water may spook a bonefish or tarpon and will surely send a permit flying. Try for an eight- to ten-foot lead, allow the fly to sink to or near the bottom, and begin a stripping retrieve. If a fish moves towards the fly at the first strip or two, chances are three to one that you're going to have a hook-up. Flats fish never turn down an easy meal if they're not frightened.

The temptation to move the boat is great; you see a lot of fish "just over there, a hundred feet away." Resist moving until you're absolutely convinced you're tied up at the wrong

Unless it's a potential record-class fish, bonefish are usually released. Here Captain Frank Garisto is about to give an 8-pound bone its freedom. He'll hold the fish by the tail until it swims free after being "pumped" back and forth to force some water through its gills.

spot. A slight change in tide movement, resulting in more or less water at your position, can change matters in a hurry. One final reminder about "waiting": try to avoid unnecessary noise. Talking won't affect matters at all but too much stomping on the deck and rattling around in the drink cooler can be heard for hundreds of feet through the water.

The bonefish has but one thing on its tiny brain when hooked: get away from wherever it happens to be—in a big hurry. It won't jump, it can't dive for the bottom, it can only run and run fast. There's nothing to do at first except hold the rod at a 45-degree angle and allow the reel spool to turn. You'll suddenly understand why 200 yards of backing are needed on a bonefish reel. When it stops running begin the pump-and-reel routine. The fish will make another run or more, each run being shorter than the last.

Bonefish wear themselves out quickly as a result of their speedy runs. When they are at boatside, and turn on their sides, they're easy to slip into a net. When your companion or guide lifts the net, drop the rod tip and strip a few feet of line from the reel. This allows some slack for fly removal. No one keeps a bonefish unless it's a record-class catch or the sport wants to have his first one mounted. Though delicious, hardly anyone eats bonefish, because, as the name implies, they are jammed full of wiry bones.

If you handle the unhooking chores, hold the fish by the tail for a minute or so, and pump it fore and aft at a slow, methodical cadence. This is the time for photos. The exertion of the battle takes a lot out of the fish and it needs to regain its equilibrium before being released.

STALKING THE FLATS

There are times when taking a boat onto an extremely shallow flat, where the water is two feet or less in depth, is not advisable. Breaking your propeller or grounding your boat is not pleasant if you happen to be some distance from port. Stalking fish in such situations is the right way to do it. Many anglers prefer stalking over chumming. No boat is necessary, if the flats are close to shore.

Stalking bonefish and other flats species is not unlike fishing for trout that are feeding on dry flies. The difference is, instead of rising to take surface food, the bonefish is grubbing on the bottom and betrays its presence by stirring up mud and occasionally thrusting its tail above the surface. That tip of tail will sparkle like a flash of bright silver in the sun. When you spot the mud "blossom" or see the "V" of a tail, walk slowly and directly towards the signs until you are within comfortable casting distance. Move slowly and steadily without creating a visible wake. Pounding through the water like a little kid galloping into rain puddles is not good form.

When you are within range, determine which way the fish is headed and drop the fly about six feet in front of its nose. Wait a second or so, and begin to strip the fly in two-inch increments. This is important. A too-fast retrieve may spook the fish. There are differences of opinion on this, but most of the time short hopping strokes will bring more strikes than long, sweeping pulls. The idea is to make the fly suggest a back-peddling crab or scooting shrimp. Bonefish love them both.

TACKLE FOR THE FLATS

The same 9-foot rod and 9-weight line recommended for Atlantic salmon is a perfect choice for bonefish and all other flats species except tarpon and sharks. For these much larger fish, a 12-weight rod and line is better suited. Some very large tarpon and sharks have been caught on lighter rods but it *does* take a while to subdue a hundred pounder!

The big-game fly reel used for offshore species is the choice for tarpon. A dependable, smooth drag and a spool holding 250 yards of

Stalking a bonefish on the flats is as much like hunting as it is fishing. This angler, almost too close to the shadowy form of the bonefish in the foreground, has knelt in the water in an effort to prevent the fish from seeing the movement of the rod.

John Randolph with a 7-pound bonefish about to be released. Wet wading is a cool and effective way to stalk bonefish in the shallow flats. Don't do it barefooted—wear sneakers. Jellyfish sting and sharp coral are equally dangerous and painful.

30-pound backing are required. For bonefish and most other species that generally weigh less than 50 pounds, a somewhat smaller reel will suffice, but again, be sure the reel will carry at least 200 yards of backing. *More* is always better when it comes to backing. Reels for bonefish and all other flats species must be as durable as those used for bigger fish. The fast, long runs and violent tugging these fish are capable of will quickly destroy a bargain basement reel. Some experienced anglers choose 15- or 20-pound-test backing for their flats reels as a way of adding extra yardage. If you want to try this trade-off, fine, but I'd stick with 30-pound Micron or something similar for all saltwater work at first. It's easier to handle, easier to tie knots in, and lasts longer.

The correct leader for tarpon and sharks is precisely like that used for offshore species. A monofilament shock tippet is suitable for tarpon since they don't wear vicious dentures. Sharks require a *wire* shock tippet, as do barracuda. It's best to have several leaders of both types tied in advance and ready to go in Ziplock bags with fly already attached. Tie a surgeon's loop on the end of the butt section of each of them. When you need a different leader or a new one, it's quick and easy to interlock the loops.

Bonefish leaders cast better if they are tapered much like a trout leader. But they don't have to be quite so sophisticated. Begin with a 20-inch piece of 40-pound material. Next, add four sections of pound-test 30, 20, 15, and 12, each measuring about 10 inches. Finish off the leader with a 30-inch tippet section of 10-pound test. This should add up to about the length of the rod. If you want to go lighter reduce all sections by a few inches and add a smaller diameter tippet. Keep in mind that if you are interested in logging an official record catch, the class tippet must be at least 15 inches long.

TARPON

The tarpon is the unquestionable giant of the flats for the fly rodder. The odd shark may show up in shallow water that will outweigh the largest of tarpon, but thus far few sharks have been boated by the fly rod that weighed over 100 pounds. (Master angler Stephen Sloan caught a 184-pound blue shark in the Atlantic Ocean, and Steve Abel subdued a 140-pounder in California waters.) Tarpon of over 150 pounds are regularly caught on the Gulf side of Florida and at other locations. Tarpon in the 75- to 100-pound range are commonplace.

Chumming tarpon does not seem to work well. Oh, they'll come to the sweet smell of cut-up fish, but when they get there, taking a fly does not seem high on their list of priorities. Whatever the reason, tarpon much prefer to grab a live baitfish in shallow water and, surprisingly, will take very small flies at times. While this may appear to be a disadvantage, it isn't. Setting a small hook, say a 2/0 or 3/0, is easier than driving a 6/0 point and barb into a tarpon's jaw, which has the resistance of a truck tire.

A preferred technique for tarpon is to anchor within casting distance of a channel or pocket of slightly deeper water where tidal currents

Few fish fight with the wild abandon of tarpon. When first hooked they almost always jump and then head for some distant port.

attract schools of baitfish. It's the guide's job to know where these tarpon hotspots are. If you own a boat and are already an experienced skipper, you can find them by spending some time cruising about. But finding a tarpon "alley" today or at a particular point of the tide, doesn't mean it will produce tarpon tomorrow or next week. For the first several tarpon-seeking adventures it's best to hire a guide. Whatever you choose to do, don't do it alone. To gaff a tarpon while handling the rod is possible, but not likely. Such a solo performance can lead to calamity or worse. A 100-pound fish cannot be scooped up in a landing net!

Captain Bob Marvin (left) with the author's biggest fly-rod tarpon to date. Caught off Florida's west coast near Homosassa, it was one of twenty fish in a tarpon "daisy chain."

Hooking a Tarpon

Let's assume that you're with a competent guide who has chosen to toss out the anchor at the edge of a passageway through a submerged coral bar. The outgoing tide is moving the water through the "cut" and the guide figures that tarpon will pass by as the water recedes. This isn't just a guess on the guide's part. He knows where and when fish move in his part of the flats and he's anchored in such a way that should provide a shot at some cruising fish. He also won't be guessing much about which direction they'll come from. He'll ask you to make a cast or two to get the range.

After watching you cast, the guide may reposition the boat. He'll know instantly if you're a 50-, 75-, or 100-foot caster by watching you do your stuff. (This is double-haul territory, and if you haven't read the chapter on casting, you should do so right now.) When the tarpon cruise past your location, you'll false cast (once or twice) to shoot some line on the backcast, followed by a forward cast that shoots enough line to drop the fly about ten feet in front of a moving fish. It's not unlike shooting clay pigeons. The cast must be timed to have the fly at the fish's swimming depth before the retrieve begins.

The angler may be required to stand on the bow deck for several hours or only a few seconds before seeing fish. Casting about randomly is a waste of time and energy, and with a 12-weight rod, tiring. Do the practice casting another time.

Alright, you're ready. Surplus line is resting in loose coils on the deck, the fly is in your hand, and enough line to get a cast started droops from the rod tip to barely touch the water in front of you. The guide is at your left shoulder peering at the water as anxiously as you are. He nudges your arm and points at four dark shapes that have entered the cut and are coming at an angle that will need a 60-foot cast. If these are the first tarpon you've ever seen in the water, you will probably think they look as big as tele-

Harry Kime with a big tarpon that he hooked at the Casa Mar Camp in Costa Rica. Shortly after this picture was taken Harry was captured by Nicaraguan revolutionaries and held captive for several days. He finally convinced them he wasn't a spy, just a crazy American angler.

phone poles. You will also have a sudden misgiving that a fly rod seems terribly inadequate for the task at hand. You may even be a bit frightened. Don't worry about this. Most first time tarpon anglers go through periods of self-doubt. This is angling excitement at its peak. If your heart doesn't go into overtime at this moment you are probably better suited for golf or chess.

The chances are at least 50-50 that some-

thing will go wrong when the guide says "cast now." Your double-haul technique will fall apart, a loop of line will have found its way around your ankle or a wayward gust of wind will send the fly somewhere you do not want it to go. All of these terrible things can happen at once including some you've not dreamed of. In short, the whole situation can come unglued.

But the goof-ups eventually play themselves out and this time the fly fishing gods smile and your fly drops perfectly in front of the fish leading the pack. The fly sinks to just in front of its nose and you begin to strip in one-foot pulls. Keep the rod tip low, almost touching the water, pointed directly at the fish. The tarpon changes direction slightly and wags its tail in a half-dozen quick strokes. It gulps. You gulp. The fly vanishes into a huge mouth. So far, so good.

The next move should be made with the hand that's been doing the stripping. Pull on the line until you feel resistance. This may require an extra strip—try not to move the rod hand until you feel a pull. At this moment, jab sideways with the rod and pull with near equal force with the hand holding the line. Now you'll feel some serious pressure. Jab three or four quick times. One stroke is seldom enough to sink the steel. At this point, the tarpon will realize that whatever it grabbed is not lunch and will go into a head-shaking frenzy and probably jump clear of the water, then start on a mad dash for somewhere else. Allow the surplus line to slide through your fingers, keeping enough tension on it to sort out the kinks and curls. What's hoped for here is that the line will clear the deck, your feet, and everything else, and eventually be coming directly from the reel. If all goes well it will and the tarpon is running madly, jumping and doing a great impression of a runaway freight train.

About all the angler can do in the early stages of a tarpon battle is to watch, keep his hands away from the reel handle and remember to lower the rod tip when the fish jumps. The jumps and the surface thrashing are exciting to watch and cause apprehension as well. The fish may come unstuck at any moment if it wasn't hooked soundly. The leader may break or be cut on a protruding shard of coral. Anything can happen. These are accepted risks because the reason a big fish like this can be subdued on a fly rod with a tippet of 16 pounds or less is because of its frenzied behavior. In the shallow water of the flats such huge fish can't dive into

the depths to slug it out. Their frantic antics to escape wear them out—with help from the relentless flex of the long rod.

As with large fish anywhere, allow the tarpon to run when it will and reel up slack when it gives it back to you. Keep the pressure on at all times and a deep arc in the rod. This is vital with tarpon. These fish have rudimentary lungs and must surface from time to time to gulp air in order to retain their equilibrium. If they are kept busy working against the pressure of the rod and don't get much of a chance to suck in some air they will tire much sooner. Pulling them constantly to one side instead of straight up keeps throwing them off balance. Individual fish vary considerably, but most tarpon can be whipped in less than an hour. It just seems longer!

When the fish begins to "show some belly" and coasts to the top on its side, its about ready to be gaffed. It's now much weaker, but its sheer bulk makes it difficult to force close to the boat. This is where the lifting power of a rod is appreciated. If the tarpon simply lies there, slowly fanning, it will regain some strength. By reeling and pumping steadily, you must bring the fish within a few feet of the gunwale. When the moment of truth arrives, the guide or your fishing partner drives the point of the gaff down through the tarpon's lower jaw and sticks it into the underside of the splash rail of the boat. This is a positive, no-turn-back move. It must be done swiftly. Once impaled and anchored to the boat, the tarpon will thrash about for a few seconds before giving up. It's not dead, just worn out. At this time it can be raised out of the water for a few seconds for picture taking and fly retrieval. Pull out a silver scale as a souvenir and slide the gaff free. Practically all tarpon are released, except a record-class fish that might be kept for a wall decoration. Of course, any fish over 75 pounds looks very big, but remember, the record fly-rod tarpon is over *175* pounds. That's a *monster* tarpon.

Some fish fight harder than others and some

are not so quick to recover when released. It may be necessary to hold the fish upright for a few minutes, working it back and forth in a way that forces water into its gills. The only tarpon I've ever seen go belly up after release didn't last long. As it swam away, sort of half on its side, a huge bull shark appeared out of nowhere and ate it in four bites. The tarpon weighed somewhat over 100 pounds, so you can imagine how big the shark was. I was not anxious to fall overboard at the moment.

Smaller Tarpon

Not all tarpon are huge. There must be small ones in order for there to be big ones. The smaller fish tend to travel in larger groups and some of the lagoons and backwaters of Florida, Central America, Mexico and all around the Caribbean rim are loaded with them. Technique is pretty much the same except for the length of the fight and the size of the gear. For school tarpon of no more than 25 pounds, a 9-weight fly rod will do nicely. If the tarpon available are really little guys of under 10 pounds, a 6- or 7-weight fly rod is a sporty alternative. But you'll still need plenty of backing on the reel just in case one decides to run into the next county. And then there's always the chance you'll hook something much bigger—no matter where you are in salt or brackish water.

The Tarpon "Daisy Chain"

In some tarpon waters, the distinctive mating ritual of large tarpon offers the chance of stalking these fish. From April through June the female tarpon of the Western Hemisphere eject their eggs and the males jostle for position to fertilize them. The males seem to know when a gravid female is "ripe," or ready to drop her eggs, and several of them follow her for a week or longer waiting for the event to happen. This usually takes place in shallow water, just deep enough to

cover the fish. If the angler is lucky enough to be at the right place at the right time, it can lead to the most exciting fly fishing possible.

A group of a dozen or so male tarpon fall into single file behind a female and follow her until she begins to swim in a tight circle. The males follow suit until what's known as a "daisy chain" of fish is formed that looks very much like an aquatic merry-go-round. When one of these circles of huge fish is spotted, it's possible to approach it in a boat, if it's propelled by pole or electric motor. While the tarpon are concentrating on romance, the angler can cast his fly to a spot on the periphery of the daisy chain. When one of the fish approaches the fly, it's stripped slowly away from the chain. If a fish shows interest, the retrieve speed is increased. If the fish breaks away from the pack and appears to be in earnest about grabbing it, the fly is moved a bit faster. If the fish is going to take it, don't worry about moving the fly too fast. It'll be engulfed in a eye wink.

If the fish doesn't move far away from the chain and goes back to playing the mating game, cast again. There's almost always one fish in the group that's more interested in eating than in mating. If the one that turns toward your fly happens to be the female, chances are she'll be the biggest one in the chain. Daisy chains are where the record-size tarpon come from. Several huge fish are hooked each year off the west coast of Florida in this manner. Hooked that is. The percentages of boating a 200-pounder are not high, but just seeing a daisy chain of big tarpon is a thrilling sight.

Flies for Tarpon

Every angler with considerable tarpon experience behind him has positive ideas about which style flies are best. There is, however, a general consensus that long, flowing tails and/or wings that undulate are more productive. The eel-like heads of patterns such as the Chinese Claw and

Typical saltwater flies (left) that will catch a variety of species. Prominent eyes are good additions to any fly and so is a dash of red and silver. Flies for tarpon (right) should be tied with the long feathers attached near the bend of the hook.

the Stu Apte style are very popular. These flies don't have a wing at all. They are mostly head and tail. The "head" extends from the eye of the hook to just aft of the midpoint of the shank. It is tapered from rear to front. Painted, plastic, or chain-bead eyes are usually added. The flowing feathers, hair, or synthetic tail material extend rearward for another hook length.

Wings attached near the eye of the hook, in conventional fashion, don't work well on tarpon flies. When the soft feathers are wet they tend to wrap around the heavy hook and cause the fly to look tangled and dead in the water.

Barred rooster feathers or grizzly hackles are highly effective on tarpon flies. In the natural, speckled state or when dyed yellow, green, blue or red, these mottled feathers do indeed suggest small fish. They present a lifelike appearance that is unmatched by any other natural material. Some anglers swear by all-red flies, others prefer blue and silver and, for turbid water (which is often the case in Central America),

all-black and black and red are well thought of.

The axiom followed by many anglers is bright fly for bright days and dark fly for dark days. This can also be applied to clear water and cloudy water. It's true that dark flies show up better under reduced light conditions. In my experience, smaller flies are also more productive on tarpon in very clear water and on bright, sunny days. In conjunction with smaller flies under such conditions, a fly with somewhat less wing and a thinner body seems to work better. Perhaps clear water magnifies the size of the fly to a tarpon's eye. At any rate, they don't appear to have any trouble seeing a rather small fly if they're inclined to grab it.

For such hard-fighting fish, hooks should be of well-tempered steel and resist bending. This is seldom a problem with commercially tied tarpon flies. Saltwater hooks from most of the major hook makers will serve the fly tier well. Try bending a hook in the fly vise if you want to be sure. Tie a section of 25-pound mono to the eye of the hook and see if you can put a permanent kink in it by pulling down. You probably can't. If you can, buy another brand of hook.

Sizes 2/0, 3/0, and 4/0 will prove most useful for tarpon flies with a 1/0 being needed at times for very clear water. Unless the fly must be fished in more than six feet of water, larger hook sizes are counterproductive. They are more difficult to set well and are more difficult to cast.

As with other matters pertaining to tarpon fishing, your guide will have tarpon flies on board and chances are he'll want you to use them. You should. He knows what's best in his water, so take his advice.

PERMIT

The third member of the Big Three of the flats is the permit, found about everywhere that bonefish and tarpon are abundant. There aren't as many of them in most places and even where they are fairly common they are never easy to catch on a fly. The truth is, they are not easy to catch on anything including live bait. In deep water, permit can sometimes be chummed to the surface and may hit almost anything with abandon, but on the flats it's a different story. These fish may spook from their own shadow when they're in shallow water. To catch one on a fly is the goal of many saltwater fly rodders.

Permit may come to a chum spread laid out for bonefish or they may be seen while stalking the flats. They occasionally cruise past a tarpon "waiting position" or when you happen to be looking for something else. At times, particularly off the coast of southern Mexico (on the Gulf side), large numbers of permit will magically appear and take any fly cast with total recklessness. Then again, they act like an aloof house cat and refuse even to look at a live crab, which is their favorite food. Strange fish.

It's the elusiveness of the permit that makes it so desirable as a fly rod trophy. But if you hook one, you'll discover another reason that puts these

The slab-sided permit is the most difficult of the flats sportfish to catch on the fly. In fact, it's not easy to catch a permit on anything. Very shy and highly selective, a permit of any size is a trophy worth talking about.

fish into a special category—they run even faster than a bonefish, and have the endurance of a marathon runner. In short, they fight like hell!

The best type of fly for permit is one that suggests a small fiddler crab. While the odd permit has been caught on standard bonefish flies, the crab patterns have proven to be far superior. There are many variations that have caught fish and new ones are created each year. Brown and yellow are the favorite colors, with materials running the gamut. Clipped deer hair, soft leather, yarn, and many synthetics have been

Dr. Neil Rogers with a permit caught in the flats of Belize, Central America. Rogers is standing in twelve inches of water and the permit is wider than that from back to belly. As it swims in such shallow water, the black tips of tail and dorsal fin are easy to spot; but the fish is not easy to catch.

employed. Camera's Crab, an all synthetic one, is a current favorite. Best sizes are 1 and 1/0.

If a permit is spotted (an all-black tail and a black-tipped dorsal fin are the clues), try to drop the crab fly a full ten feet in front of the cruising fish. Don't begin a retrieve until the fly has touched the bottom. At that point try to make the fly move in short hops, rising and falling back to the bottom. These antics suggest a live crab.

The strike of a permit is much like that of a bonefish; it inhales the fly with one gulp, a pull is felt and the angler merely tightens up. When it feels the hook a permit takes off running just like a bonefish, except it's even faster and will peel off a lot more backing. The battle will last longer because of the frying-pan shape of the permit. Even in the final stages of the fight, a permit will turn sideways to the angler and unless the rod has some backbone, it will be a chore to pull it close enough for netting or tailing.

BARRACUDA AND SHARKS

These two fish are often encountered when chumming on the flats and are also spotted when wading. If you're equipped with a leader tied for bonefish, the urge to cast at either of them may not be contained. If they take the fly, however, you'll probably lose them in short order. Both fish will tear through monofilament of any diameter, which makes a wire shock tippet necessary. If you cast expressly for these species have a suitable leader tied and ready to go for a quick change.

Barracuda are vicious strikers—when they decide to strike. In spite of their menacing looks and great appetites, they are very cautious fish. They seldom fall for a slow or jerky retrieve. Instead, they want a fly moving at breakneck speed. In fact, an angler can't move a fly too fast for a barracuda. If you see one turn towards your fly, try to move it even faster. If it appears like a baitfish that has spotted the predator, and is making a break to escape, you may get a hook-up.

Barracuda are strong fighters for a few minutes and will usually make a swift initial run. They don't have the stamina of bonefish or permit, but unlike them will frequently make a jump or two.

Extremely long, red and orange streamer flies are the top choices for barracuda; most saltwater tackle stores that sell fly fishing gear stock some good ones. Bright green and yellow are also useful colors on bright days and in clear water. If you buy your flies, instead of making them your-

Another excellent sportfish on the flats is the barracuda. These fish will look at a lot of flies before grabbing one—they want their prey moving fast. The wolflike teeth require a wire leader.

self, stick with synthetic materials. A barracuda's teeth make a mess out of soft feathers and yarn.

While most barracuda spotted on the flats will be smaller than 20 pounds, fish of over 35 have been taken on the fly and even larger ones are seen. Hook sizes 4/0 and 5/0 are best. If you catch one on a smaller hook and the fish has taken it deeply, there's no way to get the fly back without delivering a killing bop on the head. If you don't want to kill the fish, the only thing to do is cut the leader.

Sharks are usually the opposite of barracuda in the caution department. They don't spook easily and may hang around chum as long as there is a strong aroma of food. They are always hungry but can be difficult to hook because of the positioning of their eyes. Sharks simply cannot see anything that's precisely in front of them. They may sense that something is there but they just can't zero in on it. The trick when tossing a fly at them is to retrieve the fly *slowly past one eye.* If interested, the shark will snap its head to one side and make a lunge at it. If it misses, try again. Once a shark shows some interest it can be hooked if the angler is persistent.

There's no question about red being the best color for shark flies. They sure seem to know what blood looks like and respond to it. They must see the fly in order to get excited, which makes large flies the best choice. The same hook sizes suggested for barracuda are correct, with the points touched up with a three-cornered file. Shark jaws are tough as leather. At the strike, jerk the hook home several times, just as you would with a tarpon.

Fighting a shark is a long, rod-straining ordeal if the fish weighs 50 pounds or more. It may make a long run at first, but usually settles down to a steady game of tugging and head shaking. A few species such as the black-tip may jump and thrash about on the surface, but mostly they just pull hard. Plan to be hooked up for a long time.

Handling sharks and barracuda at unhooking

Fly rods that will be used on saltwater fish that may weigh over 40 pounds must have lifting power. This shark is almost ready to gaff, but if the rod doesn't have the backbone to move it, the end of the battle is far from over.

time can be a dicey business without help. *Very* small ones can be grabbed behind the gills, across the top of the head. But don't, repeat DON'T, try this unless the fish is well fought-out. As with gaffing, don't make any false moves. When you grab the fish, grab it and hang on. Remove the hook with pliers not your fingers. Professional guides don't carry those pliers in little leather holsters just for looks!

If a shark appears to be longer than you are, get back in the boat if you happen to be wad-

ing. Your bare ankles may look remarkably like a four-course meal. Do not attempt to grab a fish of this size. Sharks have no skeletal structure. Their inner frame consists of a highly flexible cord of cartilage that can bend into a complete circle. They will bite you if they can. Use a long-handled gaff and sink the point into the lower jaw for the unhooking chore. Remove the hook with long-nosed pliers or sacrifice the fly by cutting the wire leader. Acquiring another fly is easier than growing a new finger!

16

Other Saltwater Species

Wherever there are fish that come near the surface there will be fly rodders to fish for them. Even species such as flounder, lingcod, pollock, and halibut are being taken on flies. Anglers all over the world are developing techniques and flies to catch an even wider assortment of saltwater fish. The fly fishing horizons are ever broadening.

Bluefish, weakfish, mackerel, dolphin, striped bass, bonito, skipjack tuna, yellowtail, cobia, and a couple dozen others are made to order for saltwater fly rodding. The idea of catching these on a fly rod has not been foremost in the minds of many anglers until recently. I think this has been more a case of thinking of these species as food fish instead of sport fish since many of them were targets of commercial nets and sold regularly in fish markets. A day on the water for blues, mackerel, weakfish, or spotted seatrout was not considered successful unless a lot of them were caught. That kind of thinking is changing. Quality of experience rather than quantity of fish is the new order of all sport fishing.

Because a 5-pound *anything* fights harder and longer when hooked on a fly rod than it does on 30-pound trolling or baitfishing gear, filling the fish box takes longer. So what? A new generation of anglers is also discovering that boating less on a fly rod is more fun than boating more on overpowering gear. That's what fly fishing is about!

CHUMMING

For many species in any ocean, chumming is the most productive way to coax school fish to or near the surface. In the section dealing with offshore chumming for really big fish, the basic technique was described. It's done the same way from small boats within sight of shore. Unless fish are simply not in the area, chumming usually beings results. Simply tossing some cut-up baitfish, clams, crabs, or squid overboard is often all it takes. The chum slick drifts with the tide and wind currents and the fish, like beagles trailing a rabbit, follow the scent to its source.

Another equally good method in near shore waters is to use a "chum pot." In its basic form, a chum pot is a metal can, well perforated with holes, into which cut-up chum is dumped. The

The bluefish is a fly-rod fighter that also happens to be a plentiful Atlantic species. A school of feeding bluefish will keep an angler busy for hours because boating each one hooked will require at least a minute per pound of fish.

can is fastened to a stout cord and lowered over the side. As the scent and bits of chum ooze from the can, fish that are cruising on or near the bottom rise up to check on what smells like a free lunch. If baitfish are attracted to the chum, so much the better; they will keep the larger customers even more interested in hanging around the chum pot. Of course, the fly fisherman is there in the boat, waiting, with his imitation baitfish tied to the end of his leader.

When a school of bluefish, mackerel, bonito, or other fish that feed near the surface come to inspect the chum, there is no question of their arrival. There will be some wild thrashing and splashing as they race about crazily, slashing at the chum and the baitfish. Get your fly in the water, strip it a few times, and you'll probably have a strike instantly.

The action around a chum pot or chum slick may continue for an hour or longer. However, it may last for but a few minutes depending on the number of baitfish in the area. If the larger fish scare the bait away, they'll probably chase after it and the catching stops. Hang in there and keep on chumming. School fish move about constantly, and in due time they'll be back for another look. If the baitfish return, you can bet that the larger fish will too.

When chumming, any and all of the species that hang around shallow water may be attracted. At times, even the fish that are considered to be "blue-water" travelers will appear.

Weakfish is another excellent fly-rod fish that frequently appears in large schools and can provide fast action. They can be chummed to the surface like blues. Weakies are fond of long eel-like patterns in black, blue, and purple.

Bonito, mackerel, tuna, and various sharks may come into very shallow water. Near-shore chumming can be full of surprises!

BLUEFISH

On the East Coast, the bluefish are the bread and butter species of the party boat fleet and deserve special mention. These swift, voracious, sharp-toothed fighters are plentiful and well distributed. They are also the best training fish for a new saltwater fly fisherman. Bluefish are caught from Florida to Canada at various times of the year, with the peak of the run being off the mid-Atlantic coast from late May until the end of October. As ocean temperatures warm in

Yellowtail snapper is one of the many semitropical fish that hit small, shrimp-like flies. Dozens of saltwater species may appear when chum is tossed overboard. Wish for a few yellowtails—they are one of the best tasting fish in the ocean.

the spring, the fish follow the coastline north, giving an entire army of anglers a crack at them. You'll know when a school of blues is around. The sky will be full of gulls and terns. The birds know that the fish are there and that soon a feeding frenzy will take place. The birds will be there to feed on the crippled baitfish that lie in the wake of a bluefish attack.

Bluefish tend to travel in hunting packs of similar sized companions. This may be for protection, because bluefish will feed on anything that moves—including their own kind—when they choose to. In fact, schools of ravenous bluefish occasionally attack swimmers in the surf with serious results. The teeth of a bluefish are plentiful and sharp. More anglers have been bitten by bluefish than by any other species. Do not attempt to unhook a blue with bare fingers. Use a gloved hand to hold the fish and long-nose pliers to grasp the hook.

Chasing the birds in a small boat is another

Small bluerunners may show up at anytime and snap at white and silver flies with abandon. Like all saltwater fly fishing targets, they fight harder than freshwater species on a pound-for-pound basis.

School-size dolphin are one of the flashiest fish in the ocean—literally. When hooked, they glow in the water with a greenish-yellow aura. A hard-fighting dolphin of this size is worth a ten-minute battle on a fly rod.

way to find some top-water bluefish opportunities and so is walking a beach. At any time during a bluefish season, they may come close to shore chasing schools of baitfish. If the water is warm, wet wading can be comfortable. If it isn't, wear chest-high waders. Casting in a rolling surf can be dangerous, however, so unless you are an experienced surfer, don't do this kind of fishing alone.

Fly tackle for bluefish in near-shore waters and in the surf is not complicated. The same 9-foot, 9-weight combination suggested for bonefish, pike, and salmon is the best choice. In fact, this pairing of rod and line is the most useful combination for general saltwater use. Except-

ing the species found farther off shore and the tarpon of the flats, a 9-weight outfit will handle 95 percent of the work.

When bluefish are involved, a short wire leader of ten inches or so is mandatory, solid or braided, with braided being a bit easier to handle. In time, the braided stuff will kink up, whereas the solid wire lasts longer.

Bluefish flies are nothing special. Anything will work if the blues are on a rampage—even a hank of yarn tied to a bare hook. Red-and-white bucktails tied on a 1/0 or 2/0 hook are deadly and so are green, yellow, and blue. On sunny days, more strikes will probably come to flies that have a touch of silver in them. But

Striped bass expert Stu Tinney guided the author to his first striper on the fly. This one hit a yellow and white streamer on a size 2/0 hook. Stripers don't have fearsome teeth but their gill covers can cut thin mono.

again, it doesn't matter much. When blues are on the feed they just don't seem to care.

As the fly is being retrieved, bluefish smack it so hard they are automatically hooked. The wonderful part of this fishing is the battle. Blues run fast, pull hard, and occasionally jump. For such small fish they have amazing stamina and keep on flopping even after they're in the boat. Handle a hooked blue just like any other hard-fighting fish. Allow it to run when it's first hooked, fight it from the reel and keep the pres-

sure on. The amount of pressure depends on the diameter of the leader that's attached to the wire. As with all fly fishing, learning how much pressure to apply can only come from experience. It can't be explained.

Generally, the closer to shore, the smaller the bluefish. Blues measuring less than 25 inches are referred to as "snappers," and snap they do at anything in sight. These little guys, not incidentally, have teeth that are just as sharp as the big blues. The "slammers" of 15 pounds and

Bluefish run and jump much like the larger saltwater species, which makes them a great training fish for new fly rodders. When they have been chummed close to the boat, size 2/0 flies featuring white bucktail and dashes of silver and red will be all that's needed.

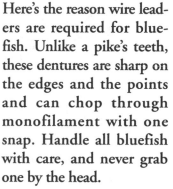

Here's the reason wire leaders are required for bluefish. Unlike a pike's teeth, these dentures are sharp on the edges and the points and can chop through monofilament with one snap. Handle all bluefish with care, and never grab one by the head.

over are the fish that cruise the surf and deeper waters. On certain days, however, some really huge blues may show up anywhere. That's why a 9-weight rod is suggested. Such a rod is too heavy for the snappers, but you never know what may strike next. This presents a small problem in deciding what size hook to use. A 2/0 or 3/0 is not too large for slammers but may be for snappers. The best plan is to have a selection of flies tied on some smaller hooks (sizes 1 and 2) in case the pee-wees get active.

These little blues, by the way, are absolutely delicious when broiled whole.

REGIONAL SPECIES

To cover every fish in detail, discussing techniques, best times to find them and so on could fill several more books. Such books would be of interest only to the anglers who are located to take advantage of the action. The larger weakfish of the middle Atlantic states are not avail-

Useful flies for many saltw ter fish include shrin lookalikes and patterns th resemble pieces of cut- chum. In saltwater fly ro ding, the bizarre often worl better than a fly that appear to match natural food.

able to others. Nor are the closely related spotted seatrout of the Gulf states. Florida has a corner on a wide variety of snappers, big cobia, snook, and other species which are found only in warm water.

California is the place for yellowtails, white sea bass, and a wide variety of lesser known species that are found only in Pacific waters. And so it goes, around the world.

The happy part of this is that all of these fish can be caught by chumming or by following the birds. The basic techniques and flies needed remain the same. Of course, there are subtle variations and local tricks used by the anglers who live there, but the budding fly angler will catch some fish by applying the basic saltwater methods described in these pages.

All of the fly types and patterns mentioned for specific species will work for other fish if the hook size is appropriate. So will all of the colors. But a reminder about the usefulness of *white* is in order. It must be emphasized that practically

all baitfish and most gamefish as well have white bellies. That's what a predator fish sees when it approaches a meal from the underside. The top side of most saltwater prey fish is dark, usually of a greenish or bluish shade. The backs of these fish may appear to be black under certain light conditions, which is also something to keep in mind when buying or tying flies. The sides of most small fish sparkle with an iridescent or silvery glow; take a clue from this as well. Then there's the dash of red or bright orange to suggest gill color or blood, and the added attraction of painted eyes or other forms of eye suggestions. All saltwater flies should contain at least one or more of these components.

Most of the time a floating or sink-tip fly line will handle saltwater situations. In deep, near-shore waters or estuaries that may be off-color or muddy, a full sinking line or a shooting head of lead core may be needed to get the fly down to or near the bottom. Freshwater techniques, as discussed in other chapters, can e put to use here. Flounders, halibut, oupers, sea bass of various kinds, and a host of sser known species are not keen about coming ose to the surface. But if the water is less than teen feet deep, such fish can be caught on flies.

There are limits, though, beyond which fly ishing in saltwater cannot be considered practical. A fly can be sunk to extreme depths by using heavy sinkers, an entire line of lead-core, or with downriggers—but then it becomes trolling or bottom fishing because it does not involve casting. When bottom fishing in more than fifteen feet of water is called for, other types of tackle are the sensible choices.

Trolling a fly behind an engine-driven boat in salt or fresh water is "fly fishing" in some waters, and it's a matter of personal choice and philosophy to do it or not do it. In lakes containing landlocked salmon, for example, trolling a long streamer fly is accepted fly fishing style. This same technique will bring strikes from many saltwater fish as well, and sometimes some very large ones. The International Game Fish Association, the official keeper of the records, does not recognize catches made on fly tackle when the fish was hooked while trolling. Rules state, "The craft must be completely out of gear when the fly is cast both at the time the fly is presented to the fish and during the retrieve." Put another way, fly fishing must include fly casting and not fly trolling. In all activities, there is some honor involved.